Penguin Books

TRETIAK: The Legend

Vladislav Tretiak was born in 1952 in Dmitrovo, a suburb of Moscow. From 1969 until his retirement in 1984, he was the starting goaltender for the Central Army Sports Club and the Soviet National team. In 1981 Tretiak was voted the outstanding player of the Canada Cup tournament with a phenomenal 1.5 goals against average. He has won three Olympic gold medals, over ten World Championships, and was named Most Valuable Player in Soviet hockey a record five times. His outstanding talent and sportsmanship have made him a hockey legend throughout the world.

Vladislav Tretiak now resides in Moscow with his wife and two children. He holds the rank of Colonel in the Central Army and is an ambassador for international sports.

Wayne Gretzky has written a foreword for **TRETIAK: The Legend.** He has come to know Vladislav Tretiak not only as a competitor, but as a friend. He has visited the Tretiak family in the Soviet Union, and had them as guests in his own home. In the foreword, he writes of Tretiak: *I am proud to say that he is a friend and I only regret that I cannot say he was a teammate.*

D0746263

TRETIAK: THE LEGEND

Vladislav Tretiak

Translated from Russian by Sam and Maria Budman

Foreword by Wayne Gretzky

Penguin Books

PENGUIN BOOKS

Published by the Penguin Group
Penguin Books Canada Ltd., 2801 John Street, Markham, Ontario, Canada L3R 1B4
Penguin Books, 27 Wrights Lane, London W8 5TZ, England
Viking Penguin Inc., 40 West 23rd Street, New York, New York 10010, USA
Penguin Books Australia Ltd., Ringwood, Victoria, Australia
Penguin Books (NZ) Ltd., 182-190 Wairau Road, Auckland 10, New Zealand
Penguin Books Ltd. Registered Offices: Harmondsworth, Middlesex, England

First published by Plains Publishing Inc., 1987
Published in Penguin Books, 1988

Copyright © Vladislav Tretiak and Plains Publishing Inc., Edmonton, Alberta, 1987
Published with permission of the Copyright Agency of the USSR, Moscow

All rights reserved.

Manufactured in Canada

Canadian Cataloguing in Publication Data
Tretiak, Vladislav.
  Tretiak, the legend

Translated from Russian.
ISBN 0-14-010918-8

1. Tretiak, Vladislav. 2. Hockey players —
Soviet Union — Biography. I. Title.

GV848.5.T73A3   1988   796.96'2'0924   C87-094863-6

Except in the United States of America, this book is sold subject to the condition
that it shall not, by way of trade or otherwise, be lent, re-sold, hired out, or otherwise circulated without the publisher's prior consent in any form of binding or
cover other than that in which it is published and without a similar condition
including this condition being imposed on the subsequent purchaser.

All rights reserved, including motion picture, television and radio broadcasting.
Representation as to the disposition of these rights is strictly prohibited without the
express written authorization of the author's representative, The Colbert Agency
Inc., 303 Davenport Road, Toronto, Ontario, Canada M5R 1K5.

CONTENTS

FOREWORD
by Wayne Gretzky

Over the years I have come to appreciate the efforts, skills, dedication and durability of many athletes from the world of sport. I have also come to appreciate the non-competitive talents which characterize many athletes – humility, availability, understanding and generosity.

However, when the realization occurs that I have met an athlete, male or female, who embodies all of the above, I become very excited. Such was the case after my first meeting with Vladislav Tretiak. Needless to say, his hockey skills were evident and awesome... but I soon came to realize that Vladislav represents so much more than merely one of the world's finest goaltenders.

On a truly global scale, Vladislav Tretiak has given more back to his sport than he has gained from it. He has always shown the diplomacy, charisma and warmth of an international ambassador. Which is exactly what Vladislav happens to be.

He has caused borders to be forgotten, political beliefs to be withheld, and cultures to be exchanged – while always standing tall in his representation of his team and his country.

I have visited with Vladislav and his family in their home, and they in mine. I am proud to say that he is a friend and I only regret that I cannot say he was a teammate.

TRETIAK:
THE LEGEND

1

MOTHER AND HOCKEY
Falling down and getting up

"Falling down and getting up, that's how you grow up."
Those are the words of the famous Dutch skater Keis Ferkerk.
When you think about it, that statement is very profound. Yes,
falling down and getting up – that is so true in real life, isn't
it? Unfortunately, mothers and grandmothers too often deprive
children of the 'getting up' part of the experience. They are
always nearby to protect the child from unpleasant experiences.
Yet it takes those unhappy circumstances to prepare the child
to cope with the ups and downs of adult life. The reality of
it all is that the many roads we travel in life are often rough
and unpaved.

I don't believe that it hurts to let your children get their knees
skinned on soccer fields or their eyes blackened from ski jumping. My brother and I were spared from over-protection, but
that was not the case with many boys and girls when we were
young. Nobody in our family worried too much about us. Our

punishments were sometimes too severe but always fair. Our parents demanded that we do our best at whatever they asked us to do. Our father was especially demanding, and I sometimes resented him for it. However, as an adult I discovered that the high ideals my father made me strive for were for my own benefit. In fact, without knowing it, my father prepared me to cope with the gruelling training that I would later experience under coach Anatoly Tarasov.

I spent my early childhood in a small town called Dmitrovo, not far from Moscow. My mother was a gym teacher. Many of the future Russian hockey stars like Bodunov, Lapshenkov, and Titarenko went through her class. When I was 5 years old, I found an old wooden stick with a funny curve at the end of it. I asked my mom what it was. She carefully took the stick from me, held it in her hands, and said, "This is my field hockey stick." I found out that she had participated in the Moscow championship for the Metallurgist team. In the 1930s all females played field hockey or grass hockey in Russia. It was a very popular game. My mother saved her hockey stick as a souvenir of her field hockey playing days.

I forgot about all my other toys when I first saw that hockey stick. I hit the floor with it, I pushed rocks around in the backyard with it, and finally, I broke it. I was afraid to tell my mother, but to my surprise she wasn't angry. She just sighed, "Well, if you like it so much and choose to play hockey, I won't object."

For the next five years I went to summer camp outside the city like most other boys and girls. We spent half of the time, if not more, in different sporting activities. I ran cross country, and played ping-pong and volleyball for hours on end. At school, I volunteered to participate in track and field, basketball, and skiing competitions. And I always wanted to be a champion. One day I announced to my mother, "I am definitely going to be a champion." She corrected me softly, "A sportsman." "No, only a champion!" Now we talk about it and smile.

As a youngster, I had a great desire to overcome my many fears. I wanted to kill them once and for all. Little did I know that this was impossible. There are no fearless people on earth. The true question is whether or not a human being can control his or her feelings.

My older brother used to take swimming lessons at the Dynamo pool. I also tried swimming, but I always felt cold and spent more time under a hot shower than in the water. I was fascinated, however, with high diving. It was easy enough for me to dive from the five-foot board, but one day I decided to climb the sixteen-foot tower. It didn't seem that high from below, but when I reached the edge of the board and looked down I suddenly felt dizzy and my knees started to tremble.

"Hey Vladik, be brave," my coach tried to keep up my spirit, "what's the matter with you? Be a man!" "The water is soft," the guys down below were yelling. "Don't be afraid, you won't get hurt! Jump!" But I just couldn't move, I was frozen. My legs turned to rubber. My heart was ready to jump out of my chest. "Vladik, the girls are looking at you. Can't you jump from there?" the boys below taunted me. My fear was growing with every second. The height was tremendous and the water appeared as solid as pavement. That same feeling is probably familiar to every one of you. It was very difficult to overcome the fear of jumping. It took me many years to understand fear, but it certainly began on the sixteen-foot diving tower.

Two of the boys in my mother's gym class were training at the hockey school. The first time I saw a real hockey uniform was on those boys. It may sound silly, but it made a startling impression on me. How I envied them! When I came home after school, I announced to my parents, "I want a hockey uniform too." "Just another passion," my mother said skeptically.

I was lucky because the next morning there was an opening for young hockey players at the Central Army Children's Sports School. Early in the morning three friends and I went to the school located on Leningrad Prospect. There were so many people there that it looked like all the boys in Moscow had decided to become hockey players. They came to the skating rink with their parents, grandparents, and older brothers – it was like a circus. I was trying to stay with my friend Valery Krokhmalev, and together we elbowed our way through the crowd. I had a feeling that if anyone would be admitted, it would be Valery. He had pictured himself in the club's uniform for a long time, but I had decided to become a hockey player only the day before.

The tryouts were tough, but there were no fancy requirements. The coaches put a young boy around our age out on the ice in full hockey gear and announced, "This boy has trained at our school for a year. Whoever can catch him will pass the test." One coach blew his whistle and the young hockey player named Sasha Volchkov (who later became a member of our National Team) took off on his skates as fast as he could – and we followed him. Following that, the coaches tested our ability to skate backwards. It was there that I used my experience from our family outings at the Park of Culture and Leisure skating rink, the place where I took my first skating lessons. The tryout was over. Four of us were asked to step aside. I was sure that we were the losers. I was wrong. I was admitted to the famous Central Army Sports Club. Naturally, I was extremely happy.

Thinking back, it may be that among those who didn't pass the exams were boys who were more gifted in hockey than

I was. Unfortunately, even today the criteria for entry into the sports schools are imperfect. I doubt that the coaches could see the special talents of some of the boys. I think I made the team only because I was a little braver than the others. I was also a lot more physically developed as a result of my involvement in different sports like soccer, gymnastics, and skiing.

We trained for an hour and a half three times a week at the Central Army Sports Club. I was a forward and always tried as hard as I could because I loved the game so much. But there was one thing that confused me. A month had gone by and I still hadn't received a real hockey uniform. "There's a shortage of uniforms," explained my first coach Vitaly Georgievich Erfilov. At that time we didn't have a goalkeeper on our team, because nobody wanted to play that position. I decided to try, so I went to the coach and said, "If you'll give me a hockey uniform, I will be the goalkeeper." The coach looked at me carefully and asked, "Aren't you afraid?" "What's so scary about it?" I replied simply. How could I know how much it hurts when the puck hits you? Or how difficult the fate of a goalkeeper is? The thing I wanted most at that moment was a real hockey uniform. And I got it!

When I began my hockey training my father was quite skeptical about my eagerness. He had little interest in either soccer or hockey. In those years, when either a hockey or soccer game was on television, he would leave the room. "So what if you are a goalkeeper?" he would say jokingly. "What will you learn by standing in front of a net with a broom in your hands? Just don't forget that if you get bad marks in school, you can say good-bye to your hockey." Those last words were said in a very serious manner. I have no doubt that he would have carried out his threat, if I had not managed to keep up my schoolwork. When we were young, my brother and I always put school first, so that my father's threat was never tested.

My father later changed his attitude towards the great sport of hockey. Today he knows the game very well. His former colleagues cannot believe it. "Can it really be true, Sasha, that you've become a hockey fan?" But the most excited fan in our family is our mother. When she sits in front of the television with a hockey game on, my father hangs an old road sign on the wall by the television. The sign has a symbol: "Horn sounding forbidden." The message is clear: Be a fan, Mother – but not too loudly.

* * * * *

Hockey is a stern game, and a merciless game for the goalkeeper. The temper and fury of the opposition are directed squarely at him. Their aim is to scare and to stun; to bewilder; to knock down; and to score. When some players shoot the puck, it flies like a missile. And the goalkeeper must catch it or deflect it with his hockey stick, goalpad, skate, whatever. Just block the shot. Always block the shot. Other players can make mistakes. If a forward loses the puck, the defense will usually come to his rescue. Any faults of the defensemen will be corrected by the goalkeeper. Only the goalkeeper can't make mistakes. His mistakes are seen by all. He is his own only hope. And he is his own judge. I like to compare the goalie to a border guard. Indeed, the net is your border and you have to stand bravely for it.

When I was twelve, I received my first serious injury. The puck hit me squarely in the forehead. I didn't cry only because I was afraid that I'd be kicked off the team. Hockey was no longer just a hobby to me by then. I had fallen in love with the game so much that I was selflessly devoted to it as only a young boy can be. The day after the injury I wasn't myself. During practice I only thought about one thing; how to dodge another blow from the puck. I forgot everything I had learned. I had to start again from the beginning. Again I experienced the struggle within myself. It is not easy to learn how to conquer your fears.

I decided that I had to learn to control myself. You can't be afraid of a hockey puck. Nor can you be afraid of your opponents, even when, with twisted excitement on their faces, they rush wildly at your net. There is only one thing that is supposed to be on a goalie's mind: Do not let the puck into the goal. The rest is not important. You must have patience, and you must think. You must think constantly about how to play better, more safely, and more reliably.

Yes, the puck hits hard. But I got used to bruises quickly. The only thing I couldn't get used to was losing. It literally caused me physical and mental pain. When I was a boy I played on a team that often lost. I remember feeling so bitter, and at the same time so ashamed.

The first time I cried was almost one year after I received my hockey uniform. We were playing the Dynamo youth team when our other goalie, Sasha Karnaukhov, was injured and had to leave the game. The coach sent me out on the ice. I went into the net and froze. I was frightened in the same way that I had been frightened on the diving tower at the swimming pool. When the puck was shot in the direction of my net, I closed my eyes. I knew how hard the puck was! The other team scored a few goals on me that night – ten, I recall. After the game I burst out sobbing and told the coach that I could never be a real goalkeeper. As if nothing had happened, Erfilov looked at me and said in a calm voice, "Congratulations, Vladik, on your baptism under fire. If you try hard, you can make it." "Are you teasing me?" I asked. "Just wipe away your tears and be at practice tomorrow," he said. I often wonder if Erfilov really believed that I would be a goalkeeper.

Do not think, however, that Erfilov always forgave us so easily. Later that same season, the boys who were born in 1950 didn't have a goalie. I was put in the net even though I was two years younger. In the last game of the Moscow Cup we played Krilya Sovetov. If we won, we would be the Champions. But the game ended in a 4-4 tie and I let in all four goals, all from the blue line. I had let my team down. Erfilov couldn't take any more. "You get a failing grade for the game," he said. I still remember that feeling of sadness and bitterness. But that day we were lucky. Only one hour after our game we were told that Spartak had lost their game and their defeat meant that we were champions.

Vitaly Erfilov was always generous of his time with me. Once, when Moscow's Dynamo was playing at the Palace of Sports, he said, "Today we are going to watch the goaltender Chinov." During the game we sat behind Chinov's net, watching his every move with great attention. It was a good lesson for me. Later we went to watch Konovalenko, Zinger, and other goaltenders in the same way. I adopted techniques, I noticed shortcomings, and I learned.

Time went by and I began to block shots fairly well myself. I spent all of my time after school at the nearby skating rink, and was very happy with my life in general. I no longer told my mother that I wanted to be champion. Maybe that was a real sign of a boy transforming into a teenager. I put the question of being a champion aside until later when I started to train with a coach named Tarasov.

2

THE MAN TARASOV

There were three goalies on the Central Red Army team in the summer of 1967; Victor Tolmachev, Nikolai Tolstikov and Vladimir Polupanov. Head coach Anatoly Tarasov wanted a fourth goalie to make the training more efficient. At the time I wouldn't even have dared to dream about playing on Tarasov's team. He had such great players as Konstantin Loktev, Alexander Almetov, Veniamin Alexandrov, Anatoly Firsov. How could a fifteen-year-old think of playing with them?

One day, Tarasov said to the coach of our junior team, "Let this boy come to practise with the seniors." Then he pointed to me. I was stunned! Shortly after that I began my training with the famous Red Army Team, who had been USSR Champions many times, and who supplied the majority of players to the National Team.

I tried hard at every practice. During the games I tried to stop every shot, even the impossible. "OK, try harder," Tarasov would say, patting me on the shoulder approvingly. Coming from him, it seemed to be the highest of praise, especially since I already knew how little praise he gave. Often, however there was criticism mixed with the praise. He was probably afraid that I would become overconfident. "Don't listen to compliments," he reminded me. "When people praise you, they rob you! And if I criticize you, it likely means that I need you."

I loved doing my physical exercises with the rest of the players. I brought apples from our orchard to my new friends on the team. Believe it or not, I even started to walk pigeon-toed, copying Evgeny Mishakov! In conversation, I used the favorite words and expressions of my idols. I even carried their hockey sticks. I wanted to look like I was one of them in everything I did. I was proud to be living in the Red Army Sports Pension on Peschanaya Street, and proud to be changing in the same locker room with the legendary hockey names. But this inconceivable luck lasted for only fifteen days. By the middle of July, my holidays were over. The Red Army Team left for the South. Naturally they left without me.

That year, I continued to play on the junior team, and we won the Moscow championship. In the city of Novosibirsk, I received a trophy as the best goaltender for the first time. I was also the backup goalie at the European Junior Championships in Helsinki. We ended up in second place in Helsinki, but our performance was considered a failure because everyone expected us to finish first. Any other place but first meant defeat.

A year later we returned to the European Junior Championships in Garmisch-Partenkirchen, West Germany, and won. After that championship was over, I went down to the Palace of Sports to watch the seniors on the Red Army Team practice. Tarasov was there and he called me over. He probably wants to congratulate me, I thought. But the coach looked at me very sternly and simply asked, "And you, young man, why aren't you on the ice? Hurry up!"

Still not fully aware of what was happening, I rushed to the locker room. From that day on a new life began for me. Tarasov established a task for himself; to make Tretiak the best goalkeeper. "The best in the country?" I asked. Anatoly frowned at me. "In the world! Remember this once and for all: In the world!" he said.

We started to work, and work we did. Now, looking back, I sometimes can't believe that I stood up to that tremendous workload. Three practices a day! They had me doing incredible new exercises invented especially for me. And then MCO – 'maximum consumption of oxygen' – which was, in simpler terms, a wild run around the arena grounds. Faster and faster! My teammates, feeling sorry for me, said compassionately, "Well, Vladik, it seems unlikely that you'll die of natural causes. These practices are going to kill you."

During the on-ice training, pucks flew at my net, sometimes more than one at a time. I tried to stop them all. All! I was fanatical about stopping them all. Almost every day I played in different games for different teams; one day for the Junior team, the next day for the Intermediates, and the following day for the Seniors.

And if I let in just one puck, Tarasov would ask me the next day, "What's the matter?" If it was my fault (and it usually appears to be the goalkeeper's fault), my punishment would follow immediately. After everybody else had gone home I had to do hundreds of lunges and somersaults. I could have cheated and not done them at all, since nobody was watching me – the coaches had gone home too! But I wouldn't even have considered doing one less lunge or somersault. I trusted Tarasov, trusted his every word, even when he criticized me for letting the pucks in my net during practice. There was a method to his madness. My coach didn't want me to be indifferent to being scored on. He wanted me to feel that each puck in my net was a personal defeat.

At the Red Army Sports Club training camp which is located in a suburb of Moscow called Arkhangelskoye, I shared a room with Vladimir Lutchenko and Nikolai Tolstikov. Probably because of my long neck and high voice, they gave me the nickname 'Gosling'. My mother asked the waitress at the Sports Club, Nina Bakumina, to look after me, and she certainly did. She always gave me the most delicious and plentiful meals.

It all seemed like a dream at the time. Still a teenager, I was beside our country's most famous hockey players. The veteran Alexander Pavlovich Ragulin shared a room with Viktor Kuzkin. I remember that when I was on duty at the Sports Club I was too timid to even enter their room. And I was even worse with Tarasov. I was scared to come across him! But I wasn't the only one. The veterans were afraid of him too. Tarasov's demands never seemed unreasonable to me, however, because I understood, then as now, that Tarasov had only one goal: to make Soviet hockey the best in the world.

Anatoly Tarasov was a very well-organized person. He knew his purpose in life and didn't like lazy people. I owe very much to that man. Even what some people called the Tarasov's 'moodiness', I consider to be the peculiarity of his fatherly talents.

Valery Kharlamov told a story about Tarasov's moods. Once during a practice, Valery's skatelace became untied. He stopped and knelt to tie it. When Tarasov saw him, his eyes grew wide and his face angry. He began to yell at Kharlamov. "You, young man, you just stole ten seconds of hockey from me, and you can never make it up to me!"

I recall once, after receiving new goal pads, sitting and sewing them with a large needle. Anatoly noticed it. "Do you

want to use them in the next game?'' he asked. ''Yes, I do,''
I said, standing quickly to attention. ''Very well, Tretiak,
tomorrow you will do your dry-land exercises wearing those
pads.'' It was raining outside the next morning. Everybody
was astonished to see me in running shoes and goal pads. But
there was a simple explanation to it. Tarasov knew the rain
would stretch and soften the rough skin of the pads, preparing
them for the next game. Only he could have known that it was
going to rain that day!

When Tarasov called a player by anything but his first name,
or when he spoke very politely to him, everyone knew that
it meant trouble. In the fall of 1969, after a playoff game
for the Championship of the USSR, he called me into his
office for the first time in my life. ''I'd like to talk to you,
young man.'' I was scared. I couldn't think of anything I'd
done wrong. ''Do you know why I called you here?'' ''No,
I don't.'' ''Then go out and try to think about why!'' Confused,
I closed the door and left. In an hour I was called again to
stand before his frightening stare. ''So, did you think about
it?'' In complete bewilderment now, I shrugged my shoulders.
''OK,'' he said, suddenly changing his anger to friendliness.
''Take a chair and sit down. Don't be afraid, sit over here.
Yesterday you let in two goals under your right foot. Why?
Let's think about it.''

Tarasov insisted that I always think. He wanted me to analyze
every mistake, every failure. ''Vladik, have you ever thought
of yourself as a crab? Think about this. A hundred legs and
a hundred arms! Look.'' He stood in the middle of the room
and demonstrated what, in his opinion, a crab-goalkeeper would
look like. His idea hit home. That is how we worked. I can
honestly say that there wasn't one practice to which Tarasov
came without new ideas. He amazed all of us every day. One
day he had a new exercise, the next an innovative idea, and

the next a stunning combination to remove the effectiveness of our opponents.

"Do you think playing hockey is difficult?" asked Tarasov in the early days of my career. "Of course," I answered, "especially if you play with the best." "You are mistaken!" he said. "Remember, it is easy to play. To practise is difficult! Vladik, can you practise 1350 hours per year?" His voice was rising. "Can you practise to such extent that you may end up physically sick? If you can, then you will achieve something!" "1350 hours?" I couldn't believe it. "Yes," said Tarasov sharply.

During the practices he could get us into a mood that made it easy to overcome his monstrous workloads. "Practise until you drop," Anatoly would demand, laughing. The severity of our practices could be judged by the response of hockey players from different teams who practiced with us. They would leave after the first day, massaging their hearts. We laughed at them. Once we were joined by a famous Swedish hockey player, Svedberg, but he didn't last long either. On the third day after dinner, noticeably pale, he started to say good-bye to everybody. "We Swedes don't grow up to practise like this. I don't want to die," explained our guest before his premature departure.

I will never forget Tarasov's lessons. Now, looking back after many years, I clearly understand that he was not only teaching us hockey, he was teaching us life.

I remember Anatoly suddenly quizzing young Valery Kharlamov in the middle of a practice. "Tell me, please, when you have the puck, who is in charge?" "Of course," answered the talented Kharlamov, "I am in charge." "Wrong!" said Tarasov angrily. "You are a servant of your teammates. You play on this Soviet team to benefit your comrades. Be happy for their achievements. Don't put yourself first."

He taught us to be noble and proud of how hard we worked. He had a saying; "To work like a miner," which in real life meant to practise his way.

Anatoly was constantly reminding me that I alone was worth nothing, and that my success was the success of the whole team. I believed in that without any doubt. If I hadn't, I don't honestly think anything worthwhile would have become of me.

Let me pass along a couple more examples that show the essence of Tarasov's coaching abilities. Anatoly believed that the worse the weather was, the better it was for us to forge our abilities. One day, when we were supposed to play our traditionally strong rival Dynamo, the temperature was thirty degrees below zero. We were leery about going outside for our dry-land exercises. We could easily have all caught colds. Standing in the crowded hall of our Sports Club waiting for Tarasov, we hoped that he would cancel the outdoor workout. Finally Tarasov appeared. Pretending that he didn't see anybody else, he approached me, the youngest. "Why are you here, young fellow?" he asked. "But everybody is here," I replied. "That is of no concern to you. You were supposed to be outside a long time ago, working with the tennis ball." Everybody left the hall, as if they had been swept out by a storm.

Tarasov trained me always to carry a tennis ball with me and never to leave it, even for a moment. Wherever I went, I had to throw and catch it all the time. I remember once we were swimming in the sea and Tarasov asked, "Where is your tennis ball, young fellow? You have to carry it in the water, too." And he wasn't kidding! Not at all. Nikolai Tolstikov and I were forced to make pockets in our swimming trunks for our tennis balls. Now you might get the impression that that was too much. But, who knows what would have happened to my life without that tennis ball, which undoubtedly sharpened my reaction speed and my hand-eye coordination?

Once my teammates used tennis balls for a practical joke. Mishakov and Firsov were studying at the Institute of Sports, and were preparing to take an anatomy exam. The professor asked them, "Are you ready to take your exam?" They weren't sure about how ready they were. "The exam is important – you must be prepared," said the professor. He pointed at a skeleton in the corner of the classroom and told them to study it thoroughly.

"Can we take it to training camp?" asked Mishakov. "We will study it bone by bone in our free time." They loaded the skeleton into their car and brought it to Arkhangelskoye. I was at a movie at the time. When I returned to my room, I saw a pile of bones on my bed. The skull had my toque on it, and the skeleton's hands were each holding a tennis ball. It was their way or telling me that Tarasov's demands were going to kill me! It may not have been the best joke, but I laughed along with the rest of the team. Mishakov was an expert at practical jokes. It wasn't a coincidence that the Red Army team became quieter when he left us.

Inspiration was always one of Tarasov's main motives, and his training procedures were based on solid principles developed over a long period of time. He had an excellent idea of what the perfect goaltender should look like. I once heard Anatoly himself telling a story about the perfect goaltender:

"The first time in my life that I met a world class goalkeeper was in 1948. He was a Czechoslovakian named Bogumil Modry. Not long before, Modry had been named the best goalkeeper at the World Championships in St. Moritz, Switzerland.

"At that time, our best Russian goalkeepers were not tall, and probably because of that there was a false impression that goalies had to be short. Modry presented a different picture.

He was a six-foot giant with hands like shovels. He amazed me. Every time I met him, I shook hands with him, just to see the size of those unbelievable hands.

"He appeared to be a friendly guy, and he spoke Russian fluently. Bogumil offered me technical advice without any hesitation, introducing me to his on-ice workout and his dry-land exercises. They were very interesting, but I repeat, the size of his body and his hands impressed me the most. 'What form of practice helped you to become such a great goalkeeper?' I asked. 'I play soccer, tennis, and, of course hockey,' smiled the kind Modry. 'What about weightlifting, or gymnastics?' I asked. 'No, I just play . . . .'

"Modry had developed his hockey skills simply by playing the game itself, and, combined with his natural talent, had made his way to the top. At that time you could develop naturally. But we Russians, we had to catch and surpass the Czechs, Swedes, and Canadians. There was no other task before us, so what did it mean to us? It meant that Modry's way was not for us. Time was not on our side.

"I studied with attention all of the remarkable goaltenders whom I met," continued Tarasov. "For example, Harry Mellups, the native of Riga, demonstrated to me his inner seriousness, his ability to critically analyze his own game. Grigory Mkrtchan distinguished himself by his constant aspiration to search for new methods, to experiment. Nikolai Puchkov was possessed with exceptional fearlessness and had very high self-esteem. He would clench his teeth and defy anyone to attempt to score on him. It was a pleasure to work with Viktor Konovalenko. He was the epitome of absolute tranquility. Konovalenko was always courageous, reliable, and respectful of his rivals. I don't ever remember him complaining of unfairness. After letting the puck into the net, he would only say, 'Outwitted, outwitted . . . .'

"Later I met Jacques Plante. The legendary Canadian goaltender proved that the efficiency of the goalkeeper could be higher if he chose not to play close to his net, but to cover a large area. I remember in 1967, the National Team of the USSR played a game with the Montreal Canadiens Juniors. On four occasions our forwards went one on one with the Montreal goaltender, and those were great forwards. Alexandrov, Krutov, Almetov, Mayorov! But all their best attempts went for nothing, because standing in the net for the Juniors was Plante. Because of him we lost 2-1. Four times – one on one! We became believers in Plante. He won our entire team over. After the game the Juniors carried him away on their shoulders.

"I studied Plante and noticed that he was using a technique of recoil. He would skate far away from his net to meet the puck carrier, thus decreasing the angle of the shot, and then would recoil back to his net as the player approached. Aha, I thought, we can use this technique. I was also stunned by his faultless ability to study his rivals. His intelligence was obvious. He knew how to play each forward that he faced from our team."

Anatoly continued his story. "Gradually in my consciousness, I was developing a concept of the ideal goalkeeper. I moulded it slowly, avoiding borrowing automatically the traits of other outstanding goalkeepers. I tried to study and improve every aspect of the game, critically looking at the old established teachings of goalkeeping school, and questioning them.

"I thought more about Jacques Plante. His method of skating out to meet the opponent was undoubtedly a formidable weapon. But what would happen if, tomorrow, the rival became a little more innovative himself? What if he chose not to shoot the puck, but to pass it to a teammate in a better position? Would Plante be caught flat-footed? I came to the conclusion that it was necessary to make the goalie more maneuverable, and ready for all surprises. He would have to be an acrobat! He would have to have the ability to skate in the open ice along with our forwards!

"Although Modry was a good goaltender, God be my witness, the Czechoslovakian player was neglecting his athletic training for no good reason. Craftsmanship will shine in its fullest only when it has a strong base. Speed, endurance, strength, and dexterity are needed in every hockey player, but the goalkeeper has to develop these qualities in a different way than the forwards. He must do so in relation to the specifications of his position."

Tarasov concluded, "I decided that it was absolutely necessary to upgrade the overall level of play of our goalkeepers in order for them to gain more respect on our team. It became important for them to develop a high sense of intelligence and the ability to analyze our rivals quickly. The goalkeeper had to become a major figure on the team. Just as I was coming to all these conclusions, I saw a tall boy by the name of Vladislav Tretiak. I liked his outward appearance; I immediately recalled Bogumil Modry. They looked alike, with the same mighty stature, the same huge hands. Tretiak was the person I was looking for. I started to work with him immediately. It was like he had been sent to me."

Once, Anatoly puzzled me with two questions: "What is the speed of the puck when shot, for example, by Firsov?" "A hundred kilometers per hour? I am not sure," I answered. "A hundred and twenty," Tarasov corrected me. "And do you know," he said, "that it is not humanly possible to react to a puck flying with such speed when shot from near the net? Even if you practise very hard it is impossible! Yet Jacques Plante catches pucks like that, and so does Konovalenko. The answer is not in their reaction abilities." "Perhaps it is their experience," I guessed, still not knowing what Anatoly was getting at. "Experience – that's too general. Think!" said my coach. Frankly, I was confused. What was going on? Why should one bother to perfect his reaction skills if they wouldn't be successful against the best forwards anyhow? I thought. It seemed like the goalkeeper was doomed, practice or no practice. Tarasov was enjoying my state of confusion. "The only thing that will help you to get your mind out of the vicious circle it's in is your intelligence! You are going to have to learn to read people's minds. Yes, yes! Before your opponent shoots the puck, you are going to have to learn where it's going!

"You have to know beforehand how the game will develop, who the forward will pass to, when there will be a shot at the net. You have to know everything about forwards! Everything about defensemen! Everything about hockey! More than any other hockey player!" said Tarasov.

I hope that you can see what Anatoly was getting at. If it sometimes appeared that the pucks were merely flying into my trapper, it was actually because I anticipated the shooter. I developed and used for many years that same feeling which Tarasov was talking about at the beginning of my career. When a forward started to shoot, my left hand was already moving spontaneously to intercept the puck.

Before my time, as far as I know, when teammates discussed the strategy of the game or when the coach gave directions, the goaltenders didn't participate. Nobody asked their opinion, and no one would have cared if they offered it. Tarasov changed this philosophy. Early in my career with the Red Army team, I started to participate actively in all the affairs of the team. When Anatoly Tarasov invited each line to talk with him before the game, I was present at every meeting. I listened to my teammates with attention and wasn't shy about speaking out. The players didn't hesitate to ask my opinion. Sometimes the forwards, having invented a new on-ice tactic to use, would ask, "What do you think – will it work?" "Yes, it's good," I would answer, "no goaltender would be able to defend against that." Or, conversely, I sometimes criticized the idea. I enjoyed having the glorified oldtimers, to whom I was like a son, listen respectfully to their boy-goaltender. This attitude of togetherness clearly shows the spirit of our team.

I was growing up, avidly absorbing not only hockey wisdom, but more importantly, perceiving the essence of such things as team work, responsibility, and courage. From the very beginning my coach trained me to think creatively of my role as a goaltender. He wanted me to put my mind to work first, and then my arms and legs. In the evenings at our base in Arkhangelskoye, Anatoly often invited me to his room.

"Come, sit down," Tarasov would say. "Don't you think, Vladik, that you have started to let pucks into your net more often than you're supposed to? Let's think about what's happening." And we would sit down and talk. The next morning at practice, Anatoly wouldn't forget to ask me, "Did you think up any new exercises? What are they? Show me."

In August of 1969 I went to Sweden for the first time with the Red Army team. We participated in several exhibition games, then Anatoly took me to a little town named Vesteros, where the Swedes had a goaltending camp. We practiced from early in the morning to late in the evening. I wanted to prove that I was equal to the other talents there, but frankly speaking it was a little bit hard to vie with them. For example, William Holmquist could run twice as fast as I could. I watched with great interest their exercises and on-ice drills and tried to remember all of them.

As a result of my attending that camp, the Swedes now say jokingly that it was they who gave me a ticket to the big time. Of course they are exaggerating about the ticket, but I really did bring back some good fundamental drills from Scandinavia, and my first successes in the international arena were related to having been at that goaltenders' school.

While I was at that camp I received a T-shirt, given to me as a gift by the Swedish star Holmquist. I considered that T-shirt to be lucky for me and I wore it until there were more holes than T-shirt. My mother got tired of fixing it all the time, but I couldn't throw it away. Eventually I had to throw it out, but of course the experience that I gained from training with the best Swedish goaltender stayed with me forever.

When we returned to Moscow, our team played in a Soviet sports tournament sponsored by a large newspaper. In the first game, we played the Traktor Team. We played well and won 3-2. In the next game we played the Champions of the country, Spartak. I was sure that our starting goalie would be Nikolai Tolstikov. But a couple of hours before the game started Tarasov announced, "Tretiak will play." My knees started to shake. My teammates, noticing my nervousness, tried to calm me down. I was quick to notice, however, that they weren't so calm themselves about having a boy play goal for them in such an important game.

The game started with Spartak storming to the offence. Luck was with me, and all of their shots were aimed directly at me. Spectators applauded and cheered loudly every time I deflected even the weakest shot. They were obviously sympathetic to the young boy who was defending the Red Army's net. We won 5-0 and I had been the luckiest person on earth.

Following that game there were very hard practices and then more games. I tried to prove to everyone possible that my success in the game with Spartak wasn't an accident – that I was a real goalie! It wasn't an easy thing to prove. Many people were surprised by my age. There had never been a seventeen-year-old goalie in international hockey.

Before the beginning of the traditional Izvestia tournament in Moscow, a tournament that gathers the best amateur national teams in the world, Tarasov recommended to the council of coaches of the Soviet Hockey Federation that they include me on the National Team. Anatoly didn't get much support. Tretiak is too young, they thought. Can you rely on such a youngster? But Tarasov insisted, and when he insisted, they listened.

Thus, I ended up on the National team in the fall of 1969. I have in my possession a very valuable newspaper clipping of an interview with Tarasov:

"What did you like in the young goaltender?" the reporter asked.

"First of all," replied Tarasov, "his diligence and fanatical loyalty to hockey. His ability to work hard. His strong intelligence. Vladik can analyze his actions, and make the right conclusions."

"What is the difference in Tretiak's style, as compared to other goaltenders?"

"Tactics. Vladislav maneuvers boldly in all directions. All his actions are thought out in advance."

"Could he really become an outstanding goalkeeper?"

"Right now, everyone is counting on him. But the boy is just seventeen years old. He has to grow up a bit. Then Vladik will be able to solve all his minor problems, and manage his success. Personally, I think he can do it. I believe in Tretiak."

Of course I was very lucky that Tarasov had noticed me as a boy, that he had started to teach me, and that he had patiently made me a goaltender, day by day.

"Always learn – every hour, every minute; be hard on yourself; don't deceive yourself with your success; find the root of your failures. March forward step by step!" Since then these words of Anatoly Tarasov have served as the personal rule for all of my activities in life.

3

EARLY THOUGHTS ON COURAGE

Until my very last game, I never considered my hockey education complete. There is no end to perfection, and I tried to learn a lesson from each day of my life.

Reporters have a rule of thumb: Don't write until you are surprised. What this means is that whatever it is you are going to tell the reader, it must touch your heart first. Only then will your pen write something worthwhile. This is probably a very good rule. But what it brings to my mind is this – the first step in educating yourself is to be amazed by outstanding people and their deeds. Certainly, I was lucky to meet such people. I was probably luckier than anyone else has ever been. I was taught by wonderful teachers to handle a hockey stick and a trapper, and to keep cool.

In my sports club I grew up among legendary aces of Soviet hockey. If I had to count all of my mentors, I would have to name almost all staff of the Red Army Club at the end of the

'60s. I was never ashamed to borrow all the best I saw in others. Experienced hockey players generously shared their knowledge and secrets of their craft with me. They didn't look down on me. Jacques Plante told me once that throughout his career he had to learn from his own mistakes; there was nobody to help him. In my case I consider myself lucky. I was always surrounded with good people.

My first mentor on the Soviet National Team was the terrific athlete Viktor Konovalenko. Now picture this situation. As the starting goaltender of the National Team of the USSR during the sixties, Konovalenko had been a World Champion seven times, and twice an Olympic Champion. He was in his thirties and very highly respected. All of a sudden Viktor was told that his backup would be a clumsy, puny, seventeen-year-old boy with a long chicken neck. What was a glorified veteran supposed to do in this situation? How should he react to his new partner? At our first meeting, Konovalenko looked me up and down, shook my hand as if we were equals, and said, "Keep it up, keep it up." As I remember, those were his only words at the time – nothing to wonder at. Viktor was a very quiet man. His modesty was legendary. He never asked for anything or complained. He always tried to be invisible.

From our first meeting, Konovalenko patiently began revealing the secrets of the art of being a goaltender. The famous oldtimer was thoughtfully preparing a beardless boy to stand on his own feet. He hurried to give me everything he knew, everything he had gained during his legendary career. That knowledge proved to be very valuable to me.

But Viktor Konovalenko's own fate had not been so fair. To help his family, he went to work at fourteen in a Gorky automotive plant. He played soccer on a junior team named Torpedo, then he tried out for a hockey team at the plant and became a goaltender. Although he was later taught by famous coaches, he had to learn everything on his own, especially at the beginning. He had his ups and downs. There were times when nobody believed in him anymore, but nothing could break that goaltender's spirit.

Well-built, thick-set and clumsy-looking, Viktor changed instantly when he took his place in the net. Apathy gave way to lightning reaction speed. He had a wonderful intuition. And he never lost his coolness – that was the most important thing. It was only because of pitiful misunderstandings that he never became the all-star goaltender in the World Championships. No goaltender in amateur hockey had as many titles as he had at that time.

I don't remember anybody more respected on our team than Konovalenko. He was respected for his loyalty to his club Torpedo (Viktor played there all his life, despite invitations from different Moscow teams). He was respected for fairness and his devotion to hockey, for his courage, and for his strength. He brilliantly continued the work of his predecessors – such great Soviet goalkeepers as Nikolai Puchkov, Grigory Mkrtchan, and others.

In 1970 I participated for the first time in the Senior World Championship, which took place in Stockholm. The starting goaltender was Viktor Konovalenko. He played wonderfully. In my opinion, Viktor should have been named best goaltender. I especially remember one episode from the game with the Swedes. We were losing 2-1 in the second period. A Swedish hockey player was heading towards our goal, but he pushed the puck too far out in front of him. Viktor desperately dove to knock it out. The Swede, unable to stop, continued to rush forward. His skate crashed into Konovalenko's face, and the goalie was taken to the hospital. I went into the net and let in two very easy goals. I was probably worrying too much. We lost the game 4-2.

The next day all the newspapers announced that the injured Russian goaltender would have to forget about hockey for a long time: "There were fourteen x-rays taken. They show that the bridge of Konovalenko's nose is seriously damaged. Besides that, he has heavy head injuries. One of the best players of the USSR National Team is bedridden."

As people were digesting all this information, Viktor was already on the ice practising. In the evening, the Soviet team took the ice for the next game against the Finns; Konovalenko took his usual place in the net, and played the first two periods. By the time I replaced him in the third period, I believe the score was already 10-0 for us. There was no end to the amazement of the Swedes. Early the next day, newspapers notified everybody that the personnel of the hospital had been astounded by the courage of the Russian goalie.

Our fate in the Championship of 1970 depended on the results of our second game with the Swedes. If we won, we would be World Champions. If we lost, we would have third place only. Viewers were bursting with applause when Viktor Konovalenko, cool and slow as usual, stepped onto the ice. Of course, we won that game. We were met by hundreds of people at Moscow's airport; relatives, friends, hockey fans, and reporters.

I was approached by a radio reporter, who said, "Tell me, what did you feel when you became a world champion?" "I never felt so happy in my life," I replied. "What lessons did you learn in Stockholm?" asked the reporter. "Lessons? Thanks to Viktor Konovalenko," I answered, "I now know what courage is."

Real courage. In this book, I'll be using these words often, because we are talking about hockey. Also determination and strength. These qualities have always attracted me, and always will attract me. They are necessities for a goaltender. Without them no goaltender, no matter how talented he is, can do anything. I often think about the nature of courage, and about examples of this wonderful virtue of the human spirit. I can not forget those examples – I witnessed many of them myself.

"Only real men play hockey." These are the words from a popular song that appropriately became the anthem of ice arenas. Yes, only very brave and courageous men can play the hockey that you watch on the screens of your TV sets. To lay down in front of a puck that is flying with the speed of a bullet and block it's way to the net; to collide with your rival on the boards; to fight a violent power play; to disregard any traumas or injuries; to be in the center of a play and not lose your head – all of this takes tremendous courage. I've never met hockey players who were cowards. But, of the kind who could be examples of courage, I know many.

Alexander Ragulin was a World Champion ten times. He was the most reliable defenseman in world amateur hockey. Goaltenders were safe behind his mighty back! I recall a time, at the beginning of my sports career, when we were playing a hockey team from Leningrad. It was an ordinary game, there was nothing special in it for us, and I believe we were leading 7-1 anyway. One of the Leningrad players suddenly got into a good position, and forcefully shot the puck at my net. The situation was such that only Ragulin could save us from a goal, protecting the net from the flying puck by himself. And he did so without hesitation, despite the fact that the puck almost hit him in the face.

After the game I went up to him and asked, "Why did you do that? We were winning anyway." "I didn't think about whether we were winning or losing at the time. It was important to cover the net," answered Ragulin. "But you could have been injured," I protested. "You know, Vladik," he interrupted me, "if you think all the time about when you have to be brave, nothing useful will develop of you. You have to be brave all the time! If you avoid the puck once or twice, you could lose all your courage.''

Our army coaches especially liked to show off Evgeny Mishakov as an example to young athletes. This hockey player was amazingly selfless and brave. It seemed as though he didn't feel any pain at all, as though he was made of steel. He had had very complicated surgery on his knee, after which most people can't walk for months. But Mishakov started to practice only two weeks after the surgery.

On our National team we had another such 'Iron Man'. It was Valery Vasilyev of Dynamo. In 1976 in Katowice, Poland, his little finger was shattered during the game. ''Go to the locker room quickly,'' ordered Kulagin. ''See the doctor.''

''No, I can play,'' replied Valery stubbornly, and he remained on the ice. It was a difficult moment. The championship wasn't going so well for us, and Vasilyev understood that his teammates needed him. In the locker room after the game, we gasped when he took off his glove – it was almost full of blood.

Valery Kharlamov was in a car accident for the first time in 1976. He survived, but, my God, just barely! There was no way he could ever play hockey again. But, when we were visiting him at the hospital, he repeated over and over again, ''On ice, as soon as possible, on ice.'' And we trusted him more than we trusted all the doctors.

As soon as he could stand on his feet, Valery came to practice. Limping and grimacing with pain, he put on his skates. And do you know what happened? Within the first minute, I believe, Lyosha Volchenkov inadvertently shot the puck directly into the unhealed wound on Valery's leg. There is probably no pain like that which Kharlamov felt. He was carried off the ice. ''That's it,'' we thought with sorrow, ''he won't be back for a long time.'' But the next day

Valery took his hockey stick and went out on the ice.

He suffered from his injuries for years after that. He limped a little bit, he was in constant pain, but nobody ever heard him complain. And he was always in the middle of all offense.

I am convinced that real courage has a very solid base. A rat will never show courage. Pugnacity, yes; dashing behaviour, probably; recklessness, maybe; but we are talking about real things. We are talking about displays of courage for the sake of others; about bravery in the name of an important and noble achievement.

Determination, courage, and strength are, for me, inseparably linked with such notions as patriotism, loyalty to traditions, honor of the flag, selflessness, and respect for the rival. But there are contradictions to this. What about the Canadian professionals? They are brave fellows too, but there is no selflessness or respect for the rival on their part. What can I say? It's true that they are brave. I've heard that Bobby Baun scored a decisive goal in the Stanley Cup finals of 1964, playing with a broken leg. I would say that the difference in their bravery is the price. They are professionals. They work and even accomplish heroic deeds for the sake of money. There is a price tag on everything in their world, even on courage.

Several years ago, I received a letter from a boy who asked me to advise him on how he could transform himself from a coward to a brave man. The boy explained in his letter that other boys his age didn't want to be friends with him, and girls teased him because he was timid, and had been born that way. Yes, that's exactly what he wrote, "I was born a coward, and it's probably incurable." There was something else in his letter about a rabbit who will never be a lion. In a few words, that letter breathed with endless sadness and melancholy. But I smiled when I read it, remembering myself on that sixteen-foot diving tower, my fear and my embarassment. There is no such thing as being born a coward. I told that boy that he would eventually gain victory over his own fear and timidity, and he would look on the world from a different point of view. "You have to start at one point, "I wrote, "and it's better not to leave it until tomorrow."

By the way, I did dive from that sixteen-foot tower.

In the end, it's the man alone who makes himself a hero or a grey mouse, a brave man or a coward. But even the bravest man must have the strength to back up his courage. Otherwise, his bravery will only get him into trouble.

A friend of mine, Ruslan Aushev, who is a Hero of the Soviet Union, received his Golden Star at the age of twenty-seven for performing his international duty. He told us how difficult it was in the Afghanistan mountains, where you have to depend not on the power of military equipment, but mainly on the endurance, hardiness, and strength of the people, and their ability to overcome any adversity. Ruslan told us astounding things. Once his battalion walked through the winter mountains for more than a week, making roundabout maneuvers. The soldiers, in snow above their waists, crawled over the cliffs, carrying their arms, ammunition, and food rations – a load of sixty to eighty pounds.

I met Ruslan while he was studying at the Frunze Military Academy. He visited us several times at our training camp, telling us about Afghanistan and his army comrades. I saw him later among the viewers at the Palace of Sport in Luzhniki, where naturally, he cheered for the Army Team. Three times a week, Ruslan practised combat for a few hours, ran cross-country races, and played soccer. He was in such good physical shape that many athletes would envy him. In 1985 I found out that Ruslan was once again in Afghanistan. He graduated from the Academy with the highest marks and asked to be sent back to his battalion. As an honors student and Bearer of the Order, he could have asked to be sent anywhere, but Major Aushev was convinced that he was a soldier and a protector. He was needed there, where it was the most difficult and dangerous.

Courage isn't always marked by rewards and decoration. In the Winter Olympic Games of 1976 in Innsbruck, our fifty-kilometer skiers didn't get any medals. But I would have given a medal for courage and daring to the skier who took twelfth place, the leader of our National team, Vasily Rochev.

He started out very well. Not intimidated by Olympic Champions, Rochev took the lead at once. He wasn't gliding, but flying through the snowfall and wind. After fifteen kilometers, Vasily had the best time. After forty kilometers, he was still in the leading group. The victory seemed to be close. The finish was near. But too much strength had been given to the fight. The marathon is not only a test of craftsmanship, but also of experience, and that was what our skier lacked. He had probably estimated his strength incorrectly. Not far from the finish, Rochev was about to lose consciousness. Spectators watched as the skier in the white outfit, overcome by his weariness, staggered and fell, then stubbornly continued his race. People on the sidelines stood from their seats, trying somehow to help Rochev, to support him, but what could they have done? The regulations of competition forbid anyone from helping the participants. There were hundreds of people around him, but he fought for the victory alone.

All his strength had been left on the ski course. He couldn't see anything, he strained every nerve. Staggering, no longer pushing with his ski poles, but rather supporting himself with them, Rochev slowly finished. He could have stepped aside, as sixteen other sportsmen had done that day, but he preferred to cross the finish line. Defying pain and exhaustion, he finished the competition. He didn't finish on his skis, he finished on his character.

Our team doctor, Boris Sapronenkov, was working with skiers at that time. He told me that he had never seen a man so exhausted. Doctors had to spend several hours trying to help the skier to regain consciousness. Rochev won a grand victory that day, but he received no reward except the applause of several hundred people.

Our coaches always had their own exercises for cultivating strong will in the players. Again I recall Anatoly Tarasov, who included boxing, wrestling, and jumping from high walls in our exercises. Anyone who showed even the smallest weakness was in deep trouble.

In 1971 in Switzerland, after the skating warm-up, Tarasov left Shadrin, Zimin, and myself on the ice. He said to the forwards, "One of you will shoot at Tretiak's net, while at the same time the other one will push the goalie, hit him, and try to prevent him from catching the puck. Is that clear?" The guys looked confused. "How can we possibly hit Vladik?" "What is it, my friends?" screamed Tarasov. "Don't be sissies!" Oh, what fell on my lot that day.

I was young then, and inexperienced. After every practice I left the ice-covered with bruises and scratches. It often happened that somebody would shoot the puck directly at me, and I would wave my stick in resentment, "Do you want to kill me?" But there was Tarasov. "Oh, so it hurts, young man? You should play with dolls, not hockey." Then he would soften a little. "Remember, you must not feel pain. Forget the word 'hurts'. Be happy to practise. Be H-A-P-P-Y!" Afterwards, I recalled these lessons with gratitude.

There is still a story on the National Team which qualifies as a legend. It is about how Anatoly Tarasov taught his hockey players to be brave. Once, after a long and exhausting practice, he suddenly announced, "We are finished on the ice. Let's run to the swimming pool." The swimming pool was twenty meters from the Palace of Sports. We ran there, changed, and were waiting to see what would happen next. Tarasov pointed to Boris Mayorov. "Following the famous captain of the team, everybody on the sixteen-foot diving tower! Go! And from there, head-first dives! Go, Boris!" Mayorov stood up and went hesitatingly to the tower, but Sologubov whispered to him, "Ask Tarasov to show us first."

Boris said to Tarasov, "But Anatoly, we don't know how to dive head-first. Can you show us?" Everybody was sitting on the bench, watching with interest. Our coach, who later told us that he had never dived in his life and was afraid of heights, went onto the diving board. It was a lucky coincidence that on his way up he met a real diver who told him, "Don't repel yourself off the board, just fall down head-first into the water."

Tarasov stood bravely on the edge of the diving board for a second, then jumped. Of course, he did a belly flop. But, following him, everybody dove, and not only once. Even one hockey player who couldn't swim climbed the tower. We tried to talk him out of it, telling him that it was not necessary for him to jump, but he didn't want the coach to think that he was a coward. The whole team fished him out afterwards.

There is also a story about how our mentors taught defensemen to block the puck. Coaches would put the player into the net, in full hockey gear, but without a stick. They would then shoot at him from the blue line. The defenseman was supposed to deflect the puck with his own body. Everybody went through it. And that is why Ragulin, Davidov, Romishevsky, Kuzkin, Brezhnev, and Zaytsev were able to deflect the puck by themselves so fearlessly.

Hockey is a tough occupation in itself, and if you've got a badly-behaved rival, you have to stand up for yourself. There is a rule of thumb among goalies: Whatever is going on on the ice, stay in the net and don't interfere. Both teams can fight on the ice, but it seems that goaltenders rarely get involved. They watch from far away and hold back their feelings. I always tried to follow that rule. I am not a fighter by nature.

A long time ago, in 1971, we played a series of exhibition games overseas with an amateur national team from the USA. The Americans happened to be pugnacious. Nearly every play, they got into a fight, starting brawls and fist fights. Once, when there were three of our players and four rivals left on the ice, they started another brawl. The referees were too hesitant. I saw that things were getting bad, and that our players could get hurt. That time, I regret, I couldn't stand it anymore, and I defended my comrades. The initiator of the fight and captain of the American team, Christiansen, will probably remember that game for a long time. I believe I struck out of him the will to ever swing his fists again. Of course, this was an extraordinary case. I can't recall anything like that happening again. And that's good.

The ability to overcome pain and fear is a necessity for everyone, not just for hockey players and athletes. Life checks us for strength at every step. By the way, Soviet hockey players may feel better than our other athletes in hard times. And do you know why? We are helped by the glorified past of Soviet hockey. It's like a rich, very well-fertilized soil for the roots of a mighty tree. When you remember the brilliant victories of your predecessors, when you are brought up on heroic traditions, then your strength and courage double in your efforts.

4

GOOD-BYE JUNIORS,
HELLO NATIONAL TEAM

"Falling down and getting up." I can't say that I was 'falling down and getting up' very often when I became a member of the Red Army Club. Reliable friends carefully watched over me, supported me, shared their experiences with me and cheered me up during difficult times. To the veterans I became somewhat like a son. They taught me lessons of kindness, friendship, and cooperation. I can flatly assert that there isn't any other team like ours in the whole world. I don't only mean the collection of trophies and decorations, won by the players of the Red Army Club, that could fill an entire museum, but also the demanding but surprisingly benevolent and creative atmosphere that always reigned over the club.

Special care of a young goaltender was taken on by a gloomy-looking but soft-natured man, Vladimir Brezshert. "Don't upset Vladik," he would say to the other players, "or else you will have to deal with me." Naturally, no one even thought of upsetting me, it was just that Brezshert liked being the guardian of a green rookie. "How's it going, son?" he asked me every day. "Did you do your homework?" And I would reply, "Everything is OK, Uncle Volodia."

Upon the recommendation of Igor Romishevsky, our Communist Youth League organizer, I was included in the Komsomol Buro, the Communist Youth League branch of our team. Immediately it made me brace up and become more mature and responsible.

In 1969 I completed high school. Romishevsky asked: "And now what? Are you thinking of continuing your education or not?" "I would like to," I replied, but I don't think I sounded too confident, because our Komsomol organizer immediately began upbraiding me. "You will never become a great hockey player unless you constantly expand your horizons," he said energetically. "If you remain within your intellectual boundaries, your range of interests will narrow down to the size of a hockey puck. Then, as a result, your sports talents will also stop growing. Keep this in mind: Everyone in the Central Army Sports Club is attending either university or a technical college." "Yes, I know," I said, "I do want to study, but I am not sure if I can handle both hockey and the Institute." "Not to worry," he reassured me, "we'll be right beside you. We'll help."

That fall I successfully completed entrance exams at the correspondence faculty of the Institute of Physical Education. Of course it wasn't easy to study. After practice, so tired that I could not even hold a book in my hands, I would force myself, with the help of coffee and cold showers, to get back to my studies. Homework, homework, and more homework. Five years later, I successfully completed the course.

Igor Romishevsky had been right when he talked of how it is impossible to be great in sports without an intellect; without deep, versatile knowledge. Romishevsky, by the way, completed his hockey career in our club, then wrote his master's thesis and was the head of the faculty. Another well-known hockey player, Viacheslav Starshinov, wrote his thesis in Pedagogics. Vladimir Ursonov, one of the coaches and a former member of the Russian National Team, had successfully completed his courses at the Faculty of Journalism at the Moscow University, as well as his degree from the Institute of Physical Education. These are just a few of many such examples.

Watching my older teammates everyday, I tried to copy their obvious love of hockey, their habit of working very hard. Just being there in the same dressing room with the older masters of the Central Army Sports Club was rewarding enough. I felt a festive sensation – something emotional, something big. Sometimes I woke up in the middle of the night with the thought that I could not wait until morning to get back to the team and its festive atmosphere. This feeling was with me for a long time.

In my attitude towards practices, I modelled myself after the great hockey star Anatoly Firsov. No one worked harder than he did. He was built of resilient muscles, and his rage was irrepressible during the game. As soon as he stepped on the ice, the audience would begin to roar in anticipation of a goal. Goalies dreaded the Firsov slapshot. He shot the puck with such force and speed that it was practically impossible to follow it.

We especially appreciated Anatoly for his ability to lead the team during difficult times; to unite it. He was a captain of the Red Army Club, and the playing coach. It's a shame that he never got a chance to play against the Canadian professionals. It would have been a breathtaking duel – Firsov vs. Esposito.

In my opinion, Anatoly should have been included on the 1972 USSR National team. He was superb. At the beginning of the year he became an Olympic Champion for the third time, but unfortunately due to other circumstances he wasn't able to go across the ocean.

Anatoly began his career in sports as a field hockey player on the team sponsored by the Red Giant plant. He was twelve at the time. Later he played for the Moscow Spartak, and in 1961 he became a member of the Red Army Club. While under the supervision of Anatoly Tarasov, he developed his spectacular talents. This is how Tarasov himself referred to the talents of this great forward of the sixties: "In his play, Anatoly's speed astonishes me. First of all, the quickness of his thinking is such that it sometimes seems that his play consists of continuous bright thought. When he suddenly finds himself in a difficult situation, he comes up with the most unpredictable solutions. Second, I am amazed at how quickly he can react during the execution of a move or a pass, or in going around an opposing player. Third, he is one of the fastest skaters I have ever seen. Firsov's style of play combines quick thinking, lightning reactions, and fast skating."

He was the first player on our hockey club to master the 'skate-stick' trick. During the game, he was willing to play physically. It was not only his talent that was responsible for his success, it was also his fanaticism for hockey. It was from him that I most often heard the request for extra ice time to work out with his line during the practices. He even had a set of weights at home, and those weights never had a day off.

During the 1971 World Championships in Switzerland, Anatoly got a bad cold and was forced into bed with a temperature of thirty-nine degrees Celsius. Our team needed a win in the next match and Anatoly was able to convince a doctor that he was well enough to play. How could anyone play with such a temperature? Firsov did. He wasn't thinking of himself, he was thinking of the team.

Some who read this will doubt whether it is worth it to endanger one's health in the interest of success in sports. This is a tricky question, and there is no simple answer to it. But it was made absolutely clear to me that in any situation Firsov would do it again. He thought first of his teammates, and then of himself. He was a team person. He was ready to do anything for the sake of others. That is how it should be done, no question about it.

My Red Army teammates nicknamed me, 'Dzurilla', after the Czechoslovakian star goalie, Vlado Dzurilla. I suppose they did this because our first names were similar. I had nothing against it. It was even flattering that my teammates were putting me, indirectly, on the same level with a great goaltender.

The first goalie at the Red Army Club was then Nikolai Tolstikov. With great pleasure, the new goalie 'Dzurilla' carried not only his own but also Nikolai's stick. He taught me a lot but, in the long run, the pupil was an ingrate – he pushed the teacher off the top.

Even today I feel somewhat guilty towards Nikolai, towards Lapshenkov, towards Adonin; not willingly, I had blocked their way to the top. Psychologically, they had a hard time forcing themselves to work full thrust, knowing almost certainly that Tretiak would remain the top goalie. Objectively, though, it was their fault. I would not have got in anyone's way if all of a sudden someone started playing better that myself. Even after I became the first string goalie on the Central Red Army Sports Club, I kept on carrying Nikolai's stick. Nobody among us was a bit surprised. It is a habit for us to respect our elders.

In 1971, in Switzerland, my confirmation as being the first-string goaltender of the USSR National Team took place. I went to the preliminary game of the World Championships in Bern as number two, and two weeks later I left Geneva as number one.

I still remember the feeling of strength, freshness, and confidence that I had for the rest of that season. Everything went my way; during the national championships, during an unofficial international game, during the main tournaments, everywhere. That was quite a season.

At the end of December, 1970, I went overseas with the National team while the Junior team went to the European Championships in Geneva. The goalie of the Junior Team was Viktor Krivolapov. Unforeseen circumstances forced Viktor to return home, and the hockey officials decided that I was to replace him. On December 31st, I flew from North America back to Moscow. On January 1, I was on my way to Geneva, and the next day I stepped onto the ice.

I still remember the long, stunned faces of the Czechoslovakian Juniors when they saw me in the dining room. What a surprise! But, I though to myself, we've got the edge! Lebedev, Anisin, and Budonov were playing for the Junior Team then, and the coach was M. Epstuim.

I had already participated in the European Junior Championships three times. In 1967 we took second place, but after that we brought back nothing but the gold. The Geneva tournament was no exception.

Two and a half months later, it was the Alps again. Again, the familiar and comfortable rinks. The main goalie, as usual, was Viktor Konovalenko. But at that time, he was having problems with his game. Both matches with our main opponents, Czechoslovakia, were unsuccessful. The first game was a 3-3 tie, and in the second, the USSR National Team lost 5-2. I was entrusted to play against Finland, whom we defeated 10-1, and against the Germans, whom we defeated 12-2.

Finally the time of the deciding matches had come. Tarasov had notified me that I would play against the Americans. I wanted to play, but I couldn't. A few days before, I had caught a bad cold. My temperature was almost forty degrees. Playing sick in the goal is not always an act of heroism. I could easily have let the team down. Let one goal in, then another, and before you know it there is nothing anybody can do to fix it.

Did I ever get into trouble with the coach! "You should take care of your health, watch it carefully. This is your commitment as an athlete. Good health is an indispensable condition of your life." That, in a few words, was Tarasov's angry speech. Emotionally, I had experienced enough. I was afraid to raise my eyes.

At last we reached the decisive moment; the match with the Swedes. We had to win. If we did, we would be the champions. If we lost, the main prize would be on its way to Prague. By then I had almost recovered. The day before, Tarasov had told me, "You're playing tomorrow." I could not sleep for the whole night. It seemed that my soul was on the line. It was either then, or never. But what I dreaded most was the thought of letting down my comrades and not being able to fulfill the expectations of the coaches. I was not even nineteen yet.

Even if they did beat us, the Swedes could not have got higher than third place. They did not even come out to warm up before the game. Psychologically, however, they had the upper hand. They could play freely, without pressure. They did not have the weight of a tremendous responsibility on their shoulders.

Right away, we took a 2-0 lead, and I didn't have a lot of

work. But it seemed that our forwards had settled down rather early. The Swedes had no intention of giving up without a good fight. One after the other, two pucks went into my net, and a bit later, one more. What an outcome.

During the intermission in the dressing room, Tarasov berated us. Everyone got a piece of it, even the most famous veterans. I was the only person who was pardoned by the angry coach. He patted me on the shoulder and said, "It's all right, boy, everything is OK, just hold on." Then our assistant coach, Arkady Ivanovich Chernyishev, took over. Chernyishev never raised his voice. His well-balanced, wise, calm and confident manner of conducting himself had a calming influence on the team.

Nothing could spoil Chernishev's easy-going nature. Looking back, I remember one incident during the Olympics in Sapporo. One of the opposition players, probably looking to provoke us, threw the puck at Chernishev, who was standing by the bench. He did not even change his position. As before, he remained still, leaning on the boards. But our guys taught that player a good lesson.

Tarasov and Chernishev complemented one another perfectly. They were a sparkling union of wisdom, experience, temperament, teaching talents, and faithfulness to their job. The entire sports world had never known such a coaching duo, and probably never will again.

And so, that time in Geneva, Chernishev had found a few happy words, woke us up, and made us smile again. "You are strong, you little devils. There is no other team like you."

We won, six to three! For the ninth time in a row, the Soviet hockey players had become the Champions of the World. And another record was established in Geneva; for the ninth time, Alexander Ragulin, Viacheslav Starshinov, and

Vitaly Davidov were proclaimed the Champions.

"Well done, Vladislav," Tarasov shook my hand, "you're now the main goaltender of the USSR National team. And there is pleasant news from Moscow; the board of the Sport Committee has conferred on you the title of Honored Sport Master of the USSR."

My first Olympic tournament was in Sapporo, in 1972. That was the best Olympics – without the barbwire, high fences, tough regime, guards; everything that has since made its appearance due to the constant threat of terrorism. The Games in Sapporo went by without guard dogs, and were accompanied by an atmosphere of friendship and kindness. At first, though, there was some speculation that the 'White Olympics' would be white in name only. Until February, there had been no snow on Kuido, but just before the opening day the skies literally opened up. The snow fell for several days in a row but as soon as the Games were over, it warmed up drastically and started to rain. Within a few hours all the snow had melted, as if it was never there.

My backup during the Olympic series was thirty-year-old Viktor Zinger from the Spartak team. Shortly before the Games he was injured during a practice and sent to hospital. The coaches' committee appointed a second goalie, twenty-seven-year-old Alexander Pushkov from the Dynamo team.

What was most memorable in Sapporo? The match with the Swedes, which ended in a 3-3 tie, was the only one that had cost us a point. Before the hockey tournament, the newly appointed Swedish coach, an ex-professional named Billy Harris, had self-confidently promised to make the Swedes the champions. After the tie, many thought that Harris might keep his word after all. But the Swedes' hopes did not last too long. They lost to Czechoslovakia and to Finland.

Then the rough boys from the USA made the headlines.

They beat the Czechs by a score of 11-5. Following that game, journalists wrote about the Americans' 'goon' tactics, and warned that even the Russians should be aware of their sharp teeth. "Beware, they bite" was the headline of an article in one of the local newspapers. But they overestimated the American resources. Without any special effort, we beat them 5-2.

That also happened to be the score of our last game at the Olympics, against the Czechoslovakian team. Early on, Dzurilla made three mistakes (very nearly a record for him) and we took a 3-0 lead. In the third period our opponents tried drastically to change the momentum. They did not succeed.

Shoulder to shoulder, Alexei Ragulin, Anatoly Firsov, Alexander Yakushev, and other members of the team that had captured the Olympic Gold for the third time, came out onto the ice to receive their medals. I had managed to become the most successful goaltender in Sapporo.

I was once asked, "How is it that you're so successful, and yet you're such an easy going fellow, always smiling, always kind? Where do you get all this?" It was all the outcome of Tarasov's school. I wondered why people put me in a pedestal. Did they think that fame and decorations give me the right to be arrogant, or to consider myself special in any way? No, fame has obliged me to think twice before making a decision, before saying a word. Fame is like a magnifying glass that allows other people to examine you from head to toe. Always be ready.

Sometimes I look with sadness on the following scene: A well-known athlete is walking towards his bus after a game. Boys overcome their fears, begging him, "Could you please give me your autograph?" But our athlete, barely acknowledging them, says through his teeth, "Leave me alone." This is absurd! Who is he playing for? For these kids. With sports, we help to bring them up. They see champions as their idols, and they want to be just like us. And that player says, "Leave me alone." For those kids, it is a catastrophe. What are they going to believe in? In whom? Unfortunately, there are such athletes.

I believe that it is our duty as athletes and public figures to be friendly and open with our fans, and not to lose our good humor, even in the most trying situations.

5

"SHATTERED MYTH" –
The '72 Canada-USSR Series

1972 was a special year for hockey fans worldwide. It was significant because, after long negotiations, doubts, and arguments, the strongest amateur hockey players in the world faced off against the best professionals in the world. Without any exaggeration, 1972 ushered in a new era in the history of international hockey. Those days in the fall of 1972 were the most memorable of my life. Montreal, September 2, 1972 to be exact. I still get goosebumps whenever I think about it.

Soviet hockey players first played against professionals back in 1954 at the World Championships in Stockholm, where the Canadian team used two former professional players from the Boston Bruins, Zungel and Shill. The Soviet National Team beat Canada 7-2. From 1955 to 1958 our teams played in Great Britain, France, Sweden, and Holland. Those European teams also had former Canadian professionals playing with them.

The Soviets had sixteen victories in that period. Against Canadian amateur teams the results were different. Prior to 1961 the amateurs representing the Land of the Maple Leaf were ahead in wins. Only at the Winter Olympics in 1956 did they lose to the Soviet National Team. After 1961, teams from the USSR, Czechoslovakia, and Sweden presented a more formidable opposition.

Until 1969, Canadian amateur teams had participated in almost every World Championship. However, they ignored that competition for many years afterwards. Why did they refuse to play in these important events? Perhaps because in 1969 the Canadian players were delivered a humiliating blow from which they couldn't quickly recover. At that time the Soviets, who were touring Canada, won ten out of ten games on the tour. In Ottawa, on January 24, 1969, the game ended 10-2 for the Soviets as Anatoly Firsov scored no less than six goals!

Long before the 1972 series, a lot of people tried to predict the outcome of a USSR-NHL matchup. They analyzed the game from every conceivable point of view. Nobody questioned who was stronger. The experts were merely trying to decide how much stronger the professionals were, and by how many goals they would beat the Soviets.

Personally, I know of two opposite predictions. The first came about in this way. In the summer of 1968, Vladimir Dvortsov, a hockey writer with TASS, asked six-time World Champion Boris Mayorov to play a hockey game between the Soviet team and the Canadian team on paper. Boris used a scale of one to five, one being unsatisfactory and five being excellent. Let me illustrate Boris Mayorov's rating system with the following table:

Area of Comparison	Soviets	Canadians
Physical Training	5	3
Puck Control	5	4
Passing	5	3
Number of players gaining the offensive zone before the opposition	4	3
Shooting	3	4
Physical Play	4	5
Goaltending	3	5
Defense	3 1/2	4
Skating	4	4
Individual Puck Handling	4	4
Playing Shorthanded	4	4
Offense	4	4
Game Strategy	5	5
TOTALS:	**53 1/2**	**52**

You will note the comparison of goaltending, where Canadians got the higher rating without question. Mayorov explained his comparison this way: "The overseas goalkeepers are phenomenal, they are truly magicians. Two of the best are Montreal Canadiens veteran Lorne "Gump" Worsley and his backup Rogatien Vachon."

The best prognosis came from former professional player Carl Brewer of Toronto. He told the Soviets in 1968 that if they played a series of matches in Canada they would win the first couple of games. Later the Canadians would win their share. Professionals in North America would not see any threat from the Soviet amateurs unless they were beaten, said Brewer. That meant they would not play to their potential at the beginning of the series. The dominant opinion of the hockey experts was that the Soviet amateurs would inevitably be crushed.

Before the series started, almost all Canadian newspapers reiterated their opinion that the weak spot on the Soviet team was the goaltender Tretiak. They had very good reasons for saying that. It just so happened that NHL scouts had come to Moscow in August, 1972 and attended an exhibition game between the Soviet National team and the Army Club. That day I played one of my worst games ever, letting in an extraordinary number of goals – nine.

Experts from Canada who were watching wrote in their notepads, "It seems that Tretiak is still too inexperienced to stand up to the NHL sharpshooters. He is not confident with his ability in tight situations. The goalkeeper is definitely the weakest link on the Soviet team." Those words later appeared in most Canadian newspapers.

In addition to that, the newspapers printed a number of other interesting items. It looked as if journalists from Canada and the United States had started a competition between themselves to see who could frighten the Soviet team the most. In one article someone claimed that the Canadian superstars were puncturing hockey boards with their shots. In another, a reporter promised to eat his newspaper if the Soviets scored even one goal. A popular Canadian sports writer wrote at the same time: "The greatest hockey team of Canada is ready. Everyone is certain the team will be absolutely dazzling. We should be preparing now to light candles for the Russian players' funeral."

I don't wish to judge such obvious self-assurance too harshly. Canadians had always considered their hockey players to be totally invincible – indeed, many generations grew up with this belief. No one in North America took us seriously. No one was interested in finding out what kind of hockey people were playing on the opposite side of the world. There was probably not one individual in all of Canada who would have had any doubt of a Canadian victory. And these views were not held only in Canada – almost all Soviet fans favoured the Canadians! In the Soviet Union they had heard so much about the many legends.

Ken Dryden, the Canadian goalkeeper, was the only professional player I had seen in action. He had been a backup goalie on the Canadian National Team in 1970. When we played them in Vancouver, Dryden let in nine goals.

On September 2, 1972, the day of the first game, we came to morning practice at the Forum. Our rivals were already on the ice. They were shooting pucks so fast that we thought there were bullets in the air. The speed of the Canadians was also incredible. It looked as if they were flying slightly above the ice. We still had some time before our practice, and were sitting quietly watching them. Everybody was thinking, "We're going to get it today." Seeing that we were nervous, our coach Vsevolod Bobrov said: "Come on you guys! They're just showing off in front of us. How dumb of them. We'll just have to beat them, won't we!" We woke up with his words.

Shortly before the beginning of the game, we had a visitor in our locker room. It was Jacques Plante, the famous 'Pucktamer', the best Canadian goalkeeper of all time. Plante came into our room with an interpreter and amazed us by sitting with me and explaining in detail how I should play against the likes of Mahovlich, Esposito, Cournoyer, and Henderson. "Be careful," said Plante, "when Frank Mahovlich is on the ice. He shoots on the goal from any distance and from any position. Come out of the net as far as possible. Keep in mind, Yvan Cournoyer is the fastest forward in the NHL, and Dennis Hull has scored from the red line. And remember, the most dangerous player on our team is Phil Esposito. This guy shoots the puck very quickly and can pick any corner of the net. Don't take your eyes off him when he is in the crease." To help me visualize it, Plante showed me everything on a blackboard. Then he said goodbye and left. I am still puzzled by what motivated him to do that. He probably felt sorry for me, the little guy, in whom Esposito was going to shoot holes. I don't know, but I will always be very grateful to Jacques Plante, whose suggestions helped me so much.

We took to the ice. I had warmed up as thoroughly as always. When we were introduced, our names were met with silence. When the announcer started to introduce the names of the Canadian players, the crowd began roaring with such enthusiasm that my knees started to tremble! I actually felt fear. But when I went to the net, it disappeared.

In his book *Face Off of the Century*, Gilles Therroux wrote, "When Tretiak let in the first goal after only thirty seconds, everybody started to yell, 'We'll eat them alive! What the hell are they doing here?'" Therroux was right. There was so much noise – I remember the crowd going crazy; people were roaring, laughing, whistling, yelling. Phil Esposito, who scored the goal, patronizingly tapped me on my shoulder and said "OK." It was a clear message: Take it easy, don't forget who you're playing against. "OK," I answered automatically.

The sirens were screaming, lights were flashing, the organist was playing "Moscow Night". I still wonder why we weren't confused. When Henderson scored their second goal after just six minutes, the crowd flew into a triumphant rage. The organist played a funeral march. Nevertheless, we had the last laugh that night, because shortly after that everything fell into place. We adapted our strategies to the situation and won handily, 7-3. It plunged our rivals into a state of shock. We truly felt sorry for them. Spectators cheered silently, their way of congratulating us for the victory. We had done it with speed, skill, and grace.

The next morning Valery Kharlamov was offered one million

dollars to play in the NHL. "I can't come and play without Petrov and Mikhailov," replied Kharlamov jokingly. The Canadians didn't understand his joke and consequently assured Valery that both Petrov and Mikhailov would also receive the same amount of money!

Also the next day, the Canadian journalist who had promised to eat his newspaper if Canada lost was getting ready to live up to his promise. He sat down on the steps in front of our hotel in Toronto, put a bowl of soup beside him, and asked me to place the newspaper in it. I didn't feel comfortable, so I refused to do it. He kept insisting. From nowhere, T.V. reporters appeared. I didn't want to participate in this questionable show, so I left. The journalist crumpled his article into a ball and started to mix it with his soup as I walked away.

Newspapers everywhere changed their attitude after our victory. Each tried to outdo the other in praising us and blaming their recent favorites. In writing about the game in his book, Therroux remarked; "Tretiak made several remarkable saves to prevent what should have been certain goals. Frank Mahovlich couldn't hide his frustration at this outstanding young goalkeeper. He told me, 'Every time I try to score, it's almost like Tretiak can foresee my every move in advance. It's like we have played against each other since childhood.'"

Incidently, I remember Frank Mahovlich very well. Later, in a game in Vancouver, when the Canadians were losing by three goals, I nearly started a fight with him. Our opponents were very frustrated at that point in the series. The puck was shot in my direction and Mahovlich tried to get it, but I was there first and shot it up ice. Mahovlich proceeded to knock me off my feet and then sit on me. There was no whistle, and the game continued. I tried to stand up with all my strength, but Mahovlich was a big man and I couldn't move him. I decided that when I finally could stand up, I was going to punch him.

But just then the Canadian crowd started to yell and whistle at Mahovlich, so he rolled off me and quickly skated away.

Almost overnight, nobody wrote anything more about the Soviet goalie who was the weakest link on the Soviet team. I was approached by one of the Canadian writers who had been present at the exhibition game between the Soviet National Team and the Army Club in Moscow. "Why did you let in nine goals that first day? Was it a ruse? Did you want to bewilder us?" "No," I answered laughingly, "it just happened that I was getting married the next morning and couldn't concentrate on the game." "Aha," answered my interrogator with astonishment, "it all makes sense to me now!"

In those days, the experts in professional hockey were extremely surprised that we didn't crumble, particularly at the hands of the Canadians' power play, which was a very important aspect of North American hockey. The previous summer, however, we had had special training during which our coaches invented a lot of different strategies to defend against the power play. They taught us not to be afraid of taking the body on someone, and we even took boxing lessons.

As the '72 Series progressed in Toronto, the Canadians won game two 4-1. In Winnipeg we tied 4-4, and in Vancouver we were again victorious, 5-3. I remember in Vancouver when the Canadian fans actually started to boo their home team. After the game, Phil Esposito was interviewed on television. I honestly felt sorry for him. Tired, sweating, and confused, his eyes deep in their sockets, he spoke angrily into the microphones: "We gave two hundred percent tonight, and you're not happy. We have never quit on anyone! Who could have imagined that the damn Russians would be so strong? We have been told all our lives that they are amateurs, but in reality any NHL club would sign any one of them to a contract today," said Esposito.

When we returned to Moscow we were happy; probably too happy. We still had four games to play and some players on our team were already convinced that we were stronger than the Canadians. They thought that since we won two games in Canada, we should be able to win all four at home. But it is well known that any overconfidence, even the smallest amount, is extremely dangerous in sports.

On September 13, one week before the first game in Moscow, the Canadians flew to Stockholm, Sweden to play two exhibition games against the Swedish National Team. These games were intended to get the Canadians adapted to the climate and the large ice surfaces. The Canadians won the first game 4-1, and in the second avoided defeat by only forty-seven seconds. The Swedish newspapers strongly criticized the visitors for dirty play. The Swedes were shocked that professionals would even fight during a period intermission – right at the entrance to the Swedish locker room. Boris Mayorov deliberately went to Stockholm to scout those games, and returned with the message, "The Canadians are coming to Moscow in a very angry mood."

We won the first game in Moscow by a score of 5-4. The next two games were characterized by unusually fierce and aggressive combat, and ended up in scores of 3-2 and 4-3 for the Canadians. Those games gave the Moscow spectators the opportunity to see first-hand the inside of professional hockey. The dirty tricks, punches, threats to the referees, and after-the-whistle hits were all tactics that the Canadians demonstrated without any trace of shame. Our fans, who were used to a different kind of competition, were literally shocked. Many of them demanded an immediate end to any further competition with the North American professionals.

The last game in Moscow was very dramatic. After the second period we led 5-3, and the outcome of the game appeared certain. But Esposito and Cournoyer managed to tie the score due to our sloppy play. Seven minutes remained in the game. If it ended in a tie, the difference of goals scored in the series, which was on our side, would allow us to be considered the victors in the entire series. Thinking back now, I believe that our players probably thought this way and changed their usual offensive style to a more defensive one. "Instead of the constant offensive play that never failed them, the Russians started to hold back," Canadian coach Harry Sinden wrote in his book *Hockey Showdown*. "This gave us more opportunities, and now, more than ever before, my players could taste victory. The Soviets were trying to play for the tie. We weren't! And, with only thirty-four seconds left, Paul Henderson put Canada ahead 6-5." I will always count that goal as the most maddening of all goals scored on me in hockey.

The Series ended, but the excitement that it stirred up wasn't going to settle down for a long, long time.

"The '72 Series was magnificent," was what the American Christian Science Monitor wrote, "and its final game was one of those rare moments in sports when all previous records, strategies, and boastful claims are discarded as the competitors play to their maximum abilities, and beyond, until the final siren. This is the highest level of competition in sports, and it demands a supreme effort from every player – extreme concentration and energy, backed by an unwavering determination. Canada, digging down deeper than ever before, broke the tie literally seconds before the end of the game. Victory was had for our side."

Despite losing the series, the Soviet National Hockey Team gained a tremendous amount of prestige in the '72 Canada-USSR Series. From the physical conditioning point of view, the Soviet players showed their superiority throughout. Their remarkable individual skills were obvious at every level of the game. The Soviets made an unforgettable impression on millions of television viewers around the world. The Canadians showed us commitment, intensity, and extreme pride. They would not be denied.

Most importantly, I believe that those games were conducive in bringing together the peoples of the USSR and North America. There would be more such games, and hockey fans around the world would be the true winners.

6

VLADISLAV TRETIAK VS.
BOBBY HULL

Two years later another series of meetings was held between us and the Canadian professionals, but this time it was against the World Hockey Association. After that series, the documentary film *Vladislav Tretiak vs. Bobby Hull* was released. The producers had not stressed my duel against Hull by accident. Bobby Hull was by far the greatest danger to us.

But let me get back to my story. We flew to Montreal, where we had to change flights for Quebec City. The airport was invaded by journalists. Questions were thrown at me from everywhere. "Do you do anything special to prepare for the professionals?" "Sure, the same things the professionals do to get ready to meet us." "What do you think of Bill Harris's team?" "I don't. We have absolutely no idea what this team looks like, or how strong it is." "What do you think the outcome of these games will be?" "Successful for Team USSR."

After I said that, I kept my eye on the Canadian reporters.

Two years ago this remark would probably have drawn sarcastic grins. But now their faces remained absolutely impassive, as if I had said something that was already known. Later in Quebec City, we read in Canadian papers that a great defeat was predicted for the professionals. Since even Team NHL couldn't handle the Russians, the papers suggested that Team WHA was out of their league.

From the Hilton Hotel, where we were staying, we went right to practice. What a sight. Our bus, surrounded by police officers riding powerful Harleys, moved non-stop through the city. Sirens were wailing and lights were flashing. At every intersection we were given a green light. No one was able to pass us. People on the streets and in the cars were all looking at us.

During the practice, the arena was filled to capacity. The entire WHA team came to take a look at Team USSR. Our head coach, Boris Pavlovich Kulagin, pointed towards them; there was Gordie Howe. Others we recognized ourselves – Frank Mahovlich, Henderson, Stapleton – we'd met them two years ago. The Canadians were calmly chewing their gum, and quietly looking at the ice. "Let's show them what we can do," said Boris Mikhailov.

What a practice! We gave it all we had. I played goal as if it was the deciding game. "Look what you're up against!" was the message we were sending the professionals. Our players were in an excellent mood. The only concern was not to lose all this fiery enthusiasm.

September 17 was the day of the first game. The Quebec Coliseum was filled to the roof. The game had not yet begun, but the audience was already roaring. The electric organ played, horns sounded, pots and drums banged. It all resembled a real psychological attack, like the one we had experienced two years ago. The only difference was that in '72 we were astonished by all this commotion, and now we were calm. Roar if you like. Personally, I liked to play when there were many fans. When the passions of the crowd ran high, I felt something special and uplifting. I could feel the excess of energy, the inspiration.

The game began with the home team on the attack and they took an early 1-0 lead. During the intermission we received orders to ''wear out'' the opponent with speed, speed, speed. The game resulted in a 3-3 tie. I had to work so hard that if someone had asked me how the game went, I could not have given a detailed description of it. The whole game had turned into a non-stop bombardment. It seemed like there were at least ten pucks on the ice, and the Canadians never stopped shooting them at me. I think, however, that the Canadian goalie Gerry Cheevers experienced the same, if not worse. He was superb.

A few incidents were especially memorable. Bernier shot the puck from a very good position. When I made the save, he broke his stick on the boards, as if it was the stick's fault. Thirty-six seconds before the final whistle, one of the Canadians, I think Frank Mahovlich, suddenly got a breakaway. I kept my cool, as usual, and moved out to meet him. Mahovlich got set, shot the puck, and missed. Bobby Hull scored twice on me. The legends about him are told for a reason. What a shot! I didn't even see it coming. J.C. Tremblay was a very reliable defenseman. And our best, of course, was Kharlamov. His individual efforts and striving should have been filmed and shown in every hockey school and all the way up to the big leagues.

It seems to me that Valery Kharlamov had something in common with the cosmonaut Yuri Gagarin. He was equally unaffected, bright, and modest. Fame did not influence his character – he remained benevolent, open to all, cheerful, and always smiling. Both died young, but left bright memories;

the cosmonaut is remembered by people around the whole world, the hockey player is remembered by those who love the sport, and who are not indifferent to the display of talent.

Kharlamov's hockey life was similar to mine. In 1962, when he was thirteen, Valery and his gang went to the Central Army Sports Club ice arena. Among his friends, he was the only person accepted to the sport school. At that time, Kulagin was in charge of picking out the young hockey players. Tarasov completed Kharlamov's hockey education.

We began together on a junior team, where he was better than everybody. His talents, as they say, were God-given. Many times I admired how easily he handled opponents. He could do practically everything; a smart play, a tricky pass, a precise shot. And everything he did looked so easy, so elegant – as if there was nothing to it. The Canadians had singled him out among all our players. After that first game on September 2, 1972, he became an idol to many Canadians.

"I like to play beautifully," Valery often repeated. This was so true. His execution of hockey was aesthetic. It amazed millions of people. When he showed up on the ice, goalies trembled and spectators vigorously expressed their enthusiasm.

But bad luck followed Kharlamov. In 1976, on his way home late at night, his car went out of control and crashed. He and his wife were rushed to the hospital. Multiple fractures of the ribs and ankles, and concussion of the brain were diagnosed. It was not going too well for him. Just married, and now this – a honeymoon at the army hospital. For a long time doctors could not predict whether or not Valery would play again. He spent two months in bed.

Five years later there was another car accident. This time it was fatal. The news of his death reached us in Edmonton, just before the second Canada Cup tournament. I will never forget it. The entire Coliseum paid their last respects to the great Soviet athlete with a minute of silence. With bowed heads, the Canadian professionals stood across from us. Eighteen thousand viewers stood still in sorrow. We all probably felt the same thing. Kharlamov and his unique talent belonged to the world he was a part of; all who loved hockey.

For the rest of our time abroad, Canadians came to us on the streets to express their sincere condolences. Many TV stations showed clips of Kharlamov's most memorable plays. Everyone understood that the loss was irreplaceable.

It is impossible to talk about Kharlamov without mentioning Boris Mikhailov and Vladimir Petrov. Valery's superb linemates helped him to discover his talents. It seemed that they were born to meet and become the greatest hockey line in history. I know that during difficult moments I relied only on them. Many times they changed the momentum of an unfortunate game. They drew the game towards themselves, and scored the deciding goals. They were great for many years. Over the course of time the first line was 'diluted' with other players, and in my opinion there was always something missing.

The oldest among them was Boris Mikhailov. On the team he was the fighter of all fighters. His favorite place during the attack was in front of the goal, the most dangerous place to play. This is the spot where nobody is safe during the hot moments. Mikhailov was not very big and strong, but in his character, and in his will power, he more than made up for it. Though he was not as talented as Kharlamov, not as fast as Balderis, and not as powerful as Petrov, he was still very effective. He was our captain and leader. Everybody looked up to him, tried their best for him, tried to be like him.

Mikhailov changed noticeably after he was appointed as a captain. He became more demanding of himself, more responsible, and more patient towards others in his words and actions. Sometimes when I let in an easy goal, Boris would lose his temper and say, "What are you here for? To let the pucks in?" But as the team captain, he would skate over, hit me on the pad, and say, "Don't worry, we will retaliate with two goals."

What distinguished this trio was their thirst for goals. They did not care who got the credit for a goal or an assist, the important thing was to score. They could not bear defeat, even when they played soccer or pool. They only wanted to win, and that was it. Their style was to stun, to crush, to confuse the opponent in a crazy roundabout way, to make them panic, and then to score a beautiful goal, taking advantage of the opportunity. Each trusted his linemates as he would himself. They never looked back. Even during practice, our first line did not like to give in. You should have seen it! They melted the ice with their speed and pressure.

There are some players who do not care about public opinion, who do not value their name. Today they may play well, and tomorrow, terribly. So what? They do not care. Boris Mikhailov, Vladimir Petrov, and Valery Kharlamov valued their names a great deal. As any other great masters, they were picky about their game. To play carelessly, not giving it their all, was not their style. They could not do it.

That line no longer exists. Kharlamov died, Mikhailov and Petrov became coaches. Although new, talented players came to replace them, it wasn't the same.

* * * * *

Let me return now to the '74 Series. The game in Quebec was over. Weak and drained, we sat in the dressing room. It was dead quiet. What a boilerhouse, I thought. It looks like these meetings will be a lot more difficult than previous ones. Who said that we would be on easy street in Canada!

The players who hadn't dressed for the game walked in

looking extremely excited. During the game they had been sitting in the stands. The goalie, Volodia Polupanovos, was ecstatic, "What a game! This is..." He could not find the proper words to describe his feelings. "It is fantastic!" As for us, we were sitting quietly; "Let us catch our breath, Volodia." Yuri Sepelkin shouted, "I have never seen anything like this game!" From the door, my backup Alexander Sedelnikov chimed in, "Boy, Vladik, you saved the team so many times!"

But we were sitting quietly, dead tired. Later that night Bobby Hull commented on TV: "The Russians have a very good team. They're disciplined and united, just like an army platoon. Each knows his responsibilities. As for us, we were too nervous tonight. Mackenzie told me that just before the game his knees wouldn't stop shaking. But now we will get a hold of ourselves. Our team will win this series."

"Well, we'll just have to see about that," said Sedelnikov, shutting off the TV. As usual, we were sharing the same room. We didn't usually talk too much. It was not because we had nothing to say to each other. No, the reason was that before a game I immersed myself in thought. I became silent and isolated. Alex knew this, and tried not to disturb me with any idle talk.

The second game was to take place in Toronto, the Hockey Capital of Canada. Hockey here is a divinity that is admired by every age and gender. Hockey! Hockey! Hockey!

Just like two years before, we were defeated in Toronto by a score of 4-1. I still wonder what went wrong with our defensive game. What happened to our defensemen? Strategically, they didn't play well; Vasiliev and Gusev weren't covering for each other. Of course, we were unaccustomed to the conditions. The rink was too small for our style of play. Our players like to skate behind the nets to pass the puck, but there was not much room to maneuver; the space behind the nets was only about a meter wide. Nothing went our way. When Petrov finally got the puck past Cheevers, it bounced out of the net before the referee saw it, and the goal was disallowed.

That game exhausted me. I lasted for two periods, then for the first time in my life I said to the coaches, "I'm not sure if I can last much longer." They replied, "Hold on, Vladik, you're our only hope."

Not well rested, I went back on the ice. In the first seconds, Mackenzie, like a raging bull, broke through towards my net. Everything came back to me, I forgot about my weariness. All I saw was Mackenzie. In his eyes, and in his wind-up I tried to guess where he was aiming the shot. Then it all started. A shot, another shot, and another. It was almost unfair. The majority of Canadian attacks ended up somewhere senseless. They just went to the net and shot. They could have tried to trick me, make a move on me, get me away from the goal. But no, they put everything they had into the shot, as if they wanted to shoot through me. But, I guess that is what we call the unrefined style of Canadian hockey.

I don't know what happened to my fatigue! I was playing as if I was in a state of amnesia. Something that I cannot describe came over me. Perhaps it was an inspiration. Yes, I think it would be best to call it an inspiration. Everything inside me was extremely sharp. I could not allow myself to take a break, even for a moment, but I think it was for the better. If I was to relax, even for a second, I could lose my touch, my inspiration.

In the third period, the Canadians got a penalty shot. I watched as a tall fellow skated to center ice. Hull? No. Howe? No. It was a Canadian who was totally unfamiliar to me. If they have confidence in him to take this shot, I thought to myself, he must be their most skilled player, a real expert. I found our later, it was Mike Walton.

Usually in such cases I wondered whether or not I would make the save. But now my mind was clear. All I saw was the opponent and the puck, nothing more. Until the attacking player crossed the blue line, I was not allowed to move. But as soon as Walton did, I immediately rushed towards him in order to cut down the angle. The Canadian had not expected my sudden move. As a result, he got intimidated and rushed with the shot. I can handle that kind of a shot. Viewers roared, either in disappointment or in delight. Walton skated over to me and said, "Good game!" And I replied, "Thank you."

When we got back to the dressing room, my legs gave out and I collapsed on a bench, totally exhausted. Everything was over. Only the deadly fatigue remained. Hundreds of questions went through my mind. Would I be able to withstand such a brutal assault again? Would our defensemen finally start playing up to their potential? Would the Canadians keep on going at such a hurricane pace? How could I handle Hull? Why had the Canadian referee, Brown, disallowed the goal scored by Petrov?

On the plane from Toronto to Winnipeg, I asked Brown why his objectivity had failed him. "Please don't remind me about it, Mr. Tretiak," he shook his head. "I feel bad enough as it is. Of the twenty thousand people who were present at the game, I was the only one who didn't see the goal."

Our players handled such obvious misjudgment with dignity. We were accustomed to accepting the word of the referee as law. Just out of curiosity, I wonder how the Canadians would have reacted if it had happened to them?

Yes, our opponents were strong. So far, they had definitely played better than us. They played with enthusiasm and dedication. Each and every one of them was willing to block shots with his body, even the aging veteran Gordie Howe.

I thought that they had chosen a very effective tactic. From defense they quickly moved to the offense, exactly as we had done two years before against the NHL team. I was still not certain that our opponents could keep up this hurricane pace to the end. I had my doubts that they would continue playing on such a high note.

It is hard to describe the chaos that reigned before the third game. Tickets that normally cost ten dollars were being sold by scalpers for $200.00. The mood of the Canadian press had changed drastically. Canadians had started to believe that Team WHA could beat us.

Winnipeg was the home of Bobby Hull, one of the greatest, and one of the kindest hockey individuals in Canada. Hull could be considered as a model of endurance and self-control. He was thirty-five years old, but his game hadn't lost that freshness and spark. He was able to do anything. With his past, how could he not? He was four years old the first time he picked up a stick. At eighteen, he became a professional. An interesting fact is that out of all of Hull's teammates, he was the only one who attended all the Team USSR practices and studied them very carefully.

Hull, as well as forty-six-year-old Gordie Howe and other great hockey players from Team Canada '74, stayed in modest rooms, just like other Canadian players. Hull and Howe were first on the ice during practices. Their impressively modest behaviour constantly reminded younger players of how real hockey players must conduct themselves.

Our usual strong team showed up for the third game. Kulagin said to our younger players who were eager to get some action, "Just hold on, fellows. Let us win a few games. Let us show that we're stronger. Then I'll play all of you." I don't know about the rest of us, but the coach was pretty sure of a victorious outcome. Harris played the backup goaltender, Don MacLeod. According to the newspaper, Cheevers had decided to take a break. It seems that the first two games hadn't been a picnic for him either.

The ice in Winnipeg was terrible, all covered in bumps and puddles. By the way, the look of this blue on silver-white on green ice can be deceiving. From above it always looks ideally smooth, but the secret of how to make perfect ice is known by very few. Even a small pothole, or bump can decide the outcome of the game.

From the beginning, it was clear to me that our forwards were in top form. They smashed the opponents. The Canadians, as I had predicted, could not keep up their fast pace and had begun to slow down.

In the second period, Walton gave me a shot in the stomach with his fist that made me grimace in pain. I felt so sick that the team doctor had to give me a pill to kill the pain. As the second period ended the score was 7-2 for Team USSR. Well, I thought, now that the game is almost done, Sedelnikov will take over. But no, I had to get back into the game. I suffered for about ten minutes, but did not let in a goal. Then I went towards our bench where the doctor had already prepared liquid ammonia. I smelled it and looked at the coach. "Maybe now they'll replace me," I thought. No, I had to finish the game. I felt pretty bad; I could have lost my consciousness at any time. As a result, I let in three goals in the last three minutes.

The first was scored by Henderson. It was rather interesting that during the course of the game he'd had few opportunities, but as soon as he did, he would take a shot. He should either have played the goalie or made a good pass, but instead he kept shooting, as if someone had put a spring in him. I'd had no problems blocking his shots, and now it was him again, racing towards me. I noticed that our defense had fallen asleep at the perfect moment. That meant that it was all up to me. To the right of Henderson was another Canadian who was in an even better position to make the shot. Well, I thought, now he will pass the puck. He must think it would be stupid not to! So I started to move towards the other player, opening a corner of the net. But Henderson again had no intention of passing the puck. He shot again. He didn't miss that corner.

Bobby Hull gave me the most problems. Often when he took a shot, I did not even see the puck. He fired it like a bullet. But that was not the worst of it. Usually, when a hockey player takes a wrist shot or a slapshot, he has to wind up. The experienced goalie can decide, according to this wind-up, the direction and the strength of the shot. A good player has a wind-up that lasts only a split second, but the goalie has enough time to cover the spot where he is aiming. Hull did not have to wind up. His devastating shot was done strictly by the wrist. He had scored many goals, probably because his teammates always played to set him up.

Then, Mackenzie and Lacroix raced in. They were vigorous, fast, and bold, but frankly, I wasn't worried about them. I was looking for Hull. Where was he? Aha, there he was, heading towards my net as usual. Mackenzie and Lacroix passed to each other, but I swear neither of them ever thought of shooting. They had that magical faith in Bobby Hull. He was to shoot, only him. When he finally got into the perfect position, the puck was immediately passed to him. He scored.

In Moscow he would score just one goal; he would be closely covered. But in Canada, he already had six goals. From game to game I tried to find a counter-maneuver against the Canadian, and at last I came up with an idea. Instead of waiting until he got into our zone, I would go towards him, just as he got to the puck. That is what I did for the rest of the games.

The fifth goal was scored by Walton. The shot was very hard. I caught it, but the puck somehow got out from my glove, and, as if it was alive, flew into the net.

It was hard in Winnipeg, but, despite my weak play in the third period, we won convincingly and beautifully. The score was 8-5. One Canadian paper said: "Only a fool can believe that we are playing against anything less than a good hockey team. We haven't seen a single Russian player who would have any trouble playing the best professional clubs." Naturally, it was very flattering to hear such high praise. It was good to realize that we had solved what was once considered the mystery of Canadian hockey. Now we understood its traditions, its tactics. We found its weak spots, and tried to take advantage of them. Even the Canadians quickly learned the lessons we gave them. The majority of the Team WHA players were trying to play the combination style. This team's tactics were much more diverse those of the team we played two years ago. Harris taught players quick, sneaky moves, and team play. Hull and Henderson were the only players faithful to the old style.

Surprisingly, the majority of Canadians preferred to play without helmets. Once I asked one of the professionals about it. "This is a thoughtless and stupid habit," he replied. "It is partly due to this habit that we get most of our injuries. Every year, we pledge to wear helmets, but when the new season comes, everything remains the same." The problem was that professional hockey players had never worn helmets. It became a sort of trademark of theirs. The tradition would be very hard to break, but even then, I did not doubt that in the long run, common sense would take over, and that's what happened.

I was fascinated by the goalie Gerry Cheevers. He was fearless, skillful, and calm; a very good goalkeeper. As an individual he was one in a million. Before the game he would come over and hit me on the pads with his stick, his way of wishing me good luck. What I could not understand was that he smoked. Even just before the game, he would stand in front of the dressing room with a thick cigar in his mouth. Once I asked, "Gerry, why do you smoke?" "It helps me to relax," he replied. In his contract, it was stated that he was allowed to drink beer during the intermission. Amazing! I think that this was just as reckless as playing without a helmet.

Then there was Johnny Mackenzie, who liked to play rough. He was always looking for a fight, looking to hit someone. He did not even try to hide it. "Yes, I play rough," he said, "but I will not argue with you if you play rough against me too." Personally, I don't like this philosophy. I did not even like Mackenzie. After the game in Vancouver was over and passions had settled down, the players shook hands and skated towards their respective dressing rooms. I stretched my hand towards Mackenzie. He pointedly turned away and, as if unintentionally, jabbed me with his stick.

Game four in Vancouver resulted in a 5-5 tie.

Then there were five games in Moscow. I will not give too many details, except to say that luck was entirely on our side.

By now, because of our conditioning, we were having an easier time than the professionals in this series. We won the fifth and deciding game. With each game, we became more confident. As for the Canadians, they became flat, exhibiting less and less their former style of play.

Just before the seventh game, the coaches of the USSR team had heard rumors that the Canadians wanted to 'take Tretiak out'. In other words, they wanted to hurt me so badly that I would not be able to continue the game. "Protect Vladik," instructed the coaches, just before the players got onto the ice. "If someone even touches him with a finger, get him." But everything went well.

I did not play the last game. Instead, my wife and I sat in the third row, and for the first time I watched the game not as a goalie, but as a spectator. My heart trembled, that is how much I worried for my team, especially for Alex Sedelnikov. However, the professionals were no match for our young goalie. Had it not been for Cheevers, we would have won even more persuasively. So far, we had four wins, three ties, and one loss. The ratio of goals for and against was 32-27 for the Russian team.

Not only had two national teams met in the arenas of Canada and Moscow, but also two completely different styles of hockey. Our victory meant that our hockey was more up to date. It meant that we had been on the right track all those years. During those games, we had to give all, even more than all. We had shown the better conditioning of Soviet athletes as well as teamwork, dedication, unity and the will to win. In my opinion, the Russian players looked a lot better than the opponents in every aspect of the game, especially when it came to speed. The Canadians obviously could not handle the tempo set by our players from the very beginning. The professionals were often left vulnerable by their unimaginative play, their tactical limitations. Our hockey turned out to be more creative, more artistic.

After a space of three months, we were once again on our way overseas, this time as the Red Army Club. This time we were up against amateurs, not professionals. I recall this tour for the reason that, frankly, we thought of this trip to Canada as a break of some kind. We had not planned to waste much strength playing against the foreign amateurs. As it turned out, however, our opponents tried their best to beat the Red Army Club, as if they had made a pact.

At first, we were taken aback. Every game was a battle for each goal. Later, we were told what had happened. A victory over our club meant that the players of the Canadian club were true men. It would improve the club's reputation drastically. Taking into consideration that members of these clubs were eighteen to nineteen-year-old fellows (future professionals), their determination was even more understandable.

The first game was in Hamilton. The arena was so small that the only thing it was good for was a children's sandbox. The lack of space was so uncomfortable that we managed to win by only one goal. The next day the coach of the Toronto Maple Leafs walked over to me. "Well, how did you feel last night during the game?" he asked. "Not too well," I replied. "Yes, I know what you mean. It probably would have been better to play in a telephone booth." We also had a hard time against the local Toronto team. The Canadians were fighting as if they were playing for a million dollars. Thousands of spectators came to see it. The Russians gave good hockey lessons. They exhibited beautiful, correct, modern play.

While in Toronto, we visited the Hockey Hall of Fame. One can find everything about hockey in this excellent museum. Even some of our famous athletes and coaches are included in the exhibition. One of the central places is occupied by a wax model depicting the last seconds of the eighth game between Team USSR and Team NHL – that exact moment where, the score tied at 5-5, they had scored the sixth goal that decided the outcome of the whole series. Among the exhibits we saw a stand dedicated to Anatoly Tarasov, a hockey stick signed by Yakushev, and my sweater, which had mysteriously vanished from the dressing room in Vancouver in September of 1972.

We played a total of seven games in Canada. We won all of them, and, completely worn out, we returned home. It had not been the nice break we had hoped for.

Once back in Moscow, just before our practice, I was stopped by a man who introduced himself as an employee of the state publishing company. He handed me a package; "This is a book written by the Canadian goaltender Ken Dryden. We have published it in Russian, and we would like to know your opinion of it.'' The book was called *Face-off at the Summit*, and was devoted to the '72 Series. I swallowed it with joy, experiencing once again the events of three years ago.

I stumbled on one paragraph and read it over again and again: "It is absolutely evident that the Russians are very interesting people. It would be nice to talk to them about hockey, but somehow I never get a chance to. I would like to know what they think about professional hockey players. Did we impress them? If so, in what way? Too bad that I cannot find out about it. During the press conferences, I could only get diplomatic answers, and to me they don't mean anything. There they are, fellows who have only now gained our respect, sitting just twenty yards away from us, and yet we cannot even talk to them, even though we do communicate with each other through hand signals.''

You're right, Ken. We all had the same feelings, I know. Too bad that our communication was limited to the boards of the hockey rink. We could probably have told each other quite a few interesting stories. 'Sport was meant to unite people'; I have never considered that to be just a beautiful phrase. But let's be frank until the end, Ken. Back then, in 1972, the language barrier was not the only problem. Many of your friends could not overcome their wounded pride. You looked upon us from above. It took some time for us to gain your respect, you said so yourself in your book.

What do we think about professional players? I extend my notes to answer Dryden's question. We think that they are splendid masters, and, with some exceptions, excellent fellows. We also think that we can play equally well. In regular meetings of two hockey schools, the goal is progress for amateurs as well as for professionals.

7

WHAT GOALIES ARE MADE OF

The 1974 World Championships were held in Helsinki. They began with our loss to Czechoslovakia, 7-2. The mood was horrible. I remember after one of our games, a reporter asked me, "Tell me please, Mr. Tretiak, would you have become a goalie if you were to start your hockey career again?" I was taken by surprise with the question and simply shrugged my shoulders. "I don't know." "Seriously," insisted the reporter. I thought about it, but still escaped from giving a direct answer.

It was actually impossible for me to give a direct answer to his question. By that time I had had more than enough bumps and bruises. If someone had told me then, that I was going to play for another ten years, I would never have believed him.

When I was playing for the juniors, one of our forwards suddenly got sick. It happened just before a very important game, and there was no one to replace him. I was asked to put on his uniform and play forward under his name. Of course, it wasn't very sportsmanlike. In truth, it was the purest form of fake substitution. However, since it happened a long time ago, I should be forgiven. I really enjoyed being an attacker. But would I want to remain being a forward? I'm not sure.

In 1971 Jacques Plante gave me his book, *The School of a Goalie*. He wrote on the cover, "I think you will enjoy reading this book, since we became friends during your last trip to Canada. You are one of the best young goaltenders that has ever come to us. I hope you play for many more years and become the best goaltender in the world." This book was not only exciting, it was also educational. I even marked a few interesting passages, for example: "Intensity, this is the name of a goalie's game.... People will never understand how great this intensity really is."

Once during dinner, a famous professional goalie threw a beefsteak at his wife. That is how intense he was before a game. Not long after, he decided that he had had enough of hockey, and left the game. I often wonder what his reaction would be to the curved sticks and raised shots that are very common today. And then there was 'Mr. Goalie', Glen Hall. He usually arrived at the arena deadly sick. Glen Hall's nervous system was so overloaded that very often he could not control his nausea, and yet he still remained in the net until the end of the game.

"You can have an upset stomach," continued Jacques Plante, "you can shake as if you have a fever. Most of the time, these symptoms will disappear as soon as the game begins. But if they remain, or if they occur too often, you should leave hockey, as many goalies before you have done. Their overexertion gave them ulcers."

It could be that Plante exaggerated a little, but overall he is quite right about goalies suffering from stress. During the last years of my goaltending career, I experienced many of those unpleasant sensations which Plante had described; upset stomach, insomnia, pain. I felt that there was not a single healthy spot on my body.

Continuing with Plante's book: "At times, sitting in the dressing room in a state of perplexity, you ask yourself: How did I get here? Why did I choose to be a goalie? Other players will laugh and make jokes about your struggles. They cannot think about the game the way you do, they are not going through such intensity. If players make a mistake, they might apologize to you, but it might also be too late. You cannot say a word to your defense when the referee digs the puck out of your net. Everyone will be looking at you as if to say, It's your fault. Why did you let in the goal? Fans may boo you, be ready for it. That is your job.

Plante is right that most of the coaches do not have the slightest idea of what the goalie has to do, let alone the players. "Nobody among them," Plante noted bitterly, "is capable of understanding what the goaltender goes through before and during the game. After the final whistle, goalies are forced to explain the reasons why they were scored on. Usually, they take all the blame. But when they try to point out the mistakes of others players, they are accused of looking for excuses."

Yet another opinion is that of Bobby Hull: "I would say that every goalie, of either a highly-skilled or a beginner team, is made from a special mold. Even with my love of hockey, I am glad that I never had to test my courage by playing in the net. Every coach knows the value of a good defenseman or of a good forward, but you cannot put a price tag on a good goaltender."

Once, I came across a newspaper clipping about a North American journalist who was writing a book about goalies. Dressed up as a goaltender, this fifty-year-old man played five minutes as a goalie for the Boston Bruins, against Philadelphia.

The clipping said that during those five minutes he allowed one goal, but made three saves and stopped a penalty shot. Not too bad, considering that he had only had two weeks to practise. The point is, however, that if that journalist was to write about forwards, I doubt that he would even have stepped onto the ice.

Everyone is used to the fact that, at the beginning of the game, two players distinct from the others, take their places in front of the nets. Their bodies are locked into impenetrable (or so it appears) pads, their faces are hidden behind the masks. They hold sticks that look as if you couldn't even lift them off the ground. Everyone is accustomed to this. But, if you think about it, what could be more absurd? With all their strength, five men shoot the puck, which is as hard as a rock, at a sixth player. And this sixth player, instead of getting out of the way, tries to block the puck with his arms, his legs, his body. What a yo-yo!

Just try not putting out a goalie for a game. It would be impossible. The goaltender is practically the most important individual on the team. He is protected from the attacks of somewhat excited opponents. Before the game, he is surrounded by other players who bang their sticks against his pads for good luck, as if he was a living idol. Not many people are aware that, when Canadians first invented hockey, goalies did not even exist. Forwards existed, defensemen existed, but the place in front of the nets remained empty. Games in those days were probably very high scoring.

There are many rumors about the goaltending profession, although truth is greatly mixed with legend. Once, for example, I read that one of the professional teams had a goalie who, in 110 games had not missed a single goal, and that on his face, he had more that four hundred scars. I think that this is a figment of someone's imagination. However, I know for sure that my friend Gerry Cheevers painted stitches on his face mask to represent the scars he would have had on his face if he had played without a mask. They say that in eight years, he had painted 120 stitches.

Certainly, the role that goaltenders must faithfully play every day has an impact on their characters, as well as their life styles. Frankly, I have never met a goalie who was not a nice person. The man who is unstable, unreliable, or temperamental will never be able to play goal, not even if he has an enormous amount of talent.

They say that a goalie 'stands in goal'. This is not true. He does not stand, he plays! Unreplaced throughout the whole game, he catches and deflects pucks; he is pushed and harassed. He must dash like a sprinter, lunge and twist like a gymnast. And he remembers well that the goalie is the one person on the team who cannot make a mistake.

Leo Yashin, the famous Soviet soccer goalkeeper, has asserted that in sport, there does not exist a more benevolent position than that of goaltender. Or a more difficult one, I will add.

Quickness, deftness, impeccable coordination, endurance, and strength – these are what a goalie needs. Some people ask, why strength? Don't forget that all his movements are made under an armor that weighs 15-20 kilograms. The goalie also needs special powers of observation, the ability to orient himself quickly, boldness, temper, intuition, and will power.

The ex-goalie of a Czechoslovakian national team, Ladislav Gorski, once calculated that the soccer goaltender makes an average of ten to fifteen plays per game. The hockey goaltender makes more than forty. Sometimes, however, you touch the puck only a few times during the whole period, but the intensity is so great that at the end you're still dragging. Jacques Plante was absolutely right in saying that intensity is one of the peculiarities of the goalie's job.

Yes, this game is merciless towards the goalie. If the puck slips by, the red light goes on as a signal of disaster. Sometimes the fans are also merciless towards the goalie, and so are his teammates. That's the goalie's fate in hockey. That is why goaltenders suffer from insomnia after a game has been lost.

It is impossible to achieve success in one day in this business. The whole year is not enough. There must be many such years of hard work, failures, pain, fear, victories, and defeats. Only then, after a long and difficult road where there are more curves that straightaways, can you say, I am a goalie. You should realize this, as you reach for the heaviest stick from the pile.

But let's go back to the 1974 World Championships in Helsinki. On April 18th, we played our second match against the Czechoslovakian team. Right across from me, at the other end of the ice, the Czechoslovakian goaltender Irzy Molichek took his place. I couldn't see his face because of his mask, but I could tell from the restless shifting of his feet that he was worried. Molichek was an outstanding goaltender. He was much older than me, and he knew every little trick of our trade. It was practically impossible to score on him from close up. He had exceptional reflexes, he was bold and intuitive. His only flaw that I know of was that when he missed a goal he could become very upset and make more mistakes which could end up in more goals.

Nevertheless, the first goal in this game was scored against me when Tsygankov got a five minute major penalty. Only in the second period, after a long siege, did Yakushev equalize the score. Molichek, as I had expected, got upset and soon made another mistake. Maltsev put us ahead.

I did not miss any more goals in that game, but it wasn't easy. Czechoslovakian players forced me to jump from post to post. Their shots were accurate and hard.

Martinec got possession of the puck. He was still far away from me, almost on the red line, but I was already ninety-eight percent prepared. I knew that this player never missed from any distance. His partner moved rapidly toward me with the puck. Would he shoot, or would he make a pass? I looked at his eyes. If he looked at me, he would shoot; if he looked to the right, then he'd pass to Martinec, and he would know what to do. Sure enough, he made a quick pass to the right –hold on, goalie!

During the second intermission I could not stop sweating, even though I had not consumed much water during the game. I breathed heavily, and from the outside I probably looked rather pitiful. The coach, Boris Pavlovich Kulagin, came over. "Hold on, Vladik." Then he said suddenly, "Remember when you ran twenty laps?" I smiled, surprised that I could still smile.

Memories of the past, when I was invited to the Red Army Junior Team camp, went through my mind. As punishment for a bad performance during morning exercises, Kulagin once made us run twenty laps. Fellows who were four years older than me had no problem with the test. As for me, I lasted ten laps, and that was it, I couldn't do anymore. I felt like I was going to die, like I was going to fall helplessly. Some of the boys said to Kulagin, "Go easy on him, he's still young." "If he can make it, he will become a hockey player," replied the coach imperturbably.

I made it in the end. I don't know how, but I did. Remembering Kulagin and that incident, I don't know why, but I smiled again. It was time to go, the intermission was over.

We won that game by a score of 3-1.

Our last game was played against the Swedish team. The orders were to attack, to break the opponent's defense by any means we had. We succeeded. We scored three times and missed once. The score could have been greater, but their goalie, Abrahamsson, performed miracles. Mikhailov took several shots at him from point blank range, and each time he made the save. Christy Abrahamsson was a kind fellow, but as soon as he stepped on the ice he was transformed into a bully. Just touch him and the next thing you knew, he would scream and swing his stick, trying to start a fight. In my opinion, the goalie must lock his emotions deep inside. There is no need to get so excited.

Swedish goalies have traditionally been very well-trained. As far as I know, they feared only one forward, Anatoly Firsov. When he took his famous slapshot, goalies didn't even have time to blink before the puck was in their net. I realize now how lucky I was that Firsov played on my team, and never took a shot at my net. I know when Firsov wound up, some goalies closed their eyes and surrendered early.

Right after the game against the Swedes, we went back to our hotel in order to get ready for the final ceremonies. As I stepped into the next room where our players were assembling, I finally became aware of the enormous tension that had built up during the last few days. My head started to spin, I felt sick, and I quickly left the room.

The closing ceremonies took place at the concert hall 'Finland'. There, I was presented with a prize as the best goaltender.

I always wanted to be the best. First in my own team, then during the European competitions, then on the national team. You can call it ambition. So what? My drive to be the best never interfered with the interests of the team. On the contrary, it was entirely subordinate to the goals of the team as a whole. And my teammates, coaches, and most of all Anatoly Vladimirovich Tarasov must take credit for my success.

On my way back to the hotel I thought, no, now more than ever, don't ask me if I would be willing to exchange my goaltender's share for anything else.

"SUPER SERIES":
A Beautiful Night in Montreal

In 1976, as usual, we celebrated the New Year far away from home. Throughout the world, Christmas and New Year's are considered to be family holidays, and so it is in our homeland. Only hockey players constantly violate this tradition. When all our relatives and close friends are gathering around the table, raising glasses of champagne, and toasting one another, we are always elsewhere. We are able to hear the voices of wives, children, and parents only on the telephone. Such is life on our hockey team at the end of December, when the foreign tournaments never seem to end.

1975 turned out to be a pretty good year. My hockey career had reached its pinnacle. In the Kremlin, I was awarded by the Order of the Badge of Honor. For the second time, sports writers named me the best goaltender of the USSR. My son, Dmitri, had started to play with his hockey stick, and he kept asking me to play with him. I received letters from all over the world, consisting of congratulations, advice, requests, and most of all, a lot of questions about the game.

A number of interesting things connected with my name had happened. For instance, there was a rumour in Detroit that I was about to sign a contract with the Red Wings. Apparently they did discover a man who called himself Tretiak and spoke with a Russian accent. A thorough check showed that the real name of this impostor was Tarliff, and that he had as much in common with hockey as I do with playing the harp. I don't know what happened to him, but from what I heard, he managed to make a bundle by using other people's names before he was exposed.

A similar incident had happened in Birmingham, Alabama. I heard that a man calling himself Tretiak lived for almost a month in the house of a stockbroker, amusing him with stories of his heroism on the ice. Sometimes I am surprised at Americans' naïveté. It is so easy to fool them.

At the end of 1975, we went to Canada to play against the professional clubs. 'Superseries' – that is what these games were called abroad. Our two clubs, The Red Army Club and Krilya Sovetov (Wings of the Soviets), were to face the strongest clubs of the NHL. At the time, the Canadians were asserting, with good reason, that their clubs were a lot stronger than any national team.

Just before our departure for Canada, I finally reached my peak form. Until then, I'd had a few problems with my game, but now everything fell into place. The puck 'listened to me', as if it was trained. I felt great.

Even the veterans of our team were surprised. "Well Vladik, you look as if you've just been reborn." Once during a scrimmage I was playing goal for Vladimir Petrov's line. We were leading. "Sure," the leader of our opponents, Vladimir Vikulov, said to Petrov, "you have Tretiak, no one can score on him.'' ''It's not Tretiak, you should play better, that's all,'' said Petrov. ''Do you want to trade?'' he offered readily. So, we traded. I took my place in the net for Vikulov's team, and, now with reassurance, they began to lead.

Forgive me for sounding conceited, but that particular incident came back to me because of this Superseries story. At the end of 1975, I constantly experienced something which could probably be described as 'hockey inspiration'. How perfect that it happened precisely in December.

* * * * *

We felt a little uncomfortable when we arrived in Montreal. First of all, it was extremely cold. We also felt the time difference. Our bodies ached. We always wanted to sleep. And, for some reason, everybody was extremely thirsty. The reason for this might have been that we were unaccustomed to the cuisine. Everything was beautiful and appetizing, but it either seemed tasteless, or it had a strange aftertaste. Even the potatoes seemed strange.

We were placed at the Queen Elizabeth Hotel and, as before, we were surrounded by reporters. There was no end to their questions.

The Canadians' love of hockey is widely known. But, while their idols had once been only the local stars, now everything had changed. We felt it ourselves. Every police officer smiled at us when they spotted us on the streets in Montreal. Even Harry Sinden, an ex-coach of Team NHL who was pretty hostile towards us after the 1972 series, now changed his attitude. He commented to one of the newspapers that the Soviet team was not only strong because of team play, thoroughly worked out tactics, and precise passing, but we also had many strong individual players. He compared Kharlamov to Rick

Martin; "Besides Kharlamov, the Russians have many strong individual players. But how many Martins do we have?"

Actually, we accepted this praise with restraint, and never took it seriously. We knew that we also had our share of flaws.

Canadian and American newspapers were no longer writing that the home team would eat us alive, but the majority still preferred the professionals. We were more than a little surprised when a *Journal de Montréal* reporter predicted that the Soviets would win five times, lose twice, and tie once. "I sure would like to be wrong," he concluded. As far as I know, this reporter was one of the few Canadians who correctly predicted the outcome of the Superseries.

Our hosts treated the Red Army Club and Krilya Sovetov to a reception at the Montreal Forum. From there we immediately went for a practice, and all the players of the Montreal Canadiens followed to watch. The professionals carefully watched every Soviet player, and took detailed notes. Their expressions were a blend of respect and enthusiasm. Nothing similar had happened in the previous series. Again, I could not help remembering September of 1972. So much arrogance, haughtiness, and disregard had been shown to us by the players and the officials of the NHL. Where did it go?

We began the series in New York against the New York Rangers. Our reception left much to be desired. For a while they couldn't find us a hotel, and they didn't rush with our supper either. It made us nervous. What was it, we wondered, were they trying to make us angry on purpose?

The Rangers scored first, but this only excited our forwards. Watch out, Esposito! We took the play to them with quick, intense hockey. It seemed that our opponents didn't have enough time to understand what was happening on the ice. Even their goaltender appeared to be in a state of confusion, and could not help his team. After the game, Pete Stemkowski commented that it seemed like we were on a merry-go-round.

In one of the papers I read: "Maybe it wasn't us, but the Russians who invented hockey. In any case, it seemed that way last night on the ice of Madison Square Gardens. Boris Alexandrov showed the Rangers what hockey is all about."

But let's get back to the game. A rotten egg hit the ice right beside me and game was stopped. I looked up at the stands and saw a policeman holding one of the fans. The police officer began to hit him on the pockets, which were stuffed to capacity. Apparently, this character had brought a jacket full of rotten eggs. I hope he likes them scrambled, I thought to myself.

At the end of the game, someone threw a paper cup onto the ice. I turned around and pointed towards the scoreboard. I thought: Look at the score, you hoodlum! The score was 7-3 for us.

As we expected, Esposito was the best player on the opposing team as he had been in '72. Then, he was called 'Looking-for-Trouble Phil'. During that series it seemed that he could not get over the fact that the Russian players could be as good as the professional players. Now, he was more restrained. He admitted that the Russians could play a strong game. Phil was outstanding in '72, but sometimes he did get out of line. I can't say that we had parted as friends.

The owners of the Boston Bruins had sold Esposito to the New York Rangers. When we asked why, we were surprised to learn that the Boston Bruins had considered this deal extremely profitable for them. It is very important to get rid of an aging player, we were told. A little longer, and no one would have been interested in buying Esposito.

Yes, our old friend had changed. He was not as fast on his skates, but his superb ability to control the puck, his powerful game in front of the net, and his astounding intuition were, as always, distinct Esposito trademarks.

After the game he said, "I warned my teammates to watch out for the Russians, but they laughed at me."

The next day we returned to Montreal and went straight from the airport to the arena to practise. We knew that the most important and the most difficult games were yet to come. Our next opponents were the Montreal Canadiens, the most famous club in the NHL. They were the trend-setters, the star-makers.

Without exaggeration, I think that the whole of Canada was looking forward to this game. The excitement had reached unbelievable proportions. Everyone thought that the Montreal Canadiens would put up a good fight against the Russian hockey players. "We must show the world that the best hockey players are playing within these walls," Guy Lapointe told the reporters, pointing to the walls of the Forum.

Yes, the Forum. It has seen quite a few great players, great games. From the outside, this hockey palace doesn't present anything special. It was built, to be frank, without any architectural inspiration – a concrete cube among many other such faceless buildings. You can walk by it without even realizing that this is a holy place of Canadian professional sport, the mecca for thousands of admirers. Even though it isn't beautiful from the outside, it has everything inside for athletes, spectators, referees, and journalists to comfortably worship their divinity, hockey.

A few years ago, the general manager of the Montreal Canadiens, Serge Savard, showed me the Forum from the roof down to the basement. Savard, a French Canadian, had been a member of the 1972 NHL team. His story fascinated me. "Our stands can seat 16,076 people, and another two thousand can watch the game standing up," he said, pointing to the aisles of seats that went up to the roof. "When we played here in 1972, there were twenty-two thousand people here. The Forum was built in 1924, but it could only handle five thousand viewers. It has gone through three renovations. The last one, in 1968, made the building the way it appears now." He smiled cunningly, "If a certain Soviet goaltender was to agree to play for Montreal for a few years, we would renovate the Forum again to double its capacity.

"There are fifty games a season played here, plus all sorts of circuses and stage shows, the Ice Capades, car shows, rock concerts, gymnastic competitions, volleyball, and basketball. During the Summer Olympics of 1976, the Forum was used for the final boxing matches."

"We sell two million tickets a year," added the witty Jerry Goodman, the administrative manager. "We can even hold a rodeo here."

Savard took a drag on his cigar and willingly let his helper take over. Goodman gladly assumed the duties of a guide. "These are the cafeterias and bars. There are enough of them to feed all the spectators within nine minutes. "Why nine?" I asked. "Well, the intermission is fifteen minutes. That allows three minutes for the spectators to get out, and three to get back in, leaving the remaining nine minutes. We can open all the doors simultaneously by pressing a button on the control board. Almost twenty thousand fans can easily leave the establishment in only twelve minutes."

From Jerry Goodman, I learned that attending the games in Montreal could be an expensive hobby. On average, tickets cost $6.00, but if you wanted to get a better seat you would have to pay $17.50. Two and a half thousand people have season tickets. These people are the elite of the Canadiens' fans. Becoming a member of this group is as hard as becoming a member of the British Parliament. The seats are inherited and legally passed down to immediate relatives. Some families have been season ticket holders for thirty or forty years.

Journalists at the Forum are provided with a special press

gallery. It reminded me of a steel balcony that is suspended under the ceiling, with each place reserved for a particular hockey reporter. Right across on the other side of the ice, there is an identical gallery designated for TV and radio reporters. There are teletypes and telephones in the press center of the Forum. These provide the scores of other games that are going on at other arenas around the league. Overall, we could learn from the Canadiens everything that concerns respect for fans and players.

Savard showed me a room which was designed especially for the team's veterans. Admission to this club is allowed only to those who have played at least one hundred games for the Montreal Canadiens. These veterans can come here with their families to relax, meet with colleagues, or talk to the press. The Canadiens were the first team in the NHL to have such a place, Savard proudly informed me.

In the Montreal Forum, as in any reputable establishment, tradition is honored. The Montreal Canadiens' emblem, for example, has been unchanged for almost seventy years. There is a chair in the stands numbered 57, which is marked with a name tag, 'Jean Beliveau'.

The walls are covered with pictures of team captains; Serge Savard, Henri Richard, Bob Gainey, Yvan Cournoyer, Jean Beliveau, Maurice Richard. There were framed copies of yellowing newspapers with the reports of triumphs of the Montreal Canadiens.

On the walls of the dressing room there are beautifully done photographs of veterans. Over the pictures there is a sign saying, "To you from failing hands we throw the torch...". On the other wall of the dressing room is a list, written in gold, of all the members of the team over the years. It is these precise details that create the atmosphere of a real club, that train players to value the name and to have pride in the team.

Next to the dressing room is an exercise room, an emergency room, a sauna, a swimming pool, and meeting rooms equipped with video units. There is even a room where players' wives can relax before the final whistle. In the lobby we saw a gallery of brass busts of people who have contributed to the development of hockey in Montreal. Savard mentioned a few of their names and occupations; coach, architect, writer, journalist, player, commentator.

And so, we had a decisive game with this famous NHL club on our hands right in the middle of this great hockey citadel. Not only the arena, but the entire city was electrified. The Canadiens' desire to win was so great that even the ice-makers, so we were told later, tried to help. They made the ice sticky and full of bumps on purpose, to throw us off our game.

The fans met the appearance of the players on the Forum ice with a thunderous roar, the likes of which I have never heard in my entire life. Compared to this, the reaction of the New York crowd was dead quiet. During a game, I always tried to help my teammates by shouting advice. Here, it was absolutely senseless. I couldn't even hear my own voice.

At the beginning the Canadiens succeeded in breaking our defense, and they took the lead. The score was 2-0 after the first period. Our forwards could not organize a counter-attack. For a while, we could not play or pass. We could not act as a team. The shots on goal were 10-4 in favor of our opponents. But luckily, my teammates did not panic. In the dressing room the coaches suggested that our players skate faster and be more accurate with their passing. "And everything will be OK," said Loktev with reassurance. Our coaches never yelled at our players. Even if they were irritated or worked up, you still never heard them swear or speak harshly. To shout at the player during the game is to totally break his concentration.

We began the second period shorthanded when Zhlutkov took

a two minute penalty. That's when I had to work! The Canadiens, I think, outdid themselves. Shots followed one after the other, and all of them were hard and accurate. But we held on, and in a few minutes Mikhailov cut down the lead.

Then Solodukhin and Gusev got penalties. Although three of our fellows desperately tried to block an extremely hard shot by Cournoyer, the puck went into my net. Frankly, I didn't even see it, because there was a pile-up right in front of me. The Canadiens were on the attack again.

I loved to play when the seats were filled to capacity and the fans didn't stop applauding. The game became more challenging when the fans were cheering against us. There exists a common feeling shared by teachers and actors that comes from contact with the audience. The best way I felt this contact, this uplifting inspiration, was when thousands of people were constantly watching my net, hungering to see that little rubber disk in my goal, and I would either catch it, deflect it, or block it with my body. No, I thought defiantly, I won't let you see the puck in my net, my friends. Time and again, I would get up from under a pile of bodies, subconsciously admit to myself that I was doing OK, and open my catching glove. There it was, the puck. Then everything started all over again.

A well-known Canadian journalist once asked me why the majority of my best games were played against professionals. "Because they are professionals," I replied. And then I added candidly that the stronger my opponent was, the more confident I felt.

In this game, as in others, there were too many delays. The organ entertained the players as well as the audience during these pauses. Meanwhile, local TV was feeding its audience a fantastic amount of advertising. I thought that these delays were advantageous to the Canadiens. Our weapon was fast tempo; we could play the game with no delays at all.

Kharlamov scored a goal, and what a beauty! Breaking the sound barrier, he went through two defensemen, made a smart move on Dryden, and completed his staggering raid with an accurate shot.

In the third period, the Canadiens again threw themselves at us. They were great, I cannot deny. Pete Mahovlich, Lafleur, and Cournoyer were playing tough but fair hockey. The Montreal game made a lasting impression on us. As far as I'm concerned, this is what the game of hockey is all about; fast, full of combinations, rough (but not rude), with an exciting plot. I would love play it over again.

The last goal on this New Year's Eve was scored by Boris Alexandrov. Three to three!

Pete Mahovlich, Yvan Cournoyer, and I were named the best players of the game, and we stayed behind to get our pictures taken. The fans were going berserk. Now, years later, when I look at that picture, every little detail of that excellent night in Montreal comes back to me.

The next morning I read that Scotty Bowman, the Montreal coach, insisted that his team had more chances to shoot on the goal than in any other game that season. He said that any other goalie would have had to pick the pieces of puck from his skin like it was shrapnel. Any other, but not Tretiak. "This Russian lieutenant stole the victory away from us." To be fair, it is not quite true. I did not steal a victory from the Montreal Canadiens, I simply and conscientiously did what I had to do, and the rest was done by the others.

The Canadiens considered Boris Alexandrov the surprise of the Superseries. To us it was no surprise; two years before during practices he had scored more goals on me than even Kharlamov himself. He is left-handed – it is very hard for a goalie to get used to this kind of player. Also, he was awfully gifted and persistent. On the ice, Alexandrov constantly improvised, followed his own style, and as soon as he spotted an opportunity to score, he shot, and rarely missed. This hockey player could have been a worthy replacement to Valery Kharlamov. Could have... but his constant disciplinary violations interfered with the development of his skills.

After the game we went to the Soviet Consulate to celebrate the New Year. I think everyone was satisfied with the game; our opponents, us, and the fans. A few minutes before midnight, I turned on the TV, where they were showing the highlights of the game. Then the commentator enthusiastically covered his head with confetti and shouted, "Hurray! It's a tie! Happy New Year!" That's how that unforgettable night ended.

The next morning the Canadiens players said that they had played the best hockey of their lives the night before. The majority of people and experts said that they hadn't seen anything like it for a long time. Still, some thought that since the Canadiens outshot the Red Army Club 38-13, the home team team had the advantage, meaning that they deserved to win more than us. This thinking cannot be considered well-founded.

The whole trick lies in the distinction between the styles of the Soviet and Canadian teams. From childhood, Canadians are taught to shoot the puck as soon as they have a chance. Our players, on the other hand, shoot the puck only when they have the perfect chance. They like to 'fiddle' with the puck, to play 'cat and mouse' with the opponent's defense, as well as with the goalie.

It is hard to say whose style is better. In fact, the harmony lies somewhere in the middle. In any case, after the game with the Boston Bruins, their coach Don Cherry asserted: "The number of shots on goal will most likely remain a criterion for evaluating our players. But, in reality, what was the use of us taking thirteen shots at the Red Army Team's net if they weren't successful? As for the Russians, they took only six shots, two of which went in.''

But I am getting ahead of myself. On January 5, our team flew to Boston. One of the most important games of the Superseries was to take place here. The Boston Bruins were one of the strongest and most famous clubs.

The Boston hockey players, inspired by Buffalo's victory over Krilya Sovetov, wanted desperately to beat us. Harry Sinden, the former coach of Team NHL who was now the manager of the Boston Bruins, followed our team everywhere. Because the cooling system in the Boston Garden had broken down, our practice took place somewhere far from the city. Nevertheless, Sinden brought his entire team to one of our practices. They took their places close to the boards and scrutinized each Soviet player. This close attention forced each of us to brace ourselves, to gather our thoughts, and once again realize the importance of this duel.

We still had a few days before the game. The most important thing now was not to burn ourselves out with useless worrying. On Monday, January 8, the energy would have to be there. After practice, we spent a lot of our time walking around the city. The weather here, unlike Montreal, was warm with no snow. We gladly accepted our hosts' offer to attend a concert of modern music. We also enjoyed watching professional basketball.

We were very curious to see whether or not Bobby Orr would play against us. It was said that he was the brightest star in professional hockey, and a very nice fellow (in this we had a chance to make sure for ourselves). Our team started practising at ten o'clock, and the Bruins started at eleven. Bobby was on the ice by himself even before our practice. He hadn't played for three months because his left knee hadn't healed properly after an injury.

If you can believe the papers, each game with Orr was an event in Canadian hockey. Unfortunately, we did not get a chance to see him in action. His injuries followed him everywhere.

But we did have time to get to know this strong, not too tall fellow, whose face always had a warm, sincere smile and I remember him being unhappy about not being able to play against us. "Some people say that I simply got scared of the Soviet hockey players, and, not wanting to lose my prestige, I refused to participate in the game," Orr told us with sadness and perplexity. "But that's not true. I have dreamed of this for a long time. Who could have known that it would turn out this way?" Bobby glanced at his knee. We tried to console him by saying that there would be a lot more games in the future. "Come over to see us, we'll fix your leg in a month," our team doctor Igor Silin said quite seriously.

Usually, when I was alone, I prepared myself mentally for the upcoming game. I analyzed the actions of the opponents, I found their weak and strong points. Although we had never played the Boston Bruins before, I reasoned that it was possible, taking into consideration that this team was a colorful representative of the traditional Canadian school, to model the game. Naturally, they would immediately begin storming us. They would try to stun us, to crush us, to knock us off balance, to bombard us with pucks. Even in 1972 the professionals had successfully demonstrated this kind of hockey. This meant that I would have to be especially ready in the first few minutes of the game. They could be the deciding ones.

The hockey rink in Boston is pretty old. If I am not mistaken, it was built in 1926. It is a huge, gloomy building. But it did have one advantage (for us anyway); the ice surface there was fairly large.

As I predicted, the game began with the hosts' fearless attack. Even without Orr, The Boston Bruins were very strong. Starting in the first seconds of the game, they applied their favorite variation of play; furious pressure all over the ice. There was such a tempo that it seemed that the strength of the players would not last long. During the first period, I stopped nineteen shots. Valery Kharlamov and Boris Mikhailov replied for us with a flurry of shots, but the game was still scoreless at the end of the period.

It wasn't just a game, it was poetry in motion. The second period began with me making a crucial mistake. Forbes took a long shot which hit the end of my pad and bounced into the net. That's all it takes; just relax a little, lose sight of the puck, and the next thing you know, it's in the net. I hadn't made such an error in a long time. Kharlamov evened the score two minutes later, and from then on we took control. In the end we won by a score of 5-2. Boris Alexandrov scored the final goal with a move on the goalie Gilbert that was so smooth, even the crowd murmured in admiration. Our captain, Boris Mikhailov, also played an excellent game. He scored fewer goals that his linemates, but his drive and his dedication were obvious in all four games against the professionals.

After the game in Boston, a reporter asked me how I thought the fourth game of the Superseries against the Philadelphia Flyers would turn out. "We are in good shape," I replied. "You've seen it! If the Philadelphia Flyers play a fair game, then the result will be no worse than tonight's."

Unfortunately, the last game spoiled our good mood.

I think that the hosts had planned everything in advance. Even during the reception, two days before the game, they made it perfectly clear that they had no intention of associating with the Soviet players. The Stanley Cup winners demonstrated their highly unfriendly, if not hostile attitude. Nobody came over to welcome us. Even the local press was shocked by such blatant inhospitality.

What happened later, I'd like to forget. It certainly wasn't hockey. The Philadelphia Flyers' game could not be called clean, nor the victory deserved. Many North American hockey authorities were of the same opinion. For example, Bobby Hull said that he was indignant at the Flyers' play. "The sticks were given to us not to create a slaughter, but to entertain the viewers," he noted fairly.

Early in the game, our coaches pulled us off the ice, having decided that the game could not go on under such conditions, and we thought that we wouldn't return. No Red Army player wanted to play against the Flyers. Each of us could have been hit from behind, cross-checked, kicked – what kind of sport was this? It had nothing at all in common with the sport of hockey. In less than a month after the game in Philadelphia, we had to take part in the Olympic tournament. The coaches had forbidden us from getting involved in any fights. We had to go home completely healthy, not injured.

Only after prolonged assurances on the Flyers' part that the game would be played according to the rules, did our team decide to go back on the ice. We returned, totally frustrated. Everything was turned inside-out; we did not play, we merely skated. Philadelphia beat us 4-1, but could anyone consider it a fair victory? I don't think that the Philadelphia Flyers were the strongest team team in the NHL at the time, even though they won the Stanley Cup twice in a row. What they had demonstrated on January 11th, 1976, was considered to be their usual style. This club was the absolute champion of the world – in penalties. Even among the professionals, the Flyers were considered to be monstrously brutal.

The coach of the Philadelphia Flyers, Fred Shero, came to Moscow sometime later to study our hockey methods. He tried his best to present the Flyers' victory over us in Philadelphia as well-deserved. His reasoning totally lacked any objectivity. "The Philadelphia Flyers," he was quoted as saying, "are not a group of gangsters. We are the best hockey team in the world. We were criticized for being the best team. We simply have more guts than any other team."

That frankly bragging monologue of Fred Shero's did not get a warm reception in Moscow. The whole article, printed at that time in one of the biggest American newspapers, followed in the same tone. It had much more interesting expressions. "We handled the game with the Russians masterfullly. We showed the stuff that our boys are made of. I had more satisfaction from this game than in winning the Stanley Cup. During the weeks preceding the game, I explained to my players how they should play against the Russians; endurance was fundamental. Our endurance was rewarded, and I think that is what shook the Russians. That is why they left the ice in the first period."

Apparently, Mr. Shero understood endurance to mean cheap shots, kicking, tripping, and unnecessary hits. He claimed that the Russians were totally confused by Philadelphia's disciplined and patient hockey. Perhaps we were confused, but it was due to other reasons. We didn't know before that a pack of barbarians could put on skates and get away with hunting hockey players in front of thousands of spectators.

I may sound overly agitated about these events. Of course, we had seen the dirty play of professionals before, in 1972 as well as in 1974. But what happened in Philadelphia was an apotheosis of professional hockey thuggery. Even now, I cannot not think about it without shuddering. I am not alone. The New York Times called this game "The triumph of terror over style," and no one could consider this paper to be sympathetic towards the Russians!

In an article that appeared in the worldwide sports press, Anatoly Tarasov appealed to the professionals in no uncertain terms: "I would like to appeal to the intellectual conscience of the professionals themselves. You make your living honestly. A hundred games per season is enormous and hard work. You need good health as you do air. This 'club' that your coaches are trying to put in your hands instead of the stick of knighthood and true craft has two ends. Don't anger the opponents. Remember, their patience also has a limit."

I totally support his point of view. No one had ever succeeded in frightening Soviet hockey players.

Despite the loss in Philadelphia, we won the Superseries with two wins, a tie, and a loss. Krilya Sovetov also did very well abroad, winning three of their four games against NHL clubs. Once again, we proved that we were at the forefront of world hockey.

9

SECRETS TO THE
TRETIAK PUZZLE

Once, during a regular tour of the Soviet team in North America, I came across a newspaper article entitled "The Secret of Tretiak". The writer, absolutely serious, accused me of using the power of hypnosis against my rivals. He quoted statements made by two professional players who had played against me. One of them described his impression of me in this way: "I took the puck and skated to the Russian net. When I looked up, I noticed Tretiak staring at me. He was absolutely calm and confident, as if he knew how I was going to attack him and where I would shoot the puck. I was going to fake a shot and pass the puck to my teammate, but the motionless figure in the net radiated a mysterious force which I was powerless to resist. At the last moment, I lost my nerve, and took a weak shot. Naturally, Tretiak caught it."

For me, it was ridiculous to read such fantasies about my play. I never used any hypnosis, and I have no such abilities.

All the awards I won and the records I set were not the work of any mysterious force. A goalie achieves success only through skill, character, and hard work. I had overcome fear, I wasn't afraid of the puck. I noticed that the more confident I felt in the net, the more uncertain was the play of my opponents.

I never made a secret of my skills. Very often, journalists and experts were interested in watching me practise. I was always ready to answer their questions and to show them how I prepared myself for games. As I see it, no one can steal the methods of craftsmanship. It is necessary to feel and develop them in yourself. They are directly related to experience, and without it have no value.

Of course, every goalkeeper has his own favorite methods for each game. Naturally the goalkeeper tries to hide such secrets from his rivals, who could use them against him in the game. For example, when I first started to play hockey, there was a very good goalkeeper who played for Automobilist of Sverdlosk – Viktor Puchkov. Puchkov had his own trick. When a forward had a breakaway on him, he would suddenly dive for the opponent's feet and take the puck away. Such an attack usually caught the forward by surprise and he lost in that single combat.

Puchkov's tactic was successful until the forwards figured it out. Right away, they introduced their own methods against it. They would trick him into going down on the ice, then skate calmly around him and score. I too was forced to reject this method. I understood that, in contemporary hockey, with continually increasing speed, a goalie lying flat on the ice was incapable of correcting his mistakes.

I had to find my own ways to defend the net. It wasn't an easy search and it didn't bring immediate results. I started to deflect the puck with the outside of the skate; with the toe and hockey pad above it, to be exact. Tarasov was furious when he first saw it. "What is this, young man?" he yelled at me. "Before you, our best goalies – Puchkov, Zinger, Konovalenko – played in such a situation only with the inside blade of the skate." He showed me the not-so-simple method of turning the skate which my predecessors liked so much.

In spite of the high authority of my predecessors and the stern persistence of Tarasov, I continued to play my way. I felt more comfortable that way, and I could intercept the puck faster. Further hockey developments confirmed that I was right. Now, most goalies deflect pucks my way.

There is one secret of my play which I have never told anybody. In the last couple of years of my career, I learned to play 'by eyes'. This was probably the reason why some hockey players accused me of hypnotizing them. What is the essence of this trick? Each player has his own distinguishing characteristics on the ice. You only have to understand and remember the mechanics of his movements and then choose the right position in the net. Over a long period of time, I trained myself to foresee the actions of the forward. Coming out on the ice, I always had a mental file on the rivals who were most dangerous. These observations definitely enhanced my reliability as a goalkeeper.

In an actual game, however, the goalkeeper often finds himself in an extremely tough situation, alone against two forwards. It's easy to get confused in such situations, and a goal is sure to follow. I always tried to keep cool. I followed the eyes of the player who was handling the puck. If, at the last moment, he looked first at me, and then at the puck, I knew he would shoot, himself. Then I could forget about his partner and fight him one on one. But if he looked for a moment at his teammate, and then at the puck, I knew he would pass to his partner and I was ready for it. That's the practicality of foresight.

Hockey players from Spartak and Dynamo, who often practised with me on the National Team, somehow got to know about my ability to play 'by eyes'. Although they could sometimes fool me during practice, they could do nothing in a game situation. It's always difficult to experiment during a crucial game. When I left hockey, I tried to teach this trick to my junior colleagues but unfortunately, none of them ever adopted it perfectly.

The goalkeeper's art is not unlike that of the acrobat. To master it, you must first make yourself familiar with the basics of goalkeeping, and travel the long and difficult route to becoming an expert in your field.

For now, I will briefly explain some of my theories on goaltending. Nearly fifteen years ago, I graduated from the Regional Institute of Physical Culture in Smolensk. The title of my thesis was "A Research of Tactical Actions of a Hockey Goalkeeper". In hindsight, some assertions in my work seem to be naive and wrong. The others I developed further in the game, and they became logically complete.

My thesis started with detailed analyses of Canadian goalkeepers – influenced greatly by our games with NHL professionals. What first impressed me about Canadian goalkeepers was their amazing ability to come out of the net while under attack in order to cut down the angles. For many years, my movements had been limited and bound by the goal crease. In no way could I overcome the fear of leaving the net to come forward and handle the puck. In order to overcome this shortcoming I developed an exercise in which I would skate at top speed to different face-off spots, then backed up to my own net. Since the goalie can't turn to face his net in such a situation, I learned to find the net intuitively from anywhere on the ice.

Observing Canadian goalkeepers helped me to make one

more important conclusion: It is necessary to develop in yourself a high reserve of energy, to be able to concentrate and mobilize yourself for a lightning reaction.

A puck shot from a distance of twenty to thirty feet develops fantastic speed – such speed that even the best trained man can't react in time. My observations of the game led to a solution. The goalkeeper has to see the puck the moment it leaves the curve of the hockey stick. He must not follow the puck, but build a trajectory of its flight in his mind and be ready to set up a barricade at the point of its landing. I mastered the use of hockey mathematics many years after I wrote my thesis. It is one thing to know the theory, and another to put it into practice. Many years went by before I could rely completely on my intuition.

What does the craftsmanship of a goalie consist of? In the draft of my thesis I described it this way: "Character, multiplied by athletic ability, technique and experience – that's what makes the goalkeeper successful in a game." A bit later, I added two more qualities to this list: hard work and psychological stability. I still wonder why I left hard work out in the first place. It is widely known that talent without diligence is nothing.

I remember being astonished by a 'prophecy' of an American futurologist, who predicted that in the year 2000, a human being whose zealous attitude toward work as a duty was higher than his other values in life would be looked upon as a dangerous and harmful neurotic. According to this theory, even those who regarded their work as a mission would probably be evaluated as narrow minded egocentric people with an exaggerated sense of responsibility. What a prognosis!

For me, work was always the first priority. Back then, when I was doing my graduate work, I was probably so carried away by hockey that I couldn't separate diligence from accumulating game experience, physical fortitude, and perfection of technique. I always considered, and still consider now, the character of the athlete as the most important condition of craftsmanship. A man who is short-tempered, with no ability to calm himself down or to cheer up others, will always be a panic-monger, capable at any moment of letting down his teammates. This is especially unforgivable in a goalkeeper.

Discipline, and the ability to control one's own actions have to be in the blood of the athlete. How many talented players, who could have been world stars, were ruined by slackness, lack of self-discipline, and an unwillingness to follow the stern sports routine. Of course, to smoke one cigarette or to drink one glass of wine doesn't bring immediate ruin, but the tragedy is in allowing oneself one indulgence after another and so on, and so on, until one loses control. Sports categorically excludes alcohol and tobacco.

The goalkeeper has to be respected on his team. He must learn to manage the defense of his own team as a conductor handles the orchestra. I would even call the management of the defense one of the main responsibilities of the goalkeeper. He has to notify his players, quietly but clearly, about movements of their rivals on the ice. Jacques Plante recommended that goalkeepers never blame their teammates. They should suggest but never criticize. I tried to follow this rule. A quarrelsome character doesn't belong to a goalkeeper. I have met with many goalkeepers around the world. Almost all of them are quiet and steady people. A goalkeeper should never be reproached for his mistakes during the game. On the contrary, he should be constantly encouraged. The friendlier the mood on the team, the better and more coordinated the game.

There are other qualities that are necessary to the goalkeeper. He has to be strong physically; often he has to battle his opponent for the puck. On the Army Team, attention was always given to the athletic conditioning. Tikhonov always gave us the maximum physical workout, as Tarasov had done.

Contemporary hockey demands technical and tactical literacy from a goalie. With tactical/technical training, you upgrade the following skills: choice of correct stance and position, movement, and management of defense. Each goalkeeper chooses a stance which is comfortable for his stature. There are, of course, some general rules; the goalkeeper shouldn't lean too far forward and he should hold his catcher a little bit in front of him. The playing technique of a goalkeeper must be very simple and economical in movement. Some goalkeepers try to show off their technique, using spectacular effects. This may distract the opponent momentarily but I don't believe that it adds to the goalkeeper's reliability.

The hockey stick is supposed to be approximately twenty centimeters in front of the skates. From the very beginning, a goaltender should try to catch the puck, not deflect it. If you deflect the puck with your hockey stick off a long shot, try to kick it, not back out in front of you, but into the corners to prevent rebounds. The most insidious experts at the rebound shots are the Canadian professionals.

The hockey stick always has to be touching the ice, otherwise the puck could slip under it before you notice it. To make young goalkeepers get used to this rule, sometimes they receive a heavier hockey stick.

I don't recommend blocking shots by falling down or kneeling. There is a danger of letting in high shots or rebounds. Stand confidently on your feet. It is easier to fool a goalkeeper when he is lying down. Falling is often a sign of poor skills or no confidence.

If a shot at your net goes at an acute angle, keep the hockey pad as tight as possible against the post, otherwise the puck could find its way through a small slot and deflect off your foot directly into the net. The puck is very unpredictable, you can't fool around with it.

If you are lucky enough to catch the puck, know beforehand what to do with it. As a rule, you can handle it no more that a second. I am often asked: Is it necessary to catch pucks that miss the net? Each goalkeeper has his own answer to that. For example, I do not recommend doing this unless it is necessary to stop the game, say, for a shift change. And there is something else. There is a screen behind the net and high shot can hit it and deflect directly onto the opponent's stick. Before you know it the puck is in the goal. In this situation it is better to intercept the puck.

They used to say that if you couldn't skate, you could always be a goalkeeper. This is a fallacy. A goalkeeper has to skate perfectly. This is the base of his tactical skill. The game doesn't let him stand still for a minute. He has to be ready to rush to meet the forward and recoil the same way back to the net. He makes lunges and dashes, and sometimes participates in a rough skirmish. And all this in bulky goalkeeper gear, with a heavy stick.

The ability to skate faultlessly will help you play confidently behind the net. This is absolutely necessary for a skillful goalkeeper. However, if you haven't got enough experience, don't rush to leave your place. Only when the puck is shot from the blue line will you have enough time to get back to the net before your rival is there.

It is also important to learn how to fall down and get up fast. A goaltender has to be able to move like a 'Roly-Poly' doll which has weights attached to the base, causing it always to recover its standing position. In order to practise this skill, first you fall on one knee, then on the other. Then, twenty to thirty times on both knees at once. There is a catch here. As you stand up, the natural inclination is to raise your hockey stick off the ice. A rebound shot, and – a goal! You have to train yourself to leave the hockey stick on ice when you stand up.

There are big arguments about how a goalkeeper should play when an opponent has the puck behind the net. First of all it is necessary to cover the near corner of the net with your leg and watch the puck without turning your body. Your crouch should be lower than usual so that if the puck is passed through the crease you are able to come out of the net easily and instantly get into position, ruffling up like a rooster to protect a larger area.

'Catching bullets' is an accurate description of goalkeepers' play. If in soccer, the player taking a penalty shot has the advantage over the goalkeeper, in hockey, I believe, the goalkeeper and forward both have equal chances. As a matter of fact, I'm inclined to think that an experienced goaltender is in a more advantageous position than his opponent. As soon as the forward crosses the blue line, the goalie comes sharply out of my net, scaring the opponent while at the same time allowing for the protection of a larger area of the net. It is important not to react to fake moves. I always took into account which of the forwards was taking the penalty shot, and played them according to their individual style and character. Everybody has their favorite tricks, and rarely would they invent something new in a situation like this.

I am often asked if the height of a goalie has any significance. I do not think it is important. Viktor Konovalenko, one of the greatest goalies, is not very tall. The famous Canadian goalkeeper Gump Worsley is short too. Short goalies have their advantages. They are quicker, and it's easier for them to catch low shots. Jacques Plante agrees: "Your height is a minor thing," he says. "The main thing is that the aspiring goalkeeper be a fighter, not a coward; after he lets in a goal, he blames himself, not others."

As a tall goalkeeper, and my weakness was low shots. This

was noticed immediately by Anatoly Tarasov, and he recommended that I start to seriously train my legs. He even invented special exercises for me. For example, I hopped on one leg along the blue line, moving from one side of the arena to the other. One of my favorite exercises involved transferring the center of gravity of my body from one bent leg to the other, while simultaneously trying to pull my toes as far as possible – something like a Russian folk dance. I named this exercise 'Moiseev Ensemble', after the famous Soviet dance group. For strengthening the muscles on my legs, I also did an exercise called 'The Cross' where you jump in turns on one leg, right-left-forwards-backwards. This is best done in full goalkeeper's gear. Generally, I always tried to come out on the ice for practice as if for a game – in full hockey gear.

No sport requires a goalie to have such adroit and strong hands as does hockey. The hockey goaltender has to stop and deflect pucks that fly at the net with tremendous speed. For training your arms, pushups are very helpful.

The next quality is experience. Experience is not necessarily related to age or the number of games played. Canadians are of the opinion that experience comes to the goalkeeper around thirty. I wouldn't make such a confident statement. It is necessary to take into consideration the individual characteristics of the athlete. An experienced goaltender is one who has developed the self-assurance necessary to use his natural talent and the techniques he has learned through training. To achieve this he must seriously devote his time to perfecting his play; he must know his weaknesses and the methods for improving them; and he must be fanatical about his training. Training must be intensive and year-round.

Any practice starts with a workout. Naturally, the goalkeeper has his own special one. I recommend working more on hip joints and especially the groin muscles. Some experienced athletes recommend doing the splits. It is not a bad exercise, although I never did them.

Weightlifting can be harmful to a goaltender and should only be used for general physical development. The maximum weight used in leg exercises, for example, should never exceed forty kilograms. When he works with his arms a goalkeeper should attempt to imitate the arm movements he would use in a game. For example, the stick hand works as it does when it blocks a shot with the blocker while the glove hand moves as if to catch the puck with the trapper.

I disagree with those who assert that it is not necessary to include jogging in the goalkeeper's workout. While I never enjoyed jogging,it is an essential part of the training process. Even chess players jog. For beginners, I recommend a six to ten kilometer cross-country run twice a week in summer and fall. For intermediate and senior goalkeepers the distance should be twelve to fifteen kilometers, three times a week.

The best advice I can provide anyone is whatever kind of sports you do, make your workout diversified, not boring. The workout is supposed to reward you with strength, not punish you with fatigue.

I still remember one winter when Tarasov set up a track and field training program for us. Yuri Lebedev, Slava Anisin, and I went out to the park, did our workout as we were supposed to, and waited for further instructions. "See that hill and the tree on the top of it? You have to reach that tree from three different directions. Is it clear? Go!" Tarasov ordered.

The catch was that the hill was covered in snow up to our waists. How were we supposed to get to the top without a shovel? But Tarasov had already blown on his whistle. We climbed, squeezed and crawled our way up. The snow was under our collars and our running shoes were full of it. It was hard, but at the same time it was fun and unusual. When we reached the goal our feet felt as if they were made of lead, our breath was hot. We caught our breath and dragged ourselves back down. But from the bottom of the hill, we heard Tarasov's terrible voice: ''What's the matter, why are you young fellows idling there? No walking, just fall down head over heels!'' Slava Anisin and I still like to recall that workout, ''Do you remember, 'fall head over heels'?''

After the track and field exercises and weightlifting I began my main exercises. First, I took one or two tennis balls in hands and assumed a goalkeeper's stance. I threw the ball at the wall with one hand, and caught it with the other. This way I acquired vision and developed skills for catching the puck. Then I would complicate the exercise by putting a workload on the legs. While throwing the ball, I did the ''Moiseev Ensemble''. A further complication of this exercise was for another player to stand in front of me to prevent me from catching balls bouncing off the wall. Finally I had the other player both throw the ball at the wall and at the same time try to prevent me from catching it. Next, goalkeepers worked in pairs passing two balls back and forth while moving at the same time. From the outside it probably looked like a juggling act in the circus.

The second exercise was the so-called 'mirror exercise'. In this exercise two goalkeepers are positioned face to face. One of them does as many different exercises as he can recall. The more intensive and varied they are, the better. The task of the other goalie is to follow these exercises exactly. Partners look like doubles in a mirror. It looks more like a ballet exercise, but instead of the stern discipline of the ballet school, the emphasis here is on improvisation.

For the third exercise I would take my place in the net while the coach or another player shot fifty to one hundred tennis balls at me non-stop with a racket, alternating the blows to the blocker or the catcher. After such an exercise, a goalkeeper can confidently say he was 'under fire'.

It is not advisable to use all of the exercises described above in one practice. I have simply listed exercises which, from my point of view, will help goalkeepers to acquire skills sooner. Every experienced goalkeeper probably has his own system of practising and I don't want to impose my methods on anyone. I am just sharing my experience and some of the methods I used to get to the top.

A couple of remarks regarding goalkeepers' equipment: I have said more than once that the puck hurts when it strikes you, and sometimes pads are not enough to save you. Injuries can happen, but the better your gear, the less risk that you will need a doctor. The gear has to be in order all the time. I emphasize this because if any small part of the gear is left unchecked, it can cause a lot of trouble. Hockey is not the kind of sport where you can disregard even the most trivial of details.

Underwear, knee guards, pads, elbow and shoulder pads, chestguard, hockeypants and jersey, catcher, blocker, mask, helmet, goalkeeper's hockey stick, skates – this is the mandatory list of gear necessary for a contemporary goalkeeper. The medieval knights probably had a less complicated set of clothes. But they didn't have to face Phil Esposito either.

A goalkeeper has to know the nature of all tricks, habits, and peculiarities of forwards. All of this is developed in practice. In a psychogical duel with an opponent, the goalkeeper is not supposed to react to fake moves. It is important to concentrate, and not show any signs of hesitation or indecision. A decision has to be made fast and executed in the twinkling of an eye. A good goalie can combine relaxation and maximum concentration during the game, and must be able call upon a reserve of strength and energy whenever it is needed, however late it is in the game. Nobody can correct his mistakes; behind him is the net, and then the red light. But even that unpleasant bright flash of red light must not affect his calmness and concentration. For this reason, it is useful to combine exercises of high intensity with intervals of relaxation and rest in practice.

Probably, the most typical shortcoming of the majority of goalkeepers is their mental failure, especially during important games with a strong opponent. Some make the serious mistake of being afraid to lose, or feeling uncomfortable, before the game. Others, after allowing a goal at the beginning of the game, get upset, and cannot mobilize their skills and their will. Still others suffer from an excessive desire to show off. That's why it is so important to get in the proper mood beforehand.

Each goaltender psychologically prepares for the game in his own way. It is such a personal matter that I am not going to give any advice. Viktor Konovalenko played solitaire for hours. Glenn Hall, so I've heard, got in the proper mental condition before the game by swearing at hockey, his goalkeeper's fate, teammates, fans, at the world in general. This way he got rid of needless tension and appeared on the ice calm and collected.

I, on the other hand, shrank in myself. On the day of a game I thought about the game only, nothing else but the game. I repeated over and over again: You must not let your team down. And finally I said to myself: You have a special responsibility. You are the goalkeeper. You are the main player on the team. I tried to sleep in the daytime. My nerves had to be in ideal order. I became uncommnicative; I didn't want to break my mood with idle conversation. As the game approached, I drank black coffee along with the others. Everything surrounding me which wasn't part of the game finally disappeared.

My pre-game preparation had nothing to do with superstition

or mindless habit. All I thought about was the game at hand. Tarasov taught me this. "A goalkeeper is supposed to win the game," he said. "Do you understand what that means? Learn to analyze the opponent quickly and precisely. He might not even know himself where he is going to shoot, but you have to know where, and how to intercept it. Remember," reiterated Tarasov, "you can't be a good goalkeeper without intuition. But intuition doesn't come by itself. You have to think all the time."

As I have said the psychological preparation for a game is a very personal ritual. I once took someone else's advice in this regard and the results were disastrous. A psychologist came to our camp in Novogorsk, where the team was preparing for upcoming games. "Who shall I teach to get in the right mood to win a difficult game?" he asked. "Tretiak! Vladik!" shouted one of my teammates. "He is our last defense. He can't make mistakes."

And so, my lessons with that psychologist started. I don't remember all the exercises he taught me. The sense of most of them was self-inspiration. I had to stand in front of a mirror and repeat to myself: I am the best goalkeeper. It's easy for me to save any goal. My net is impenetrable. Even while my teammates were playing tennis, or watching TV, I locked myself in the bathroom and repeated and repeated again how great I was in front of the mirror.

At practice on the day of the game I really amazed everybody with extremely clean and confident play, kicking out the majority of pucks that were flying at my net. Later in the day, we went to play a very important game against the Czechoslovakian team. And do you know what happened? I let in seven goals. Seven! That didn't happen to me often. Since then, I count only on myself.

10

LUCK TURNS ITS BACK ON US

I would say that 1976 and 1977 were the worst years in Soviet hockey over the past two decades. We had to settle for second place at the World Championships in Poland, third at the World Championships in Austria, and we were eliminated in the first round of the Canada Cup. It seemed that luck had turned its back on us.

At the beginning of April, 1976, we arrived in Warsaw. From there, we went to the city of Katowice, where the World Championship was held. We arrived by bus. The trip was not short – we drove for nine and a half hours. I was a little bit worried. I recalled details of our last games. We had lost two games in Sweden, had one tie, and won only one game. In Moscow, players of the Soviet Army Club, which was still the base of the National team, tied the game with Dynamo and lost to Krilya Sovetov. Overall, the results were not pleasant. I was worried as well because Petrov wasn't included on the team, and, as I said before, the first line seemed to lose its power when any of its members was substituted.

Our bus finally stopped at the hotel and I put aside all my sad thoughts. Our friendly hosts greeted us with bouquets of red carnations.

I was in Poland for the first time in 1967 as a fifteen-year-old boy for the International Tournament with the Moscow all star team. Bronislav Somovich was the goalie and I was a backup. The Palace of Sports in Katowice was still under construction, and it was hard to visualize this future master-piece of architecture. We played in an old wooden stadium and, generally speaking, Katowice didn't make a very lasting impression on me at the time.

Now, however, it was hard to recognize the capital of Silezia. Beautiful modern streets were sparkling clean. There were a lot of parks. Happy and smiling people were all over the place. What a breathtaking Palace of Sports! 'Spodec', as it was called looked like a giant flying saucer, and it was spacious, bright, and comfortable. It was equally pleasing to spectators and players. The ice was perfect too. Participants in the World Championships were provided with the best conditions for efficient training and exciting recreation.

In our spare time, we were shown the remarkable sites of the Katowice area, where I saw a lot of new hockey stadiums with artificial ice. It looked as if the Polish had decided to take up hockey seriously. Remembering their progress in soccer, we were expecting serious competition on the ice. By the way, they have a good record in hockey: They won the silver medal in the Continental Championships in 1929 and 1931.

At the same time that hockey arenas were being constructed in Poland, sports clubs and schools like our Army Club School were being created. Experienced coaches, some invited from the USSR, were training even the little hockey players. The popularity of hockey in Poland was helped by leading Polish sports journalists, who wrote a lot about the game.

The Poles also learned to manufacture good hockey equipment. I was given stick labelled 'Made in Poland' and it was as good as the world's best hockey sticks.

There is a reason why I am writing so much about the hosts of the 1976 World Championships. Here is what happened in Katowice.

"Who are we playing in the first game?" one of the young players asked me. "Poland? Oh, that's nothing." I was shocked. What kind of an attitude was that? "Where are you?" I asked. "You're at the World Championships. You must play the best you can in each and every game. Do you understand?" At a loss, he shrugged his shoulders and moved aside. He didn't believe me, which was a pity.

In the game with our hosts, my backup Alexander Sidelnikov was in the net. The game started with us taking the game to them. Mikhailov, Yakushev, and Maltsev each had breakaways on the Polish goalie Tkacz, but all these duels were won by the goalkeeper. From defense, our opponent quickly changed to smart counter-attacks and succeeded in taking a 2-0 lead. From the bench I could see all the mistakes of my teammates. Defensemen were standing still! Forwards were slow in moving the puck. There was no freshness or excitement in the actions of the team. It was an unpleasant sight.

When the fourth puck went in our net, I was put in the game. But it was too late, we had already lost. Our hosts built their counter-attacks with precision. They spent no more than eight minutes on offense in the whole sixty minutes of the game. Despite our advantage, they were scoring the goals. What was it?

Never before had we given away points to the teams which we did not think were our main competitors for first place.

And now ...

"It was sensational!" was what the Polish head coach Josef Kurek told a press conference after the game. "It seemed to me that it was only in the last minutes of the game, when the score was 6-4 and the referee punished the Soviets with a penalty, that we won. Before the game I asked my players to pay more attention to defense and to prevent unnecessary goals. But my players were not only confident in defense, they were also successful in offense."

I don't know what review the Polish coach gave to his goalkeeper, but the thirty-year-old Andrzey Tkacz, without any doubt, was a major hero that night. The twenty-two-year-old rookie Weslaw Jobczyk, who was playing in his first important international game, also played very well, and scored three goals on us.

The next games were not much better. We did not have much luck in the games with the Czechs, which ended up 3-2 and 3-3. We lost our second game to the Swedes, 4-3. We lost an unbelievable amount of points but managed, by some miracle, to end up in second place.

Analyzing the reasons for our unfortunate failure, I came to the conclusion that our team, in the shape it came to the Championships, could not have counted on a successful performance. It was logical. Our coaches had put all their emphasis on preparation for the Winter Olympic Games of 1976. The struggle in Innsbruck drained too much strength from us. We became Olympic Champions, but what was the price? Our guys were exhausted, both mentally and physically. Many returned from Austria with heavy injuries. In Katowice, just at the beginning of the tournament, we lost Shalimov and Maltsev to injuries. Petrov was not playing either.

I think we should have taken our young team to Katowice – the Golikov brothers, Balderis, promising defensemen – players who, a year later, joined the national team anyway. I am not saying that the youngsters would have won in Poland, but they probably wouldn't have done any worse and it could have been a good experience for them.

After a vacation, which my wife and I spent in Crimea, I was called to the Committee of Physical Culture and Sports. "Get ready," I was told, "chances are, you are going overseas for the Canada Cup."

Frankly speaking, I had mixed feelings about it. On the one hand, I wanted to play against professionals again. It was tempting to be present at the big hockey celebration. I wanted to test myself again against those great players. But I still had some concerns. The main one was the members of our team that was supposed to go to Canada.

That summer there was an accident, and our team was left without its leader, Valery Kharlamov. In addition, many players from Spartak who, along with the Army players, were the base of the National Team, could not play because of injuries. As well, it was obvious at the beginning of the season that Shadrin's line was not ready.

It was probably these reasons that influenced the decision of the hockey management to send a so-called 'experimental' version of the National Team to Canada. This team included a few unknown and inexperienced players. The management of the team was given to Viktor Tikhonov, Boris Mayorov, and Robert Cherenkov.

As I said before, I am for tempering our youth in hard games. It is necessary to do so, otherwise we will be left with nobody in the future. But I had the feeling that the coaches didn't have a lot of faith in the new recruits. "Your task is to finish in the top three," we were told before our departure. These words could have been understood as, "We know you are not the strongest, that's why we don't demand too much from you."

This didn't inspire a lot of confidence in the players. As for me, I was in shape and the other veterans were ready to do battle as well. Our fear was that the rookies might let us down. I decided to watch them, our new ones, as soon as we got to Canada.

In Montreal we were met with excitement, noise, and an avalanche of prophecies. The air was hot, both literally and metaphorically. The weather was hot and humid; it was hard to believe it was fall. Newspapers, as always, competed with their predictions. It could be seen everywhere – Canada was very serious about this tournament. For the first time in the history of hockey, the strongest amateur teams would meet the strongest professional teams. Everybody was waiting for an exciting fight. I looked at the rookies: Were they confused by all this noise? No, at first glance, everything was all right. They were emotionally stable. We would soon see what they could do on ice.

"The sooner we play, the better," Helmut Balderis said to me. "There's nothing worse than waiting. Everybody around here is going crazy with their forecasts and questions." "That's true," I agreed, "and the only answer we can give them is with our play."

The twenty-four-year-old Balderis had been included on the team only recently. If the native of Riga worked well with his partners, and the defense of the opponents was weak, the very best goalkeeper would not have much of a chance. Balderis started skating at the age of four at figure skating school, and it was said that he was not a bad figure skater. His first coach still sighs at the thought of having lost a star of ice-dancing. But hockey found in him a star of ice battles. In 1977, Helmut was named the best hockey player of the USSR Championships, and the best forward at the World Championship in Vienna. He looked like anything but a tough hockey player.

He looked more like a typical intellectual, with his glasses and a slightly absent-minded look on his gentle face.

But first impressions can be so wrong! Take, for example Bobby Clarke the former Philadelphia Flyers star. To look at him, you'd swear that Bobby was a wanted murderer, but once you got to know him, you realized what a very friendly and kind fellow he was. He damaged his reputation a little bit in 1972, when he played in Moscow for the NHL team. He probably caught that mutually aggressive spirit which was on their team.

Four years later, during Superseries, I was given a wristwatch as a gift from Clarke. "Bobby admires your game and wants to meet you," I was told. When we met I thanked him for the present and asked him what he would like to get from me in return. "I've got everything I could ever want," the Canadian answered and modestly added, "I'm a millionaire." But when I presented him with a Russian fur hat, he was excited and tried it on right away. And when, at the next meeting, I gave him a cuckoo clock, he was even more excited.

We discussed hockey and told each other about our families. "I like to play very much," he told me once, "but there is one inconvenience; hockey doesn't let me spend a lot of time with my family. I'm away ninety-five percent of the time. Tell me, Vladislav, how far does your team travel each season? I tried to recall, "Around twenty-one thousand kilometers." "And we travel nearly one hundred thousand kilometers. We play eighty games in 179 days." "That's hard," I agreed. "You play often, but we practise a lot. Twice as much as you do." "Ah, this hockey...," Bobby sighed like an old man.

We became friends. Each time we meet, Clarke asks about my wife and kids. If our schedules are such that we haven't seen one another for a long time, he'll send his regards through someone else. A Canadian newspaper wrote of this matter:

"If sharp competition between two athletes with different opinions about lifestyles does not stand in the way of their friendship, what stands in the way of the friendship between our countries?"

The Canadians wanted to win the Canada Cup so much that even the schedule of games, contrary to tradition, was arranged to work for them. We had to play the Czechs in the first game. With all due respect to the NHL, it is difficult to believe that this was just a coincidence.

A columnist the *Toronto Star* held the same opinion. This is an excerpt from an article he wrote after the tournament: "First of all, you have to acknowledge that the games were planned in such a way as to give our 'Golden Boys' the ideal conditions; on our skating rinks, with great participation of North American referees, and a schedule which would give our team the best chance.... Soviet players were called 'robots', executioners of a giant communist conspiracy, whose aim was to take over our innocent, clear-eyed, and clean-cut heroes. But if such a conspiracy existed, its members were the Canadian organizers who made up the schedule in such a way that our team appeared in a very advantageous situation. As for innocent and clear-eyed, those were the guys wearing the USSR team uniform."

Thus the tournament began for us at once, without any chance to scout the opposition. And, alas, my fears about the rookies on our team proved to be true. They were nervous and didn't show their best play. More importantly, they didn't show the fighter's character, which was always a strength of the USSR team. I had a big burden on my shoulders. Czechoslovakian players got several breakaways on me. There was no order in our defense. We were defeated by a score of 5-3.

All the lines on the Czechs' team were well-balanced, and

there was an equilibrium between veterans and youth. It was a real mix of experience and youth, calmness and temper. I know the Czechoslovakian goalkeepers, Irzi Holocek and Vlado Dzurilla, very well. Each, by his age, could be revered as a veteran, but how marvellously they both played!

After that game, Canadian newspapers justifiably wrote that the USSR team had nineteen different players, but no cooperation. During a TV interview, I was asked what the team lacked. I gave the same answer; a cooperative game. And in front of us we saw another fortress – the Swedes. We were well aware of the strengths and weaknesses of the Swedish National Team, but now the team had professional players, and that was supposed to change their tactics. The score of this game was 3-3. We let the victory slip away in the last minutes. We lost in a very sad, unforgivable manner. Kapustin passed the puck exactly on to the stick of Borje Salming, who played for the Toronto Maple Leafs. Our defenseman Kulikov was delayed at the time, and another Swedish professional, Hedberg, received the pass, came in one on one with me, and took away our victory.

The Canadian referee was far too severe with us. Twice, we ended up with two men in the penalty box at once. I had the impression that the referee clearly wanted to influence the outcome of the game. What does it mean to be left on the ice with only three players? There are no such things as tactics for playing three against five. To leave three hockey players means, in a sense, to punish them with a goal.

Our irritation after the game was softened by a prize which was given to me as the best player of the game by Jacques Plante. He called me the number one goalie in the world. Of course, such a high evaluation from a legend like Plante was very flattering, but I would have preferred to hear such words addressed to the whole team.

We beat the Finns by a score of .11-3 and then moved on to Philadelphia, for a game against the USA National Team. I woke up in a room at the Sheraton Inn, and immediately looked out the window to check the weather. The sun was shining brightly, and there wasn't a trace of cloud in the blue sky. "It's going to be a warm day," said my roomate Sasha Golikov. "It's going to be a hot day," I corrected. The day before, the thermometer had read twenty-five degrees Celsius in the shade. The air was so stuffy at the Spectrum, where we were practising, that we felt like we were on the beach. We were in a sweat the minute we picked up our hockey sticks. But the practice proceeded as usual, and everybody tried their best. Even Viktor Shalimov, who was still feeling the effects of a heavy injury, put on his skates and came out on the ice.

I won't describe the game in detail. We won relatively easily, 5-0, and it seemed to me that the rookies had acquired more confidence. The Canadians lost to the Czechs, allowing the only goal of the game to be scored in the third period. This victory immediately put the Czechoslovakian team into the finals. As for us, the most difficult duel was still to come – against the hosts of the competion.

Again, the rookies on our team couldn't control themselves. They tried their best to play, but it looked like nervousness had bound their arms and legs. The scoring began in the eighth minute with a goal by the Gilbert Perreault. Vikulov quickly replied for us. Before the intermission, Hull put his team ahead again. In the next period, Barber added a goal to make the score 3-1. That's how it stayed. I had to stop more than forty shots, but it wasn't a problem, I could've done more. It was too bad that our players, who started out at a good pace, switched to a slow, dragging pace, which favored the Canadians.

And so, for the first time in many years, the Soviet team

wasn't participating in the final round of a prestigious hockey tournament. The Canadian and Czechoslovakian teams met in the three-game final round. It was fitting; they turned out to be the best teams at this hockey celebration.

The Canada Cup was won by the pupils of Scotty Bowman, but it cannot be said that their victory was easy. The World Champions showed fierce resistance to the Canadians. The Czechoslovakian players had a good chance to win, but a momentary fear of 'the invincibles' got in their way.

The bitterness of failure was sweetened a little bit by winning the 'Showdown', which was held in Canada at the same time. I hope that someday something like this will be held in my country. A unique idea, Showdown was a competition of goalkeepers and forwards, and was put on every year by Canadian television. The best professional players participated in it.

In 1976, before the Canada Cup, 'Intershow' was held for the first time. Here, the hosts of the competition competed with European aces. We gathered in a small town not far from Toronto. There were eight goalkeepers and sixteen players. The goalkeepers were Vachon, Bouchard, and Resch from Canada, Holocek from Czechoslovakia, Leppinen from Finland, Astrem from Sweden, and me, Tretiak, representing the USSR. I won't name all the field players, but I will mention some of the stars of professional hockey who participated, such as Clarke, Larouche, Gilbert, Lafleur (who had been the leading scorer in the NHL for the previous two years), and also the strongest amateur forwards including Alexander Maltsev and Viktor Shalimov.

The skating rink in that town was not very big, but it was cozy, and somehow reminded us of our rink at the Palace of Sports of the Red Army Club. There were no viewers in the stands – everything took place in secrecy. Television monopolized this event; everything was recorded on tape so that it could be shown to the viewers during the finals of the Stanley Cup. We gave our word not to tell anybody about the results of the Showdown until spring.

Even though we all spoke different languages, there were few obstacles in getting to know each other, or to finding mutual interests. From the outside, it looked like a gathering of members of the same team, not competitors. It was wonderful!

At first, we had to find out who was to play with whom. Forwards drew slips of paper with the names of goalies out of a drum, and goalies chose forwards. The name Larouche was written on my paper. I knew what that name meant. Larouche was a rising star from Pittsburgh, who later played for the Montreal Canadiens and the New York Rangers. This handsome Frenchman looked like he had been born under a lucky star. In a word, I understood that fighting this man off would not be easy.

After me, Potvin went to try his luck. Everyone could see how nervous he was. "Go for Tretiak!" shouted one of the players jokingly, "Pull out Tretiak's name!" He pulled out a nametag, unfolded it without hesitation, and angrily threw it on the floor. Everybody guessed instantly – Tretiak! I thought to myself that I had one less rival. Potvin had already surrendered without a fight.

Now came the time to determine who would come out on the ice, and when. Not me first, I begged to myself. I hadn't any idea what I was supposed to do. I hadn't slept the night before. I was thinking about how I was going to play, how not to let down the merit of our hockey. I rarely worried so much, even before the most important games. Naturally, I drew a tag on which was written "8:30 a.m.". In other words, I was the first. No luck whatsoever!

First, the players competed in drills to test their skating, shooting, and maneuvering abilities. According to the rules of the competition, the forwards were supposed to do several very difficult exercises, which demanded a faultless ability to handle the stick, as well as sharpshooting accuracy. Very few players completed the drill perfectly. The judges even considered the speed of the puck, which was measured by a special radar device.

Then the goaltenders took their turn. Potvin was the first to attack my net. My anxiety disappeared as soon as I took my place on the ice. The referee blew his whistle. Potvin dashed at me at full speed, while I, in turn, came out of the net to meet the Canadian. He probably got scared, and shot the puck prematurely. It went directly into my catcher. All three attempts ended the same way. I stopped the shot.

Larouche was luckier; he put two out of three shots in my net. First, he took a hard shot from far away, and broke his hockey stick, which confused me. While I was looking for the puck among the debris of the stick, it slowly slid into my net. Overall the score ended up 4-2 in my favor. I didn't know if it was good or bad, since no other goalie had been on the ice yet. Should I be happy or worried?

I changed and went upstairs. There, I could see everything that was happening on the ice through a large window. I got a cup of coffee, took a chair, and watched to see what would happen next.

Holocek came out on the ice. He was pale and very nervous. First, he let in three pucks, then another two; five in all. It was clear to me that I wouldn't finish in last place. Then Astrem had his turn. He let in three out of six shots. He wasn't any luckier than the others; he had to defend his net against two very strong sharpshooters, Clarke and Gilbert. The Finnish goalie Leppinen also let in three out of six, and he and Astrem had to play a tie-breaking round. The Swede had more luck, and moved to the semifinals.

We had dinner, and drew names again. I pulled out a tag with the name Darryl Sittler on it. Oh my, I thought. Sittler had just scored three out of three on Holocek. At the time he played for the Toronto Maple Leafs and was very strong (he confirmed this reputation later in the Canada Cup games). My name was drawn by Danny Grant, the captain of the Detroit Red Wings and a winner of the last two Showdowns.

I wasn't too worried. I stopped all five shots fired at me by Sittler and Grant scored only once, so the final score was 5-1 for me. I went to the dressing room to await the outcome of the competition between Astrem and Clarke and Larouche, instead of wasting my psychological energy on the rink. The door opened and Astrem came in. I could see by his face that he was happy. He approached me. "How many?" I asked. He held up three fingers. Three out of six? Everybody rushed to congratulate me. I moved to the finals. The Czechoslovakian forward Hlinka also became a finalist, as did the goalkeeper Stephenson and the forward Danny Grant.

In the finals, Stephenson went to the net first. Hlinka scored two goals on him, and Grant, one. Somehow, it calmed me down. I went out on the ice and thought to myself: There is nothing that would prevent you from setting a record – six out of six. Go for it! I stopped all six shots and I won first prize among goalkeepers. Ivan Hlinka won for the forwards.

Could I have guessed then that third place, so uncommon for the players in red jerseys, awaited us at the World Championships in Vienna? The World Championships were still eight months away. We returned home, and went back to our teams to take a slight rest and prepare for the USSR Championship, which lasted from October to March.

That championship didn't have any surprises. Our Army team went steadily throughout the long competition, especially in the first half, where we suffered only one defeat against

Leningrad and a tie with Spartak. There was a spirit of unity among us. Our team could have been compared to a well-tuned machine, but machines are lifeless, and without souls. I could tell a lot of interesting stories about my friends; about the fantastic perseverance of Vladimir Petrov; about the smart and subtle play of Boris Mikhailov; about Valery Kharlamov's loyalty to the club, playing his heart out, while still recovering from a heavy injury.

After New Year's, our leading players were feeling quite tired, which could explain our losses to Traktor and Riga's Dynamo. Balderis scored four goals on me, and the newspaper said that I was afraid of this native of Riga. This is not true, I was never scared of anybody. Of course, Balderis was a good forward, he was always very accurate, but those four goals were more a result of our weariness; mine and the defensemen's.

The breaking point of the USSR Championship came with our games against Moscow's Dynamo; the only team who could compete with the Army Club for the gold. The third game between our two teams decided that.

We prepared specially for that game. Dynamo tactics were well known to us; they would line up on the blue line, take the puck, and immediately begin an all out rush. It was a risky play because they could easily be caught up ice.

"Use your speed and long accurate passes," recommended our head coach Loktev before the game. "And look out for Maltsev." I didn't have to be reminded about that. In my mind, I had already replayed the tape with the title "Sasha Maltsev" on it, and recalled how he shot, and from where. He would probably dominate the whole game. Of course, his linemates were strong too. Golikov and Prirodin – I had to watch out for them!

The Dynamo players came out on the ice full of youthful

vigor; "We will show you a game now!" But they couldn't fool us. I noticed at once that they were afraid of us, and were just trying to cover up their anxiety. We lead after the first period. The second period was the most difficult. Our rivals tried furiously to come back. The pace became just crazy, the puck was dashing around the net. I didn't even have a minute to catch my breath. Maltsev surprised me by changing his tactics. In previous matches, he had tried to go around me but in this game, he was shooting and his shots were like shots from a cannon. When he had the puck, I had to be on my toes.

We won that game 5-2. Our players carried out the coaches' instructions exactly, and added improvisation and fire of their own. The Red Army Club won the USSR Championship for the twentieth time. We were successful not only because the veterans played well but because our youngsters, too, had grown up into remarkable young men. I liked to watch how our coach Yuri Moiseev trained the youth. He was just as demanding – and had as much heart – as Tarasov.

Team Dynamo won the silver, and bronze went to the Traktor team from city of Chelyabinsk in the Ural Mountains. It was their first medal and I was happy for their success. I liked to play that team; they were speedy, quick tempered, and had only one thing on their minds – attack. The players from Traktor shot a lot at the net; I liked that too. Earlier, they had been clumsy and unimaginative, but their style gradually changed. In their actions, the players showed intelligence and maturity but the most attractive feature of the Traktor team was their independent, fighting mood.

With the Championship over I could finally pay more attention to my family. In December, my daughter Irina was born. I was happy. I had so much fun taking care of her, holding her in my arms. As well there was time to go back to school and I entered the Military-Political Academy. However, this rest didn't last long because preparation for the World Championships was about to begin.

Some time later, in the middle of May, the following lines appeared in my diary:

For the first time in my life, May has deceived me. Before now, May brought me only happiness. A beautiful season! Spring, lilacs, end of the hockey season, time for awards, vacation time near. . . . But now we have a feeling that lies like a stone in our hearts. Every player probably has a need, like myself, to be left alone with his thoughts. But is it possible to hide from everybody? Wherever you go, you hear the same ruthless questions: How could you lose the game? What happened? And you can only answer in a few words why the team came back from Vienna with bronze medals. Even we weren't sure what had happened.

Time must pass to calm the excitement, to let us analyze the situation. Now, everybody is still under the influence of emotions, captivated by worries and vexation. To our fans, our third place is a tragedy, and it is understandable. They were used to our victories, used to the thought that Soviet hockey is the best and the strongest in the world.

Now, a little history. The Canadians became involved in hockey in the middle of the last century. The first hockey rules were written down in 1879. The first Stanley Cup was awarded to Canadian national amateur champions in 1893. The Europeans held their first unofficial championship in 1910. Ten years later, the first Olympic hockey tournament, along with the first World Championship was held in Antwerp. In 1926 the Stanley Cup became the exclusive property of the NHL.

In our country, we hadn't heard a lot about this game. Only in the late forties did some hockey teams start to appear, made up of soccer and grass hockey players. In 1954, the National

Team of the USSR competed in World Championships for the first time, and almost immediately became one of the dominant powers in world amateur hockey. By 1977, our team had won the World crown fifteen times. That is something to be proud of! Between 1963 and 1971 we won nine world titles in a row. Our first 'misfire' occured in 1972. But with our defeat in Katowice, and then in the Canada Cup, misfortune seemed to be following us.

How did this happen? Why?

When we went to Vienna in 1977 our mood was the same as it always was before any important competition. I did, however, feel some psychological exhaustion. I had a headache, I didn't want to think about hockey.

The season had been very difficult, and I played almost all of it without substitution – both for my club, and for the National Team.

The Championship in Vienna promised to be a very interesting fight. For the first time, professional players from the USA and Canada were allowed to play on their national teams. The Canadians did not bring their strongest team – many players were busy in the Stanley Cup playoffs – but they still had a great many stars.

We started the Championships by beating all our opponents, including the Canadians. In the first game with them we won with a really devastating score, 11-1. This team made no impression on us. The professionals lacked any sense of team play. It seemed to me that they didn't know exactly why they had come to Austria.

For the first couple of days, they behaved as if they were the champions already. They wanted everyone to see that they were the best! They reminded me of spoiled children.

Their punishment struck immediately. On the second day of the tournament, the Canadians lost to the Swedes by a score of 4-2. I think that loss was the most offensive to them. During the second intermission I saw Larouche, pale and confused, smoking a cigarette and drinking black coffee. "What's the matter with you?" I asked, "Put up more effort." "Right away, right away," he answered, "We will show them." He gulped the coffee and rushed onto the ice. But my friend still couldn't show anything. The Swedes won.

An unpleasant incident occurred at the end of that game. During the playing of the Swedish national anthem, Wilf Paiement demonstratively left the ice. I must give credit to the chief of the Canadian delegation, Alan Eagleson, for taking disciplinary action. He ran after the hockey player and almost hit him. It was a very unpleasant scene. Two days later, when the Canadians lost to us, some of them behaved disgracefully during the performance of our anthem; they left their helmets on, leaned on their sticks and generally showed disrespect for the winning team. Of course, this is not the way of true sportsmen.

On April 28, we played Czechoslovakia. That was when I felt most out of place, as did the rest of the team. Too much remained in our memories of our losses to the Czechs at the last World Championship in Katowice, and at the Canada Cup tournament. The coaches tried in vain to relieve our tension; "Calm down, Vladik, calm down. Everything is going to be alright." "I am calm," I answered, not so much to them as to myself. "Yes, I am calm."

I suppose our opponents were as worried as we were. In the first few seconds, Eberman rifled a shot at my net. Then Bubla broke in on me alone. He shot and I simultaneously put out my stick and fell down with my chest on the puck. The early going was incredibly tense. A lot depended on who scored first. Luckily, we succeeded. Six minutes into the game Kapustin skated briskly along the boards behind Holocek's net, then passed to Zhluktov, who scored without stopping. Soon after that, when the Czechs had the power play, Martinec shot from far away. I was screened, and didn't react on the shot. The score was even at 1-1!

We came out for the second period in a different mood . We felt stronger than our rivals, and we thought that we could win convincingly. And that's what happened. Kapustin scored twice, and Mikhailov and Babinov made the score 5-1. In the third period Yakushev added one to make it 6-1.

After the game the Czech player Novak came up to me. "It's obvious," he said, "that you are stronger, you are going to be the champions." "We'll see," I answered evasively. When we were going to the shower room, Eberman, clearly saddened by their loss, said, "Well, we almost won the Canada Cup, and you will probably win the World Championship. That's how it's going to be, you'll see." "You must be joking," I interrupted, "all the battles are still ahead of us."

I really meant what I said but this can't be said of some of our players and coaches. I suppose they already believed that we had won the gold. Brave interviews given to journalists; premature meetings with the fans who had come to Vienna; too much self-confidence; all this was not our style. Perhaps it was this that let us down in the end.

On May 2, we had a game with the Swedes. A victory over them would guarantee gold medals for us. Nobody had any doubt about our victory. Swedes? So what! How many times had we defeated them? No doubt, the mood of our players was influenced by the optimistic statements of the newspapers; "The Russians are the strongest." "The Championship is over – the Champions are already known."

The coaches didn't disrupt this romantic vision by reminding the players of where they were. I can almost understand their reasoning. In six games, our team had scored sixty-four goals! It was hard not to believe that we were really the strongest. With just one more victory we would be the champions!

And so the game with the Swedes began. Kharlamov almost scored in the first minute. We had three more excellent scoring opportunities in the first few minutes. As strange as it may sound, this too was damaging to us. We deluded ourselves into believing that everything was all right; we were in control and now we were going to bury them. But time passed by, and nothing close to success showed up. The Swedes scored the only goal in the first period. Our players looked like fish that had been thrown on the ice. They had a tremendous will to win, they had skills – but it wasn't enough.

In the second period, the Swedes started to play more aggressively, and our defense looked stunned. The rivals shot at my net without interruption, bravely getting the rebounds, while my teammates calmly stood by and watched. I couldn't believe it! Furthermore, the Swedes built their defense skillfully. Even playing shorthanded, they were easily cutting the possibilities for our players to attack the net, and they launched counter-attacks at every opportunity. The game ended with stunning results; we lost 5-1.

The mood of the team changed at once. Instead of complacency, there was a nervous feeling of loss. It was as if we had to participate in a chase after something which had been stolen from us. And we heard from all directions : ''You must win.'' ''You've got to.'' ''You have to.'' ''Must, must, must.'' If an outsider had heard our fans, he might have assumed that the world would end if we did not take first place. Such 'pumping-up' would not do any good, a fact that was confirmed in the next game with the Czechs.

This time Dzurilla was in the net. At the end of the first period the score was 3-0 for Czechoslovakia. I still can't understand what happened. The defense was playing very badly, and the forwards were helpless. Depressed and battered, we dragged ourselves to the locker room. We didn't want to look each other in the face. Nobody would have recognized the National team of the USSR at that moment. Vladimir Petrov caught me in the hall. "You stop giving up so many rebounds," he grumbled. "And you better help the defense," I snapped. It was not like us to quarrel during intermissions, no matter how hard the game was. This was the first sign that the team was not healthy.

The second period started with the rivals scoring their fourth goal. While our defense stood by passively, the Czechs bombarded me with shots and finally they scored. I felt something akin to panic. Let's do it guys, pull yourselves together, I begged in my mind. We have beaten Czechoslovakia tens of times. We are stronger. . . . Kharlamov, Mikhailov, and Balderis each scored, but it was too little too late. Dzurilla came out on top. And so, one more defeat.

A little while later in Moscow, I happened to hear an opinion of one psychologist about our failures in Vienna which confirmed my own thoughts. "You forgot how to lose," said the psychologist. "When you fell behind you started to panic and forgot how to play. Everyone was frantically doing something he considers necessary, working really hard, using up all their strength, but there was no team on the ice, no teamwork. The advantage in the games with Sweden was on your side, but the rivals celebrated the victory. It was absurd! I also think that the coaches managed the team unwisely in difficult moments. Instead of uniting the team, they were busy looking for scapegoats." Yes, he was right.

However, all was not lost. We had to play the next game against Canada. By then the Canadians had settled down. Perhaps self-respect overpowered them, reminding them of their professional pride. I think the reaction of the Canadian fans, who criticized their team, had an effect too. The Canadians managed a 3-3 tie with Czechoslovakia, then smashed the Swedes 7-0. They had definitely finished with anarchy and seemed determined to claim one of the medals.

However in the USSR-Canada game, which was played on May 6, they reverted to their old style. It reminded us of what happened in Philadelphia a year and a half before. The Canadians, not confident in their skills, decided to scare us, the same way they had scared the Swedes before. The psychological attack began even before the game. Phil Esposito told a reporter of the Austrian newspaper *Neue Kronik Zeitung*; "If I'm forced to jump and grab somebody's throat to win the game, I will do it."

During the warmup, a puck from the Canadian zone accidently got to our side. Gena Tsigankov, our kind and gentle defenseman only touched the puck to pass it back. The professionals were on him like hawks. The Canadians were ready to start a brawl even then, to remove anybody's doubts about how terrible and bloodthirsty they were.

The warmup was over, and one of our rivals shot a puck at me. Frankly speaking, I was shocked. In all my years of playing, I had never seen anything like this. But it wasn't the end. We went down to our changing rooms, and we could hear Canadians cursing and swearing in a way that if it had happened on the street, they would have been arrested. But this was at the Palace of Sports and our rivals were considered to be 'psyching themselves up'.

Really, it was an awful scene – malicious, twisted faces, foaming at the mouth. It's hard to believe, but that's true. After the game I came upon my old friend, Aggy Kukulovich, a former professional who for many years worked in the Moscow office of Air Canada. "Aggy, what kind of gang has been brought to Vienna?" "I feel ashamed of them myself," he answered.

In that game the scoring was opened by Tsigankov. Soon the Canadians responded with a goal of their own, and what happened next I still remember with disgust. Our rivals skated up to my net and yelled in my face, "You're going to eat the puck." They wanted to unbalance me, but achieved the opposite. I said to myself, That's it, this is the last puck in my net. And it was. They didn't score another goal on me.

It drove them crazy that our players didn't give in to their provocations, didn't retaliate. The Canadian hockey players were out of their minds with frustration. Scare tactics didn't work. The referees were firm giving out penalty after penalty. The offenders were sent to the penalty box while we sent pucks into their net.

Paiement, who was supposed to cover Yakushev, carried out his mission very creatively by hooking Sasha around the neck. Russell handled his hockey stick like it was a club in a village brawl, and when he was penalized, he went to the penalty box, threw his helmet on the ground, and began swearing hysterically. After the final siren, and the announcement that the professionals had lost 8-1, Mackenzie, in powerless anger, jabbed his hockey stick into Shadrin's stomach.

What had they been hoping for? That the referees would close their eyes? That we would get scared? That spectators would like their tricks? But the referees were unforgiving and nobody could scare our team. Fans in their turn began to despise that team. It was no wonder that the Austrian fans were all shouting in unison, "Canada, go home!"

At the time of the championship, the Canadians tried to accuse the referees of not doing their job fairly, and that's why they were nervous and fighting. These claims were unfounded. The referees made only one error: In the Canada-Czechoslovakia game, they incorrectly counted the third goal in the Canadian net. But even if the referees were mistaken, did it justify the behavior of the Canadians on the ice?

First place was to be decided in the last game of the championship – USSR vs. Sweden. A victory in this game would make us the champions, defeat would plunge us into third place. Six days had passed since the cold shower that the Swedes gave us on May 2nd. We analyzed in detail the reasons for the defeat and were convinced that it was a preposterous accident. We had to avoid making the same mistakes that we had made on that ill-fated day. We needed team play, solid defense, sharpshooting forwards, and organized shift changes. What could be simpler?

Our plans fell through before the first period was over. We forgot everything that we had promised to do. Again, we were nervous; again, our rivals were left undisturbed in the neutral zone; and again, our forwards lacked confidence. Even Yakushev managed to miss a couple of empty nets. A 3-1 loss threw us into third place.

How could we have possibly played so listlessly and with so little imagination in a decisive game? It was clear in this game how the creativity of the USSR team was suffering. We looked like fish trying to jump a concrete dam, oblivious to the open channels next to us. Were we weaker than the Swedes? No, we were stronger! But our team of stars suddenly forgot the basics of hockey. It became a problem for the team to go into the opponent's zone or to mount the power play. In Vienna, we displayed neither team play nor innovative tactics.

There were many changes after the Vienna tournament. We got a new head coach, Viktor Tikhonov. The work with the Sports Clubs was improved. There was an active search for talented young players. Anatoly Tarasov became a vice-president of the USSR Hockey Federation. All these steps were taken to lead Soviet hockey back on the main road to victory.

11

TIKHONOV – OUR LEADER
IN BATTLE

It's no secret that we were cautious at first about our new coach but once we got to know Viktor Tikhonov, we knew that we could follow him through fire and water.

Tikhonov's fate was typical of many people of his generation. He went to work when he was ten years old, in the grim years of the war. He was a mechanic in a bus depot, and worked a full shift every day. This was normal for boys during the war. He even played soccer in a yard between the stone walls of buildings. Soccer was Tikhonov's first passion; he played for the Moscow Army Team and for 'Burevestnik'. In the winter, when the soccer season was over, he tried to play a game that was new to Moscow, one that involved a strange black disk on the ice. Somehow he was noticed on the ice by one of the greatest Soviet athletes, Vsevolod Bobrov, who was equally brilliant at soccer and hockey. On his recommendation, Tikhonov was invited to the now defunct Air Force Team.

He later played as a defenseman for Moscow's Dynamo, and was an assistant coach on that club. In 1968 Tikhonov moved to Riga, the capital of Latvia, where he started to coach local hockey players (at that time, the team was called 'Daugava'). His first major achievement came soon after; Riga's hockey players fought their way to the top league and, unlike many other provincial teams, confidently stayed in the limelight. The team adopted their coach's character; they never backed down from anybody. Tikhonov could consolidate the team and lead it to a great victory. In 1976, Tikhonov's team won the Polar Cup; in 1977 they took fourth place in the National Championships, and the forward Helmut Balderis was acknowledged as the best hockey player of the Soviet Union.

Riga's players were easily distinguishable from any other provincial team by their original style and their exciting, yet disciplined, play. Viktor Tikhonov was the first of our coaches to introduce four shifts to the game. This, and his other tactical innovations, strengthened the potential of Riga's team.

Tikhonov gave himself to hockey with complete abandon. He was constantly inventing, improving, searching. He could work twenty-four hours a day and still transfer his enthusiasm to others. When he came to the Red Army Club, Tikhonov didn't make radical changes in the beginning. He didn't reconstruct all of Tarasov's educational-training processes to his liking nor did he disregard proven game concepts. All the best of our fundamentals were preserved, although some elements of training and strategy changed.

By observing Tikhonov during a game, one could see how much of a hockey fan he was, and how sensitive he was to success and failure. He was a bundle of nerves. It's a wonder that he could last to the end of a game. When we lost the Izvestia Tournament to Czechoslovakia, he was heartbroken. He was wounded so deeply by our failure that I was ashamed to look him in the eye. But he found me and tried to calm me down. "That's OK Vladik," he said, "we'll prove who is stronger."

An opportunity to see who was stronger arose very soon – at the 1978 World Championships in Prague. We didn't start out too well. Winning proved to be more difficult than we had expected. I let in many goals but Tikhonov comforted me: "Everything is all right, Vladik. It doesn't matter how many you let in now, as long as you're in top form for the finals."

There was a disturbing sense of anxiety surrounding us. It came as a result of great pressure and the wish not to let the team down. It spread from one player to another, paralyzing the team. Before I left for Prague, I told a friend, "You'll see, we will win this championship." He looked at me doubtfully. "Even in the best years of the team, you always avoided such promises."

But I was confident! And so were the other players. Isn't it strange? Two years in a row we let Czechoslovakia win. Not long before the Prague tournament, in Moscow's Izvestia Tournament, the Czechs inflicted another shattering defeat on us. Where did such optimism come from? The failures of our team only awakened a desire to prove to everybody that we were strong, that we could win. Defeats didn't burden us, but uncovered hidden reserves of power . It happened to everybody. Our unsuccessful start provoked anger in my teammates. We fought harder and harder.

For the next three weeks, every step for us was difficult. The game wasn't going right, injuries followed our players everywhere. It is a common belief that difficulties build character. This is true if you look them straight in the face; if you don't whine, but go forward. You forge yourself not in difficulties, but by overcoming them.

I didn't get mad at the defense – what would be the point?

•

They were not taking it any less seriously than I was. I told myself to think of how I could play more reliably. I asked Tikhonov to give me an exercise for rebounding pucks. The coach took shots at me, and Mikhailov finished them off – he was a great expert at that. I had to find myself again; to obtain that inner feeling which had served me loyally for many years. It was nothing supernatural; I simply had to find my usual style of play – the play which I had been accustomed to since I was a child and, more importantly, in which the team had confidence.

My worries multiplied when twice – on April 30 and May 1 – Tikhonov didn't put me in the net. "Pashkov is in the net today," the coach said before each game, simply and without any explanation. Finally noticing my depressed mood, Viktor explained to me: "I'm not trying to punish you. Take a rest. I know that you will not let me down later." I felt relieved; at least they still trusted me.

So I watched the games from the alternate bench, with players from Finland and East Germany. The Finns had won their match against the Canadians and came close to beating the Czechs. I liked their play; it was fresh and full of invention. I was sure that they would give us a run for our money but I was wrong. At the beginning of May, six of the Finnish players were hit with the flu. As well, they seemed to run out of steam by the end of the competition.

In our last game with the Finns, which we won, Sasha Golikov received a serious injury. His foot was so swollen that it was terrible to look at. We were sitting at the same table having supper and I watched him bite his lips, and tears appeared in his eyes. He pushed his plate away, "I can't take it, guys, it's a hell of a pain." Several voices in unison called our doctor. He ran to our table, "Let's move Sasha to the hotel room quickly."

The injury was treated with a massage and an ice pack. The doctor and two masseurs stayed with him during the night. I know that most people with such trauma lie in bed for ten days, but Sasha was on the ice the next morning. The doctor made him stand on his feet. This was an important moment in medical history!

The Golikov brothers – Vladimir and Alexander – were respected for their courage and their play. They were brave fellows, and loyal to hockey. They were both left-handed and thus were especially dangerous to goalkeepers. Sasha and Volodia could score from spots where it seemed that the puck could never get in.

After the game against the Finns, Yurzinov, Tsigankov, Sasha Golikov and I began preparing for our battle with the Swedes. That game would show how ready we were to fight for the gold. I practised and practised. The sweat was getting in my eyes. There were two dozen pucks on the ice, and they were all flying simultaneously at my net.

"OK," said Tikhonov, "now let's try it this way. We'll take eighteen shots and if we score less than six goals, the goalkeeper wins. If we score six or more, we win. Do you agree, Vladik?" I went silently to the net and lightly tapped my pads with my stick. Boom-boom-boom... five pucks went in my net. Good! My 'rivals', to the laughs of a few spectators, did sommersaults on the ice – that was the condition of our 'duel'.

"Let's see if you can score five goals again!", I yelled to Yurzinov. "We'll show you now!" threatened Gena Tsigankov jokingly. He waved his stick wildly in the air, as if to make the first blow. This time only four of the eighteen shots got by me, and my comrades and the coach were once again doing sommersaults. I took off my mask and skated to the boards. Sweat was running down my face, and my wet hair was matted together. My hockey stick seemed to weigh a ton. I caught sympathetic looks from the bench and the stands, as if to say, "What a burden on his shoulders!"

But the fatigue didn't disrupt my feeling that the pucks were gradually becoming 'trained', that I was close to my best shape. This was important. Now all I needed was a game to get back my confidence.

The day before the game against the Swedes, a Czech newspaper wrote: "The Swedes give up nothing without a fight. They defend their goal with an icy calm and a bulldog grip." Yes, the Swedes were a real puzzle for everybody. Not long before the championship we literally annihilated them in Stockholm in two exhibition games, but who could be sure that it was not a trick by their coach Lindberg?

Lindberg was a serious young man who knew his own mind. The Swedish coach required from his players a creative approach to hockey. The Swedish team of 1978 was a thinking team; they were flexible and had great will. In the previous championship, where they won a silver medal, they had displayed an amazing ability to launch the fast break.

Lindberg's stock rose further after they beat the Finns by a score of 6-1. "Not one of the top hockey powers could have crushed the Finns like the Swedes did," wrote one newspaper. Tenacity and concentration, reinforced by brilliant play by their goalies, were what distinguished the Swedish defense. On the day of our game, the Swedes were leading the tournament. We both had the same number of points but they had the best goals for-and-against average. They had allowed only four goals in five games! Nobody had ever seen such a defense.

Finally the time came for the USSR-Sweden game. We seemed to have finally lost that numbness that had prevented us from playing at full strength. When we came out on the ice, we saw not simply our opponents, but players who had beaten us twice the year before and, because of that, were a little too self-confident.

Our rivals didn't want to tempt fate by changing the tactics which they had used successfully against us in Vienna. Heads-up play on defense, taking the initiative at center ice, and using the fast break were the tactics which Lindberg instilled in his charges. At the same time, we studied thoroughly the video tapes of the Vienna games and we decided to test our rivals with speed, to force them to run after our players. Hegusta was an excellent goalkeeper, but he was not a magician. "You have to set up a 'merry-go-round' in the crease. You must create interference, and take more unexpected shots. And, most important – team work and pace!" Tikhonov told us.

I ordered myself to keep the net locked, and for two periods, nobody could find the key. Only when the score was 3-0 for us, Andersson saw an opening in the top and scored with a high shot. My teammates responded with three more.

I mentioned the high shot on purpose. In that game, the Swedes ended almost all their offensive plays with these kinds of shots. They probably had the idea that I let in high shots more often. Or it may have been a psychological trick, intended to scare the goalkeeper. When pucks are flying in your face all the time, it is difficult to keep your eyes fully open. In any case, it didn't bring success to the Swedes. We beat them by a score of 6-1.

When the game ended, Tikhonov couldn't hide his joy. "Fine fellows – well done!" his eyes shone as he hugged us. "You have fulfilled our plan one hundred percent." Viktor could not hide his emotions. I have always liked such people – direct, open-minded – who aren't indifferent to things happening around them.

After that game with the Swedes, I started to look differently at the twenty-year-old rookie Sergei Makarov of the Traktor team. I had watched this brave young man with pleasure, and now I was finally convinced that our National Team had acquired a valuable player. It was as if this rather small but agile forward had played against Swedes and Canadians all his life in his native Chelyabinsk.

Sergei rushed to the net when it was least expected, when all the ways seemed to be closed. He was daring on ice, and ruthlessly self-disciplined, but when he took off his skates he was a kind and gentle fellow.

His older brother took him to the sports club of a pipe-rolling plant when Sergei was only five years old. At the same time in Moscow, another youngster, Viacheslav Fetisov, laced on hockey skates for the first time. As boys they played against one another in tournaments but time went by, and they met each other on the USSR junior team which won the World Championship about a year before this tournament in Czechoslovakia. I remember that the coaches of our juniors highly praised the play of Makarov and Fetisov, and predicted a bright future for both of them. They weren't mistaken. Fetisov was later named the best defenseman of the Prague championship.

"Do you know what I like best in Fetisov's play?" Viktor Zhluktov asked me. "His way of passing. Defensemen usually pass the puck with too much force but he, like Ragulin, makes a pass gently. There are defensemen who are good at breaking up the opposing team's rush but this is no longer enough. Having taken the puck away, they must start the offensive and that's what Fetisov can do. I am very happy for him but I hope he doesn't become overwhelmed by his early success." Viktor was worried for nothing. Years passed by, and soon Makarov and Fetisov were being called our 'famous veterans'. They carried on their shoulders the main weight of the hockey struggle of the first half of the eighties.

During the World Championships, the newspaper *Mlada Fronta* published an interesting interview with the Czechoslovakian player Irzi Novak. When asked how he saw the future of hockey, he answered: "In a few years all hockey players will be six feet tall and weigh two hundred pounds. Their style will be closer to today's Canadians. I am afraid that technique and improvisation will be replaced by power and force. I wouldn't like to play in tomorrow's hockey – it could hurt." I've heard such forecasts before, but I tend to think differently: The future of hockey is in such players as Makarov, Larionov, and Pervukhin.

A couple more words about our rookies: After the championship, I happened to hear an opinion that one of the advantages of today's coaches of the USSR team is their courage in letting the young players go out on the ice. I would like to rephrase that: Coaches trusted in our team from the very beginning, even in those who had just put on the team uniform, and this trust gave wings to the youth. I remember during the intermission of the last game, Tikhonov told the Golikov brothers, "Please score a goal. Of course, you can do it!" "Right away Viktor," they answered, absolutely serious, "right away!" And they scored!

But we had a long way to go before that final game. The way to victory lay through defeat. "Penalties let us down in the game with the Czechs," I wrote in my diary. The mood was terrible. The team made a lot of mistakes, and so did I. Somehow I couldn't feel freshness on ice perhaps because of a thunderstorm that had burst over Prague that night. The air was sticky, it was hard to breathe, and my feet felt like lead. We lost that game and I felt as if I had left something unfinished, as if something important had been lost without hope of ever recovering it. All six of the goals I let in that night interfered with my sleep for a long time.

Fate continued to test us, but once again I must give credit to Tikhonov. He didn't fly into a fit of temper and try to find a scapegoat. The defeat was analyzed in a calm and businesslike manner, and we decided not to change our style.

It may sound strange, but the Czechoslovakians' victory didn't serve them well. It wasn't difficult for me, as an athlete, to understand what was happening to them. Voluntarily or not, they were waiting for us to stumble again so that the question of who was the champion would be solved before the final game. They were burning themselves up with it. This exhausted our rivals, and in the end, we had some psychological superiority before the finals.

Only once did we nearly stumble, and it was the Canadians who almost tripped us. It happened on May 8, exactly one year to the day that we had lost to the Swedes in Vienna and had to settle for third place. And now the Canadians ... .

Compared to Vienna, the Canadians in Prague were almost well-behaved. Even their coach, an older man with a sad face by the name of Howell, was avoiding risky statements. "I can only say that we will outplay at least one team of the Big Four," he said modestly to journalists who requested that he share his plans with them.

As a matter of fact, Howell had come to Prague with 'Team X'. The names of the majority of the players did not mean much, even to experienced hockey experts. Who were these Canadians? What kind of hockey did they play? What kind of goalie did they have?

Little by little, we got to know them. We learned that the average age of the Canadian players was twenty-four, and that seventeen of the players were taller than 5'9" – a team of athletes! For example, Marcel Dionne, a dashing forward, had scored 265 goals in 536 games in the NHL and was one of the highest paid players in the NHL. The defenseman Rick

Hampton was one of the gentlest players in the NHL, with only nineteen penalty minutes in seventy-five games during the previous season. His partner Robert Picard, on the other hand, had 101 penalty minutes.

In Prague, the Canadian National Team of 1978 diligently tried to use the style of play that was then accepted in Europe, and sometimes they did it well. When combined with their roughness, their ability to fight until the last second, and their great skating technique, their teamwork became a terrifying weapon.

And now, the game! "No playwright could write such a play," was how the actor Evgeny Leonov described it. After fifty-six minutes of playing time, the score was tied at one. But suddenly, with just four minutes left, Lever put the Canadians ahead. The excitement was tremendous. Lever took the puck out of the net and put it back in again three times to show everybody that it was he who had scored the goal. Everyone on the Canadian bench went wild. It looked like they were going to get out the champagne and start celebrating before the final whistle. Most people probably thought that the Canadians could hold on for the last four minutes...

But everything turned out differently. Who knows, if Lever hadn't scored that goal, the game would have ended in a tie, and we, most likely, could have said good-bye to our dream of gold. The goal seemed to urge our players on; the red light behind the net was like a beacon to them as they furiously stormed the Canadian net. The professionals, beaten, cornered and confused, could not understand what was happening. Kharlamov made the score 2-2; then Kapustin and it was 3-2; and finally Fetisov, 4-2. And what beautiful goals they were! Our rivals looked as if they had been mugged.

The near loss shook us up too. We finally realized that professionals played, and always would play, with three times more energy against the USSR team. Their games with us were of great importance to the prestige of their hockey. It became clear to us that with such opponents we could not lose the initiative even for a moment (and we lost it for the whole second period). We had to use our most reliable weapons – our speed and our character.

The second game with the Canadians, was totally different. They withstood the fast pace for a period and a half, trying to keep up with us, and then they gave up. Our team called the shots on the ice.

With the score 2-0 in our favor, our rivals tried to oppose our team work with their tested weapon – dishonest, dirty hockey. They were driven into a rage when Vladimir Golikov scored our third goal in the last minute of the second period. The corner of the rink was transformed into a wrestling ring. One of their defensemen actually began pulling Bilyaletdinov's hair.

Our players hadn't been angels on ice either. They had a total of twenty-three minutes in penalties. But the difference was that our players were defending themselves; it was the Canadians who always started the fights. The Soviet team doctor was the best witness of the Canadians' play. He was the one who applied the bandages and stitches and administered the painkillers after the game.

The Canadians who went to Prague were not a team of brawlers. They really didn't have cutthroats like Dave 'The Hammer' Schultz or so-called 'policemen' like Johnny MacKenzie. Even Wilf Paiement, who had behaved so badly in Vienna, was really relatively quiet. The Canadians knew intellectually that intimidation would not work and that the 'goons' were damaging their reputation, both at home and abroad.

Understanding is one thing, but it takes time to eradicate

habits that had been nurtured since childhood. In Prague, the Canadians lost their tempers more than once over small matters, and once their hopes were definitely ruined in the second game with the Soviet Union, which was televised, they threw aside all restraints. It seems that it will take a lot of time to change the 'gladiator psychology' of the professional players.

Sergei Kapustin scored a goal that was astonishing in its beauty. He calmly went around all the Canadians and performed a graceful pirouette in front of the goalkeeper Bouchard, who tripped and fell. Only then did Kapustin tip the puck into the empty net.

That was one of the most beautiful goals in the history of hockey. It could be compared with a classic play by Helmut Balderis in the our second game with the Czechs. Balderis took the puck in the neutral zone and went straight in on two Czech defensemen, who tried to sandwich him. By some miracle, our forward split the defense and wandered in alone to score.

The line of Kapustin, Balderis and Zhluktov, just created at the beginning of the season, was the most effective in Prague. Until then they had been ineffective and even quarrelsome but now everyone was saying, "What a line! What a play!" Kapustin, Balderis, and Zhluktov scored important goals in decisive games and, more importantly, they displayed determination and character.

There was only one obstacle left. We had to beat the reigning World Champions by no less than two goals – only then would the Soviet National Team take the gold. In preparing for the game with the tournament hosts, everyone of us tried not to talk about hockey. No one wanted to waste mental energy. One night, sitting in a movie theatre, I looked at my teammates; their eyes were directed at the screen, but it was obvious that each of them thought not about the movie, but about how they would play in this final decisive game. It was the same with me.

The movie ended and the lights went on. My comrades got up from their chairs reluctantly. A journalist approached me. "So, how was the movie?" he asked. "It was a good movie," I answered, trying to hide the fact that I had not paid too much attention to the movie, and hurried to the exit. How could I possibly tell him that I saw tomorrow's game on the screen? Interesting movie . . . .

I heard that as a part of their game preparation during the tournament, the players of the Czechoslovakian National Team had evening talks with a psychologist in the suburban motel where they were staying. We were lucky to associate with three 'psychologists' during the championship: A people's actor of the USSR, Evgeny Leonov, and two popular variety actors, Vadim Tonlov and Boris Vladimirov.

I don't know if Evgeny Leonov is familiar with the details of sport psychology, but he did charge us with optimism, that's for sure! We talked for hours. Leonov told us about his stage and film work, and we told him about hockey. "I envy you guys," said the actor. "How many fans you have! I am a People's actor, but I can't compare your popularity with mine." "Yes you can," we objected, "very much so! You would be especially successful in the role of a hockey coach." He laughed and so did we.

Our meetings with Evgeny were not only entertaining, but also educational. "To act," he said, "means to spend a lot of energy; to burn yourself out." He did not draw parallels and analogies with hockey directly, but we understood that his words applied to hockey too.

On Saturday, May 13, one of our players saw Leonov in a hotel lobby with a suitcase in his hand. "Are you checking out, Evgeny?" "Yes," answered the actor, with his usual slightly shy smile, "It's time. People are waiting for me in

Moscow." "What about us?" There was probably such distress on the faces of the players that Leonov hesitated for a moment at the exit, then waved his hand and strode back to the elevator. He stayed with us to the very end, and rightly shared the joy of victory with the National Team.

The next morning, I woke up at 8:30. There was almost no traffic noise coming from the street – the true sign of a weekend. I tidied myself up and went down to the second floor, where our team had rented a big room next to the restaurant. Almost everyone was there already. We ate our breakfast silently. I turned my attention to my teammates whose faces were strangely reserved. They were hiding their internal concentration and determination.

After breakfast was finished, everyone stood up and hurried to the door. I understood my comrades, because I too had a strong wish to be alone, to avoid unnecessary talk. I swallowed my scrambled eggs and bacon and went to my room. Our doctor caught me in the corridor. "You know," he said, "Sergei Kapustin has a high fever." "Will he be able to play?" I asked. Doctor Sapronenkov shrugged his shoulders with doubt. It looked like he had not slept the night before; his sunken eyes had dark circles around them.

I tried not to think about the fact that one of the best players on our team, Sergei Kapustin, would not be able to go on the ice. I only admitted to myself that it was too bad, and that was it. It would not help to torture myself before the game. It was better not to think about hockey at all.

Yurzin, Pashkov, Lebedev, and I, went to the rink to practise. Even there, I did everything automatically. I did not think about how, this coming evening, the arena would shudder from the cheering of Prague fans, and how, on this very ice, we would have to fight for the victory against the home town favorites and win the game by at least two goals.

Before dinner I invited Sasha Pashkov for a walk. It was chilly in Prague. White ceremonial candles were nestled in the chestnut 'crowns'. Birds sang over the Vltava river. I was suddenly struck with the thought that I didn't feel any pressure. After dinner, I fell fast asleep. I slept like a baby and woke up an hour and a half later feeling calm and refreshed. As game time approached, I felt even more self-confident.

"So, guys, you have a chance to prove that you are the strongest in the world," said Viktor Tikhonov during our pregame meeting. "You have to show your opponents right away that you are here to win; to win in their own home, in front of their fans and without being intimidated by their champion's title."

On the way to the bus that was supposed to take us to the game, I was stopped by the manager of our hotel. "Vladislav," she said, "you're my favorite hockey player and I always want desperately for you to win, but how should I feel today?" "Cheer for your own team," I said with a smile. "Oh, no, I'll cheer for both sides." Later that evening she presented me with a bunch of red carnations.

When we went out on the ice, I noticed right away that our opponents were uptight. Their faces were pale, and their movements constrained. The Czechs were not even comforted by the illness of Sergei Kapustin who, despite his fever, had come out on the ice to encourage us. Kapustin was such a courageous player!

From the very first seconds, our forwards attacked the Czechs' net. The engine of our team was working at top speed; it was the only way. On the bench, our coaches were repeating, "Lock up your opponents in their zone, force the goalie to make mistakes, fool the defensemen, and, most importantly, show your character. You've got to play your best game!"

Shortly after Balderis scored our first goal, the Czechs went on the power play. Petrov got the puck at center ice, moved forward and passed it to Mikhailov on his right. In this situation the common practice is to dump the puck into the other team's end because the most important thing when playing short-handed is to kill time. But Boris caught the puck in the air and, seeing Holocek move in front of the net, passed it to Petrov. He scored!

Then it was the Czechs' turn. In the last minute of the second period, when we were on the power play, Martinec broke away and headed to my net on the right wing. I had enough time to say to myself that if I won this duel, we would be champions. Martinec was flying at my net, and the puck seemed to be glued to the end of his stick. I had to win, to fight to the end! I moved forward a bit and deflected the puck, but the next moment we collided and he knocked me off my feet, causing a pile-up. Where was the puck? There it was, lying a foot away from the goal line.

The Czechs jumped on the ice from the benches and started hugging each other as though they had scored. "No!" I shouted at the referee. "No!" he repeated. He had seen for himself that it wasn't a goal.

In the third period, Vladimir Golikov scored, and two minutes later the Czech's captain, Ivan Hlinka, scored in my net. That goal gave them even more strength. The score was 3-1. We had to hold on for ten minutes, only ten minutes – but how long ten minutes can be! Near the end of the game, when the Czechs were attempting the last assault, and the fate of the gold was to be decided, we ran out of players. Maltsev had to leave with an injury. A puck almost knocked Lutchenko's eye out, and he had to leave too. Vasilyev had heart pains. Our doctor was running from one to the other. Who was left to play? Bilyaletdinov took a two-minute penalty and the opponents were pressing.

I never looked at the clock during a game, and I never

counted the remaining time. But that time, I admit, I couldn't help it. There were fifteen seconds left in the game. Another fifteen seconds, and we would be the champions! Those were the longest seconds in my life. I counted to myself: three, two, one. When the siren sounded, I lost control for a moment and smashed my hockey stick into pieces against the ice. I shouted something, and someone shouted back.

On the bench, Tikhonov was crying, unable to hide his emotions.

12

HOCKEY MAKES FRIENDS

The Central Committee of the Young Communist League sent us on a mission to visit the builders of the Baikal-Amur railway line. In our party were coaches Tikhonov and Yurzinov, along with players Maltsev, Shalimov and me.

The helicopter blades slowed down their rotation and the engine became silent. The pilot opened the door abruptly and threw down a short metal ladder. "We have arrived," he said. "All passengers out."

We were surrounded with the dense taiga of the Lake Baikal district. As I jumped to the ground I was greeted with the hard embrace of a local land pioneer. The man was a giant.

"I never expected to see the real Maltsev and Tretiak!" he shouted. "And where? In the remotest depths, many thousand kilometers from Moscow!" His eyes were shining. "I have a double reason to celebrate today. I have a new baby boy born this morning. What a day!"

"Congratulations," I said. "What name have you chosen for him?"

"I haven't decided yet," the giant replied.

We separated into two groups, one of which went to see the fitters and another to see the tunnel builders. Two days later we were back at the helicopter pad to return, as the local people say, 'to the big land'. And again the same giant pioneer approached me, this time with a tiny baby in his arms, wrapped in a blue blanket.

"Here is my son," he said. "I took him from the hospital today just to introduce you to him. When he grows up I will tell him that he was born on the same day that Tretiak arrived at the Baikal-Amur main railway line."

I was touched. We hugged each other and said very warm good-byes. I was already headed toward the helicopter when this happy giant called me again: "Why don't you ask me what name I have chosen for my son?"

"What name did you choose?" I called back. "Vladislav! Of course Vladislav!" he shouted. "We will always remember you."

I will always remember that visit.

* * * * *

Twice in a row I was voted to the Central Committee of the Young Communist League, known in the Soviet Union as Komsomol. I saw my role not as a passive member of the Central Committee but as an active one. I tried hard to popularize physical culture, sport and the achievements of our hockey program.

How many fans I met in those years! I met miners, metallurgists, tunnel builders and hydro builders at the many construction sites to which I was sent by the Central Committee of Komsomol. These construction projects are built mainly by young people. The role of athletes on such trips is to act as so-called 'patrons' of the construction sites, to promote the achievements of different sports and to encourage physical fitness.

But you should understand how much we, the athletes, gained for ourselves from those trips and meetings. What a wonderful experience it is to see your fans, not in the stadium, but 'on the frontier', as they say; people who can rightly be called pioneers, makers of history. You realize that these workers in different industries – in oil, construction, metallurgy, geology – are the real heroes. Your own success seems rather modest compared to their selfless labor.

Sometimes when our training became unbearable I would recall those meetings and say to myself, don't give up. Those guys are under an even heavier load and nobody sees them on TV. Be patient. So in truth it's not known who benefitted more from those visits, the hosts or the guests.

My wonderful fans. How often they encouraged me in difficult moments. They never hesitated to applaud, and generously forgave my blunders. I got a lot of praise and good advice from their letters. I always felt their kindness and their faith no matter where I played.

It all started with that memorable game, Army Club vs. Spartak in 1969, which I consider to be the beginning of my hockey career. Anatoly Tarasov put me in goal that day and even the experienced Army players did not give me a very warm reception. Never before had their net been protected by such a youngster. But the fans believed in me in that game. They applauded even the easiest of saves. Since that day I have enjoyed a very warm relationship with hockey fans, and I always enjoyed meeting them.

Hockey players in the Soviet Union are often invited to sports parties sponsored by the army or by student and industrial clubs. The halls are usually full. People want to have a closer look, to compare a player's hockey skills with his physical qualities or to check their impressions of one player or another. For the players such meetings are like a comprehensive examination.

While I was working on this book, I found it difficult to decide which of these meetings to write about. What follows is a description of a typical meeting based on my recollection of the many meetings I had with my fans.

The huge assembly hall is full of people. I take a good look at their faces through a side door. Most of them are young. I am nervous. It is not the same feeling I get during a hockey game. At a hockey game I try to concentrate on the play. I see nothing but the players and the puck. All worries disappear in the first second of the game. Here it is different. I see thousands of faces, all of whom came to see how Tretiak looks without the mask.

A pleasant surprise. Before the meeting begins the organizers show the film "Vladislav Tretiak vs. Bobby Hull" which was shot in 1974 during the games against the World Hockey Association all-stars. I have seen the film before but nevertheless I am probably the most attentive viewer in the hall. On the wide screen Bobby Hull attacks my net over and over again. The sirens wail, the spectators roar. Pucks fly by, whining like bullets. The goalkeeper holds on. That's how it was in 1974.

It seems that the movie has made a big impression on other people as well. Going to the podium I can see the emotion in their faces; I can feel the sincerity in their applause. Instantly I realize that I have already established a rapport with the audience and now it is important not to lose it. There is a large pile of written questions on the table in front of me. I take the first one.

What is the most important human quality in a goaltender?

"Diligence," I answer.

Do you have moments of fear during the game?

"Goalies are not absolutely fearless people. Only mindless fools are afraid of nothing. In the dressing room, before a game, I am sometimes afraid. However, once I'm on the ice I concentrate totally on what I must do. Nothing else, including fear, exists for me.

"That isn't to say that I can forget about the danger. There are always reminders. At practice, for example, there may be five or six pucks flying toward my net simultaneously. It's impossible to react to all of them. No pad will save you from the pain of a direct shot. Canadian players have a habit of shooting at the net from very acute angles, even from the corners. While it is almost impossible to score in this situation, it is very easy for the goaltender to get hurt, particularly if the puck hits him in the throat. The throat is the most unprotected part a goalkeeper has. Some people may have the impression that all goalkeepers must look like hit-and-run victims – covered in scars and bruises with their teeth knocked out. This is not true. For example, I have never had a serious injury in all the years I have played for the Army Club and on the National Team. I have no scars to brag about – so far. But what is true is that when the puck hits, it hurts.

Do you ever dream about hockey in your sleep?

"Never."

What is your attitude toward the referees?

"I am kind of sympathetic to them. I realize that referees have a difficult job to do and that they are ordinary people, capable of making mistakes too. Nevertheless, hockey is such an intense struggle that I cannot forgive a referee's negligence in the blaze of an argument. I can't, forgive me, I can't."

How do you perceive your own fame?

"I take it in my stride. I guess I'm past the age where fan mail, fame and a lot of attention sets my head awhirl."

Is it true that the most cheerful player on the National Team was Valery Kharlamov?

"You've got the first name right, Valery. But Valery Vasiliev, not Kharlamov. You'd never guess from looking at him that he's a joker, always so preoccupied and serious. But out of the blue he'd come up with jokes that made us laugh so hard we had to hold our stomachs."

Have your phenomenal reflexes helped you outside the hockey arena?

"A couple of times they've helped me while driving a car on a slippery road."

"How do you develop your reflexes?

"I recommend tennis and ping-pong."

Do you like the steam bath?

"Frankly speaking, not very much."

Your favorite dish?

"Mushroom soup."

What should a defenseman do in a two-on-one situation?

"This is a trade question! A hockey player has asked it. Do you have a hockey team?"

"Yes, we do!" replied the audience all together. "We are regional champions."

"Then perhaps we should have a clinic. In this situation the goalkeeper is responsible for the player carrying the puck. The defenseman watches the second player while simultaneously trying to disrupt the actions of the first one. It is very important for the defenseman not to commit himself too early."

How does your wife feel about hockey?

"Tatiana understands perfectly that if I go to a game in a miserable mood I could let down not only myself but the team.

That's why she does everything to help me. But I wouldn't call my wife a hockey fan. I'd like to add something else. Hockey is very difficult for our wives and children because we spend so much time away from home."

Have you ever taken drugs?

"Why? What for? I feel that I can play very well without any drugs."

What sports do you consider most difficult?

"I think ski racing is probably the most difficult sport."

Who among athletes do you respect the most?

"I can't name any one athlete personally. I am sure that all national, world and Olympic champions deserve equal respect. It's so difficult to be number one in any contemporary sport."

What would you say to an athlete who didn't win the first prize even though he tried as hard as he could?

"I'd tell him that he shouldn't blame himself. If he tried as hard as he could then he is a real athlete."

What kinds of shots do you consider most dangerous?

"The most dangerous shot for me is the long shot when I am screened. When somebody is screening the net, the goalie cannot always react to the puck in time."

Who do you blame when someone scores on you?

"Nobody but myself."

What is your relationship with your defensemen?

"I have always had a cooperative, friendly relationship with the defense. When defensemen get too involved in the attack or get caught napping at the wrong time, and the opposing team gets a breakaway, I don't hold it against them nor do I show my irritation. In general this is not a simple topic. The goalkeeper's job today is much more difficult than it used to be. Speeds are increasing. Today the game is much more focused on the net, a characteristic that came from professional hockey. With the use of the new curved sticks, the force and the velocity of shots has increased. As well, the majority of teams today are relatively even – there are no games anymore where you can relax, so to speak, or play at half strength. As a result of all of this, the defensive lines are no longer as impenetrable as they once were.

"I don't know exactly why, but at some point the quality of our defense fell behind from both a tactical and psychological standpoint, as well as in terms of the number of talented new players. I have the impression that some coaches have lost interest in providing the special training needed for first class defensemen. Of course, there is no crisis, but I can see clearly from my net (and I'm sure you can see it from your seats) that even our best defensemen are sometimes careless. Often they get too involved in offence and don't have time to get back to fulfill their direct responsibilities.

"I don't hold it against my teammates when they let an opponent come one on one with me. But, rightly so, it is hard to remain calm when I win a duel only to have the puck pushed past me after repeated shots because the defensemen are not awake yet.

"As a goalkeeper, the defenseman I liked best was Vasily Pervukhin because of his strict, almost error-free play. When he got the puck, he didn't pretend he was Bobby Orr. Instead he always passed to his forwards. Pervukhin clearly recognized his tasks; he wasn't very noticeable on the ice but he helped the team enormously."

Who is more dangerous for a goalie, Sergei Makarov or Wayne Gretzky?

"Makarov, certainly."

What is the difference between Phil Esposito and Wayne Gretzky?

"First of all, their size. Esposito is nearly a head taller than I am and weighs about 120 kilograms. Gretzky is a skinny boy who barely weighs 76 kilos. Their characters are very different as well. Esposito never could completely rid himself of his snobbish attitude towards Soviet hockey, whereas Gretzky always stresses that the 'Tarasov school' helped to make him great."

Have you ever had any heroes?

"If you mean in hockey, yes. I always admired Viktor Konovalenko."

How much time do you need to get into your hockey gear?

"Ten to twelve minutes."

Is it true that you received an offer to play for one of the Canadian professional clubs?

"There were several offers and the Canadians were offering millions. But I think they understood that this was pure science fiction. I am a Soviet athlete, interested only in defending the honor of my Motherland."

Which team, in your opinion, is the most popular in the Soviet Union?

"Spartak, of course, has more fans..." I didn't get a chance to complete my answer because the Spartak fans in the audience burst into fierce applause. I decided to cool them down. "It's just too bad that Spartak lets their fans down so often." There was laughter and applause."

Did you receive a lot of fan mail before you got married?

"Yes, a lot. I don't get so many letters now."

Can you be thrown off balance?

"Probably, but I'm not sure what someone should do to get me."

Why do you use a wire mask rather than a fiberglass one?

"Because it's much safer. It's easier to breathe through a wire mask. The advantages in terms of vision are obvious. Most of our leading goaltenders are now using wire masks."

Do you tire more easily during a game, the older you get?

"When I was younger, games didn't tire me much at all. As I get older, however, I almost feel myself losing consciousness during long, hard tournaments. That's when the doctors help me – salt ammonia under my nose, heart medicine under my tongue – and back out on the ice."

Do you watch the actions of the opposing goaltender during the game?

"Yes, I make mental notes about his mistakes as well as his saves."

These meetings would go on for two hours or more and there seemed to be no end to the questions. I was asked about my personal life and my plans for the future. I was asked why Spartak was not playing well, what my former teammates were doing, and what I thought of the new stars. I was even asked about the misfortunes of the Central Army soccer club.

It was always heartening to find that people were so interested in sports, that they took the losses and victories of their favorite teams so personally. However, I have to say that it became more difficult for me to talk to the fans as the years went by. This was especially true after I left the game. People still expected all sorts of information from me, about events in my personal life, my serious evaluation of contemporary hockey, my thoughts about life.

I should stress that the knowledge and intelligence of hockey fans has increased dramatically in recent years and it is now much more demanding to perform in front of these audiences. Two years ago I visited the youth workers at a steel plant in Chevrepovets. I was questioned especially sharply about the reasons for our national team's loss at the 1985 world championships in Prague. I explained that in sports there is no insurance against letdowns or mistakes. I was in Prague for the finals of that tournament and I understand our fans' unhappiness.

I arrived in the Czechosolvakian capital following the completion of the preliminary round in which our players won every game.

"Congratulations, Vladislav," said my Czech friends who greeted me at the airport. "Victory is yours. Your team doesn't have an equal here."

Indeed it was clear to everyone that the Soviet team was better than the opposing teams in all respects. One didn't have to understand the fine points of the game to see it. Mishkin, our goalie, had the best goals-against average in the preliminary round. Makarov scored the most goals. The Soviet team was the only team not to lose a single point in the first round. The team looked great. I was optimistic about our chances when I saw my former teammates. Their spirits were buoyant, they were full of strength and they believed they would win. Only Tikhonov complained about bad refereeing.

Watching the preliminary games on TV in Moscow, I too had noticed that the level of refereeing was outrageously low. I'd never seen anything like it. The tone was set by the American and Canadian referees who allowed the 'clutch and grab' style of play, the kind of play which is used by players lacking skills. Our team, in particular, suffered from the leniency of the referees.

What worried me, however, was that the Czechs had ended up in fourth place and would therefore be our opponents in the first round of the finals. The Czechs never lose twice in a row! In the 1983 World Championships in West Germany, for example, they lost to us in the preliminary round but managed a 1-1 tie in the final. Personally, I am not in favor of the playoff system because it often rewards those teams who have played poorly during the main tournament.

Nevertheless, no one predicted what would happen the next day. The Soviet team got into trouble early. At the seven minute mark Mishkin moved far out of the net to meet the Czech player, Ruzicka. As he retreated backwards to his net he slipped and fell. Ruzicka scored in the empty net. It was regrettable but things like that do happen.

Our coaches must have given the order to storm the opposition net. Wave after wave of Soviet players rushed into the Czech zone. But five minutes later the unforgivable happened. As a result of a defensive error, the puck again flew into Mishkin's net and we were at a two-goal disadvantage. Unforgivable.

The Czech coaches immediately had their players go into a shell, sending one man into the Soviet zone and leaving the other four standing reliably at the blue line. They knew that only one thing mattered – to keep the lead at any cost. The clock was running. Our players started to rush their shots and passes and, when you hurry, mistakes are inevitable. The second period was over and our players still hadn't got it together.

In the third period Khomutov got one back for the Soviet team but by this time the Czechs had stopped playing hockey. All they were doing was breaking up our attacks, preventing our forwards from penetrating their zone. Their actions were understandable. The day before they had been nearly out of the running for a medal. Now they could taste the gold.

The game ended with the score 2-1. Our team lost the next game to the Canadians and found themselves in third place at the end of the championships. They were clearly the strongest team, yet they had to settle for the bronze.

How similar this was to the 1977 World Championships in Vienna. In that series as well we received premature congratulations and became too self-confident. Eight years earlier we had needed only three points in our last four games in order to win the tournament. Each player already saw himself as a champion and was mentally trying on his gold medal. But again the strongest team and again the bronze.

Enough was written in the Soviet press about the Soviet failure at the Prague championships in 1985 that I will limit myself to just a few remarks. First, whatever they say, that failure was accidental and did not reflect the true strength and zeal of Soviet hockey. Second, I disagree strongly with those who criticized the Soviet coaches for their inability to adjust to the playoff system. These critics have suggested that the coaches should have played for points, rather than playing for the win in every game thereby saving their strength for the championship round. This is not the nature of Soviet hockey. It is against our principles. I would agree that in 1985 our players did not play to their potential, nor did they show the same freshness to the end. But these problems were related to training rather than to game strategy.

There are no other words to describe the Soviet loss in 1985. It was sad. First we gave up the Canada Cup in 1984 and then the gold medal at the world championships in Prague. But sport is sport and our opponents have not been preparing themselves just to be perennial runners-up.

"It's good that our team lost," I overheard one of the Chevrepovets fans saying. "Now we'll see more exciting games. For years the play has always been in the other team's end."

Yes, it's true that our hockey players have been spoiled by their victories. But I recall once after a very important tournament in which we won the final game by a score of 3-1, I was invited to speak to a meeting of one of our military units. A gray-haired lieutenant-colonel stood up and said with resentment: "I wish you guys wouldn't do that. It wasn't clear until the last minute that you were going to take the championship. I had to take heart pills to calm myself down while you played.

Give us a 5-0 lead in the first period so we'll be able to enjoy the rest of the game.''

And what do you know? The very next year at the world championships in Moscow we were beating the Czechs 5-1 in the first period and then increased the gap even more, confidently winning the game. A few weeks later, during a meeting with some fans, I received a note which said: ''What kind of hockey is that? With a score of 5-1 in the first period the game is no longer interesting to watch. There is no struggle.''

You can't please all of the people all of the time.

But let's return to Chevrepovets. One of the brightest memories I have came from my visit to the steel plant where I saw how they made cast iron, steel and rolled iron. We walked through huge shops; their size reminded me of hockey arenas. There were no people around – automation was at work. And that gigantic smelter. I hadn't realized that it was possible to produce cast iron while sitting in a neat, clean control room filled with various buttons, levers and television monitors. The workers in the smelter talked about their work with fascination and in detail, as if they wanted to share part of their experience with me.

We spent a lot of time at smelter number three, where the foreman turned out to be a fan of the Central Army hockey club. Two of the other workers on his shift had some specific sports-related question. As skiers they wanted to discuss how best one should prepare one's self for competition.

''Well, back to work now,'' said the foreman. ''The cast iron is ready and it's time to pour it out.''

While I could have watched this process on the monitor in the control room, it would have been like going to an arena and watching a hockey game on TV in a back room. I chose to stay by the smelter and watch the iron being poured. The workers picked up their tools. One of them handed me special gloves and asked if they were much different from goalkeeper's gloves.

And then the cast iron came out. A bright yellow stream gradually turned into a powerful river with millions of little sparks that flashed like fireworks. "How beautiful!" I said out loud.

The river of metal soon dried up. As the technicians had said, the cast iron was of the highest quality and the workers had moulded a medal which they then awarded to me. That medal is as important to me as all the awards I received in the world championships.

As a military officer and a member of the Army sports club for twenty years, it was a particular pleasure for me to meet with soldiers with whom I established a special, warm and trusting relationship. They were both fans and friends. In meeting with them you could feel the friendliness, the appreciation and the genuine interest. People listened, held their breath, caught every word. Then hundreds of hands would reach for autographs and the meeting wouldn't end until I had satisfied all their requests.

What I valued in fans the most was not their uncontrolled spirit or their eagerness, but their ability to see the real beauty in hockey, to appreciate a fine combination, a cunning pass, a noble play. There were some fans whose attention was particularly important to me. One of them was the Hero of the Soviet Union, Colonel Vasily Geleta. This veteran air force navigator was devoted to hockey and often came to the games. We had known each other since I started to play for the Army Club. What a man! I liked to listen to his stories about air battles and look at his medals and military decorations. Since then I've realized that we are all deeply indebted to those who protected the freedom of our Motherland.

I've got personal reasons for feeling special warmth and

gratitude for Colonel Geleta. Back in 1972 he introduced me to his neighbor, who, exactly one month later, became my wife.

Vasily Geleta is no longer with us; he didn't live to see my farewell game. I still go to his house to visit his family and remember that marvelous man.

It's quite interesting that my attitude towards fans changed slightly when my career as a goalkeeper ended and I began to watch hockey from the spectators' seats. First of all, I had to learn how to be a fan. Don't be surprised, I mean it. Before, I saw the game either from my net, or, more rarely, from the players' bench. To be a participant in a game, even a backup, and to be a spectator are two different things. I don't think I'll ever become just a spectator. I habitually analyze the actions of the players, especially the goalkeepers and defense. I notice mistakes and imagine myself playing in different situations.

I always worry when the Army or National teams are on the ice. I leave these games feeling ill. "Why worry?" I'm told. "Watch and enjoy it, like the others." I've tried, but I can't – not yet, anyway.

I have made some discoveries while sitting among the fans. As a player, I used to perceive the spectators' noise as something faceless, homogenous. I couldn't hear separate voices or shouts. Simply speaking, I'd 'turn off' everything that was not directly related to the game, including the yelling of the fans. Now, when I am among the spectators, I can hear their remarks, shouts, and opinions, and I can better understand how different fans are from one another.

They differ in their temperaments, in their cheering habits, in their perceptions of the game. Yes, two fans can see two absolutely different hockey games, almost from the same place. One will 'soak in' the whole game, and not miss a chance to enjoy a smart play by the rivals, and will appreciate objectively the merits of their accurate passing, their sound defense, their passionate attacks, while still cheering for his favorite team. Other fans seem not to see the whole hockey game, but only the play of 'their' team. They seem to have 'blinders' on. For these fans the whole game has only one point: the victory of their favorites. The referee only blows his whistle in favor of the opponents; only the opposing players are rude.

A fan like this is not my favorite. One has to be able to enjoy the game; that's what the game is all about, and nothing else. In Canada when we smartly outplayed our hosts, the local fans gave us ovations – they understood that they were watching first-class hockey. Even though they were hurt for their team, they respected the outstanding sportsmanship of their guests.

I am afraid that fans in Moscow have forgotten how to cheer. Sometimes, even though the house is full, it is so quiet that it seems like people have come to watch ballet, not hockey. Hockey players get bored in a game when they are not cheered. However, this is not to say that emotions should not be controlled nor order maintained.

Children are the best fans. In the first place, they are different from adults because they play hockey themselves. Secondly, the main thing is that they see the meaning of the game not in getting those silly points, but in the manifestation of skills, strength, determination, and courage. I always try to answer letters from children first, because I know how important it is to them.

Fans... how many memories are connected with them? Once we were playing a team called 'Khemik'. The score was 3-2 for the Army team when Viacheslav Fetisov skated behind my net with the puck and remained there for a little while. Suddenly, the incredible happened. The puck bounced off my leg, right into the net! The red light flashed behind me. The fans cheered excitedly. The referee pointed to center ice. Goal! My heart sank. Why? There was no rival nearby, how could

Fetisov possibly score in his own net? I looked behind and saw Fetisov standing with the puck, as he had been moments before the goal. Was it a miracle? It turned out to be a fan's joke; he threw a puck from the third row of the stands and scored on my net. The goal was not counted, of course.

Pravda once asked its readers to express their opinions about the skills and characters of the most famous Soviet athletes. The editorial staff of the newspaper showed me those letters which began with the words, "My favorite athlete is Vladislav Tretiak." There were plenty of them, and they reminded me of declarations of love. I was about twenty-five years old then, and, thank God, I was smart enough not to drown in this flow of praise, to take it as an advance payment on my future success.

I deeply respect those who really know and value sports. Our hockey cannot exist without them. I was told that in 1978, when the decisive game of the World Championships in Prague was being played and a few flights were delayed at the Moscow airport, all the passengers were glued to the TV screens. No announcements or appeals could make them board the planes; they yielded to no persuasion. The two previous years, we had lost the World Championships in Poland and Austria. We were strongly criticized then, but the main thing was that people still believed in us. And when you are trusted, you can move mountains.

13

THE CHALLENGE CUP

At the end of the 1978 season my worries turned to other matters – entrance exams for the Vladimir Ilyich Lenin Military-Political Academy. I had to answer questions on pedagogics, psychology, history, tactics, and army statistics. None of my friends were surprised by my decision to study at the Academy. They knew that I enjoyed working with people and being in the midst of public life, and that I was captivated by the problems of human development.

Oh, God, was I worried that summer, studying textbooks, notes, and statistics! I spent months preparing for my first exam, but, as always, it wasn't enough. The night before the exam, I couldn't sleep; I stayed up and studied. I thought to myself that it would be easier to play the Canadians than to take those exams. I was so worried the morning of the exam that even my knees were trembling.

I sat outside the auditorium, waiting for my turn. I opened

the pedagogics textbook, which I had read over hundreds of times but as I started to turn the pages, I realized that I couldn't remember a thing! I thought to myself that it would be better to go home than to torture myself like this, when a general came up to me. "When are you going to take the test?" he asked me. "In an hour, Comrade General," I replied, standing at attention. "Very good. I will certainly come to hear you." Things were getting worse and worse.

Finally, I was called in. There were two generals and my examiner – a colonel – across the table from me. They looked benevolent, but they were demanding. "What kind of student are you?" they asked. "We have seen how you can stop the puck, now let us see how you can think." Trembling, I took my seat and immediately my worries vanished! It was like when I took my place in the net, my only thought was how I could do my best.

They listened to me with attention and interest. I spoke of definitions, and gave examples, including some from my experience as a goaltender.

The next day somebody hung a poster in the hall which read "Tretiak won, 5-0!" I successfully passed the rest of the exams and, in the fall of 1979, I became a correspondence student of the Academy, and three years later I graduated with the rank of Major.

My reasons for taking a second diploma were quite simple. It was always clear to me that someday I would have to leave hockey. And then what? Would I exploit my past fame? Would I live on my old achievements? No, that wasn't for me. I wanted to live a full and interesting life after hockey. I wanted people to appreciate me not as a former champion, but as a competent expert in another field, without reference to my past merits.

The process of leaving sports is very painful for many players. Our lives are too limited for too many years; too many habits are implanted, which we have to break. It can take a great effort to start afresh. It is always easier for those who seriously plan for their futures ahead of time, for those who don't limit their world to a hockey arena.

Alexander Yakushev of Spartak left hockey before I did and has always been an inspiration to me. He was one of the most famous players of my generation, and he was a brilliant athlete for more than ten years. The high point of his career was in 1972, in the games against the Canadians. In four of the eight games, the Canadians named him the best player of the Soviet team. Shortly after that series, Bobby Hull claimed that Yakushev was the greatest left-winger of all time. His stick is displayed in the Hockey Hall of Fame, in appreciation of his great talent.

Sasha captured the imagination of fans with his fierce, brave play. He rushed forward without ever showing fear or weariness, and was always in the midst of a struggle. He went after rebounds courageously, and was never afraid of collisions or injuries.

I suppose what impressed the Canadians most was his truly gentlemanly behavior and his exceptional self-control. In this sense, Yakushev was a unique player. While the game of hockey overflows with excitement and emotion, Alexander Yakushev was always wise, and he always kept his mouth shut. He was well-respected for that.

We were drawn to each other, and we often got together with our families. I remember one game between the Army Club and Spartak. The struggle, as usual, was intense. Passions boiled over. Yet, during one of the intermissions, Yakushev came up to me: "Did you know, Vladik, that the Metropolitan Exhibition is on at Pushkin Museum? Let's go tomorrow." I was stunned. At that moment, my mind was very far away from art. He continued: "It's impossible to get tickets, you

know, but everybody knows you – maybe we can get through.''
He was wrong there, of course; he was just as well-known
as I was.

Yakushev's hockey career wasn't always smooth. His most
successful tournament after 1972 was in 1975, when he was
named the best forward at the World Championships in West
Germany. The next season he played wonderfully, especially
in the final game against the Czechoslovakian team at the
Winter Olympic Games in Innsbruck.

Following that, I think the mood on the Spartak team, which
was not the best at that time, affected Yakushev's play. For
two years, he wasn't named to the National Team, on which
he had played since 1963. He took it very hard, and tried to
improve his game. He practised selflessly and more often than
any young player on the team. He was included on the National
Team again in 1979, and in the 1979 World Championship he
won his seventh gold medal.

I think he is the kind of person who will always be in the
limelight. Sasha had started to prepare himself for a coaching
career a long time ago. He graduated from a correspondence
institute, read many books about pedagogics and psychology,
and watched with attention the work of Kulagin, Bobrov,
Tarasov, Chernishev, and Tikhonov, all of whom had coached
him over the years. Judging by his character, he would probably fit well into the role of a sports mentor.

And so, I studied at the Academy, while continuing to defend
my hockey net. I wasn't given any breaks in my studies nor
in my hockey. It was very hard, sometimes unbearable.

One of the highlights of the 1978-9 season was the Challenge
Cup, between our national team and an NHL all-star team.

I didn't like playing in New York's Madison Square Garden.
To me it was cold, dull, and unwelcoming, and the audience
was somehow inert. The Forum in Montreal, on the other

hand, was quite a different story. There, I felt myself capable
of miracles. At the Forum, even breathing was different; it
was easy and free. In Montreal the fans were almost like an
extra player on the ice.

For obvious commercial reasons, all three Challenge Cup
games were to be held at Madison Square Garden, which seats
17,500 spectators. The organizers of the tournament later regret-
ted their decision, because the cold New York audience could
not be compared to the rabid Montreal spectators.

The core of the NHL team was made up of players from
the Montreal Canadiens. The NHLers were headed by Scotty
Bowman, who was known to favor a more gentlemanly style
and naturally the NHL team reflected that. Nobody started
a fight; they wanted to play hockey, not break the opponents'
bones. But the desire to win this mini-tournament was more
than enough. Many of the NHL stars told the media that they
would rather die than let the Russians win this time.

We were also concentrating on serious play, although our
coaches didn't exaggerate the importance of the Challenge Cup
to our team. "Play well, with devotion, but remember that
the main competition is still ahead. It is the World Championship," they told us. We were not to get too carried away, we
were not to lose our heads, and, most of all, we were to stay
healthy.

We arrived in New York three days before the first game
in order to ensure that we would not still be feeling the affects
of jet lag by game time. FBI agents took care of us like never
before. Our dressing room was searched every day by specially
trained dogs because there was a rumor that someone was going
to sabotage us. I can imagine what noise the American
newspapers would have raised if similar security measures had
been taken in Moscow for American players.

It's unfortunate, but there were still people who disapproved of our meetings with the professional players of North America. They wanted Bobby Clarke and Guy Lafleur to despise the Russians, but instead, North American hockey heroes shook our hands before each game, and we left the ice with warm embraces.

The Canadians opened the scoring with two quick goals, and went on to win by a score of 4-2. Bowman used an intelligent strategy. He advised his players to avoid long shots at my net. He knew that if they took too many shots, I would have a better chance to get warmed up, and I would feel more self-confident. That's what happened in '72, '74, and '76, when the professionals bombarded me with shots. Bowman decided to do it differently; his players shot less often but they were always on the mark. In fact, there were only eighteen shots on our net, but each attack carried with it the real threat of a goal.

In the next game, we came out on the ice more determined to win. Our pride had been hurt, and we played without any thought of the upcoming World Championships, despite the advice of our coaches to save ourselves. The tone was set by Boris Mikhailov. When he was on the bench, we could hear his vigorous voice cheering us on. When the captain came on the ice, it was as though we had a power play.

The professionals took an early 4-2 lead, but each of us felt that the turning point would come soon. Bowman built his defense on two pairs of defensemen. All of them were tall and powerful, but they had a hard time catching our speedy forwards, and soon became exhausted. Then Dryden started to panic. In the end, the Soviet team won by a 5-4 margin.

The score of the third and final game of this series was 6-0 for us. Mishkin was defending our net, and Cheevers replaced Dryden for the professionals. Mishkin played the best game of his life. In three periods, he didn't let in a single goal. He felt no fear or confusion in front of the Canadian professionals. After the game, I congratulated him from the bottom of my heart. I always liked his self-control and determination, his friendliness and his easy-going manner.

My old friend, Gerry Cheevers, complained after the game: "The Russians had their way with me. I looked awful. I don't know if I will ever recover from the shock."

We were told that back in Moscow, fans flooded the newspapers with phone calls: "Is it really 6-0? Could there be some mistake?" It seemed incredible that the brightest stars of professional hockey could lose so badly. That had never happened before.

14

LAKE PLACID
February 22, 1980

The room was narrow; it looked like a sleeping compartment of a railway car. There was a bunk bed, and a tiny window with metal bars on it. A fan on the ceiling howled. It was cold and empty.

How long had I been sitting there by myself? One hour? Two? The book was still on the same page. I had a terrible headache.

Sounds of music and laughter were coming from behind the door. There, in a round hall, Olympic athletes were getting together after a day of battle. Some were no doubt celebrating somebody's victory or giving thanks for a silver or bronze. Others were watching videotapes of cartoons like 'Bugs Bunny'.

"Watch it . . ." I heard a voice say from the other side of the door. I'm in trouble now, I thought. Then I grinned. I realized that in my daze I had thought that the threat of a cartoon wolf was addressed directly at me. I tried to calm myself down. What's the matter? Hadn't I lost to anyone before? Hadn't I ever let in any pucks that could have been saved? Of course I had. It had happened before, hadn't it?

Yes, it had happened, but not in a game like the one I'd just played. I thought about the fans at home and wondered what those people must be going through. Again I held my head tight in my hands and clenched my teeth. This damn cell. The defeat was so heavy on my heart, and on top of it all I had to live with these jail walls, the steel door, the bunk bed.

Lake Placid, 1980. We lost to the hosts of the Olympics and literally gave up all chances for a victory, when the gold had been so close.

Innsbrück, 1964; Grenoble, 1968; Sapporo, 1972; Innsbrück, 1976; the victorious march of Soviet hockey had continued for so many years, and then – misfire.

I tried to read again, but I couldn't hold a single word in my mind. The contents of the book slurred into one grey mass. Against my will, I went over the past few days in my mind, replaying moment by moment the 'video recording' of the last fatal game.

Everything was bad in Lake Placid. Please understand me correctly: I am not saying that just because we lost. What I mean is that it didn't turn out to be an Olympic celebration. It was nothing like what Moscow had presented to the best athletes around the world six months later.

I didn't think that I could be astonished by anything. I had played in a lot of cities over the years, and stayed in a lot of places. When we arrived at Lake Placid, however, we couldn't stop wondering until the last day. This small town was located in the wilderness of the Adirondack Mountains, a five-hour drive from New York. It appeared to be one of the least fit places in the world for hosting the Winter Olympic Games. It had the quietness of a village; there were a few barns and tiny motels, and the main street could not have been more than two hundred meters long. And, for the Olympic Village, the Americans used a brand new jail.

"Was it really a jail?" many people asked us skeptically when we returned from the USA. They thought we were exaggerating. I had to verify: yes, a jail, a real one with two rows of barbed wire, narrow cells without windows, and a heavily fortified yard for the prisoners.

The cells, which everyone had to share with a roommate, were so tiny that when one person entered, the other had to leave, or lie down on the bunk bed, because it was impossible for two people to pass each other. The walls weren't exactly soundproof; when Petrov sneezed in the next room, my roommate Krutov would reply, "Bless you", without raising his voice. The nights were awfully cold, we had to sleep under three blankets, and the annoying howl of the ceiling fan kept us awake. To me, it all looked like torture.

The cells were arranged in two storeys around the circumference of a circle. Inside the circle, which I referred to as a hall before, an improvised club was set up for our delegation. Actually, this place had been designated for the guards. During the Olympics, however, we had a few TV sets, a video recorder, a movie projector, and a stereo there. Here, from morning to night, our athletes who were free from competitions and practices spent all of their time. No one wanted to stay in their cell. We hockey players were used to having a nap after dinner, especially before a game; it was our peculiar way of 'tuning up' for an upcoming game. But how could we sleep when, right outside the steel door, somebody was watching a movie or celebrating a victory?

Everybody was outraged by transportation and other problems; even the local newspapers wrote more about this than about the competitors. The only people who didn't care were the organizers of the Olympics. They acted as if nothing could be done, as if the games were going well and everyone was satisfied. It seems that most of them couldn't – or wouldn't – understand why people weren't happy, or what improvements could be made. This must be a truly American way of thinking: to suppose that nobody could do any better than what they have already done, and to stubbornly reject the opinion of the rest of the world.

The hosts of the 1980 Games didn't even try to hide the fact that the Olympics were, for them, mainly a way of making money. Residents of Lake Placid showed tremendous indifference to the Olympic competitors, but their entrepreneurial ability to raise the price of everything – from gifts to hotel rooms – broke all the records. It was highway robbery. Breakfast in a cheap restaurant cost ten dollars; one night in a bad motel was eighty dollars. Such 'hospitality' was a hair-raising experience, even for seasoned tourists. Nothing like this had happened in either Sapporo or Innsbrück.

We only had a couple of chances to walk around Lake Placid, but it was enough to feel the spirit of capitalism that prevailed there. The main street of the town – called Main Street – looked like a twenty-four hour a day fair. Here, day and night, people sold everything. Distinguished gentlemen and snotty boys did business side by side. They displayed amazing energy and enterprise. One fellow on the corner was selling T-shirts with the motto; "I survived the Olympic Games in Lake Placid". It was an original reaction to the organizational problems which were not resolved by the management of the Games.

Here is one last scene from Main Street: In the middle of the street, a scruffy boy was fussing around with a bunch of bright stickers; "Nixon for President". "Are you taking part in an election campaign?" we asked. "No, they were just laying around for nine years, so I asked myself, why not make some money on them? Everything sells here. Maybe these can be sold too.'' That's the kind of mood that was there, in Lake Placid.

But, for what happened on February 22 of 1980, we had only ourselves to blame.

Our National Team arrived in the States a week before the lighting of the Olympic Flame. There was a sparring match between the USA and USSR teams. The score, 10-3, speaks for itself. The Americans showed us only a symbolic resistance; the forces were completely unequal. Our opponents looked up to us, not hiding their respect. For them, we were the team that had beaten the best North American professionals, and not just once! Every one of them dreamed of becoming a professional player.

I remember their goalkeeper, Craig, trying to catch my eye all the time. Whenever he succeeded, he would smile and nod politely. The Americans didn't even think about winning then. The only question was how many of our pucks they would let in. They were very upset at letting in ten; nevertheless, they had a higher opinion of themselves.

Who could have known that this victory would play such a bad joke on us? It would have been better for us had we not won that exhibition game at all.

In the games of the preliminary round, nobody could spoil our mood. We easily got rid of all our opponents. We crushed the Japanese team by a score of 16-0. However there were surprises in other games. For example, no one would have guessed that the Czechoslovakian team would lose to the Americans! But that is exactly what happened on the evening of February 14. The score was 7-3 for the hosts. It was new for an Olympic tournament that the team from the USA was considered as a main contender for an Olympic medal.

Our first serious obstacle was the Finnish team who, the day before, had defeated the Canadians by a score of 4-3. Frankly speaking, at first we didn't take them all that seriously. They had already lost to the Polish team, and barely managed to get past Japan. The victory over the Canadians could be one of those occasional surprises which are so typical of the Finnish team. They can suddenly and unexpectedly trip up one of the leaders. But no, this wasn't the case. They rushed and attacked us, as if nothing but a victory would satisfy them. To make up for the blanks in their hockey education, they used impudence and pressure. Our play was very careless. With great difficulty, we wrested a 4-2 victory from them.

It was the same scenario in the game with the Canadians. Again, our opponents took an early lead. We caught up and went ahead only at the end of the game, winning by a score of 6-4. Although it was probably very entertaining to the fans, it became clear to us that something was not right on the team. Somehow, we couldn't make the game go. Why not? What happened? Most of the play during our first few games was in our opponents' end of the rink and we controlled the initiative, but we couldn't score, and kept letting pucks in our net. From nowhere, a common stiffness and uncertainty appeared. The six goals that we had allowed in two games were a result of my sad mistakes and the slackness of the defensemen.

Volodia Krutov was perhaps the only one who could not take any blame. This young pupil of the Army Club was making his debut on the National Team, playing on a line with Maltsev and Lebedev but his line didn't play nearly enough. They started out on the bench as backups, but they did their best later in the game.

Teams from the USSR, Finland, the USA, and Sweden went to the finals. The Canadian and Czechosloavkian teams didn't make it, which tells you how strenuous and unpredictable this competition was.

The Americans came into the game with us with only one point, from a tie with the Swedes. By their mood, this wasn't the same team that we had met a week ago in New York. Where had all the respect and timidity disappeared? In their eyes, we could see a great will and determination to become the Olympic champions, whatever it might take. The turning point in their attitude came after the victory over the Czechs and the tie with the Swedes. "You know, we played better than they," the American Schneider told me with amazement. "Now, we are worth something here."

Four years later, at the Olympic games in Sarajevo, I was presented with the book *Miracle on Ice*, written by two Americans, about the tournament in Lake Placid. This book contained many loose, controversial statements, especially about anything that wasn't American. The American hockey players were depicted almost as national heroes, who had awakened in the United States a new spirit of optimism and faith in American might. It was a clear exaggeration.

The American propaganda machine tried to use the hockey victory to heat up the chauvinistic mood. President Carter had contributed his effort to this as well. The authors of *Miracle on Ice*, unintentionally tell why Americans needed all this noise. They point out that for a year, the country had been in a rather shaky situation, related to economic problems, continuous inflation, unemployment, and failure of American policy in different regions of the world. The nation was feeling unwell spiritually; people were agitated, preoccupied, unhappy.

According to the book, the Olympic athletes of the USA were carrying a load of responsibility for everyone from the president to the Pentagon and from the hostages in Iran to General Motors. With difficulties in internal and external politics, and a whole series of other failures, the Carter administration grabbed at the straw given to them by coach Brooks and his pupils.

The authors of the book mention that tickets to the USSR-USA game, priced at $67.20, were being sold by scalpers for $300.00. The book admits that the real fans weren't sitting in the stands. There were only rich people there – those who could afford to pay that kind of money. These people didn't show a great deal of emotion. They probably assumed that for the money they paid, they deserved a better show.

The Americans played as if their lives were on the line. They realized that their skills were inferior to ours, but they decided to compensate with a fantastic desire to overthrow the 'Russian bear'. Coach Brooks made it clear to his team before the game that they must avoid physical fights and penalties at all costs. He told them not to be afraid to play our kind of fast-skating game, to watch out for the long pass, and not to be careless on defense. He believed that the game would be won or lost in the neutral zone.

That's how it happened. The main action actually did unfold in the neutral zone and, by the way, almost all the goals were scored from afar. The American players, following their coach's advice, willingly accepted our invitation to play fast, combinational hockey. And they really tried to avoid fights. The players zealously carried out all of coach Brooks's instructions, and played hockey as it should be played.

For us, on the other hand, the game was a disaster. We can sort out all the details of our defeat, but personally, I still can't really understand what happened.

Krutov opened the scoring. At the nine-minute mark he received a long pass from Kasatonov and put the puck neatly behind Craig. Five minutes later Buzz Schneider tied the score with a goal from a sharp angle. Then we went ahead again when Makarov slipped through the wall of defense to the net and scored.

There were two minutes left to the end of the first period . . . one minute . . . a few seconds . . . and then, the second, fatal goal was scored in our net. Christian fired a hard shot at me from center ice. I made a sloppy save – the rebound went right in front of me – but there were no opponents near me anyway. But then from nowhere came Johnson. He took the puck, which had already slid to the blue line. There were two seconds left. I was unprepared for the attack. One second . . . shot . . . goal! Where were our defensemen? Why didn't they even move, when Johnson was flying like a hawk at my net? Then it became clear; they were looking at the scoreboard, counting the remaining seconds of the period.

Yes, it was a key moment in the game, and perhaps a key moment in the whole tournament. The authors of the book *Miracle on Ice* confirm this. They describe the episode: "There were ten seconds to the end of the first period. Morrow picked up the puck in his zone and passed it to Dave Christian, who was on the blue line. He yelled to Christian to just shoot the puck in Tretiak's direction, thinking that the period was over. Christian took a meaningless shot. The puck hit Tretiak in the pads, and rebounded not far from him. There were three seconds left.

"Mark Johnson, who was at the blue line, had already turned to go to the locker room. He heard a roar from the spectators and understood that there was an opportunity to score. He saw the relaxed faces of Pervukhin and Bilyaletdinov. In the blink of an eye, he slipped between them and appeared one on one with the Soviet goalie. He was able to beat him with a wrist shot.

"But what was it? Was it a goal or not? The red light didn't flash, but the referee claimed that there was a goal. It appeared that the red light didn't go on because the green light was already glowing, indicating the end of the period. Then it became clear that there was one more second left to play. The Russians had already left the ice, but the referee told them to come back, just as a formality. They returned – without Tretiak. Eruzzione skated to Brooks: "Mishkin is in the net!" This news amazed everyone. It was unthinkable that the Russians would replace Tretiak. Everybody was enthusiastic. The opposition had no idea what a boost they had given us."

Yes, I was replaced because I let the team down, as I was told, in the heat of the moment. For so many years I had been irreplaceable, and now, I was a let-down.

Of course, I hadn't played my best, but who can say that it was a consequence of my weak will or my irresponsibility! I admit I was not in my best shape, but this can happen to any athlete. To be in good shape all the time is like balancing on the edge of a blade. For some unknown reason, since arriving in Lake Placid, I couldn't get into good condition. And now, one second before the end of the first period, I was taken out of the game. I watched what was happening on the ice from the bench. For the first time in many years, winning the gold medal didn't depend on me.

The second period began. The waves of attacks splashed rapidly from board to board. It would have been logical to assume that the Americans had already exhausted all their strength; they would give in and acknowledge the fact that we were the strongest hockey team at the Olympics. But it was to no avail.

In the third period, Johnson replied to a goal scored by Maltsev, and tied the score, 3-3. One and a half minutes later, Eruzzione put his team back into the lead. Our attempts to correct this situation were fruitless. Brooks's pupils not only played sensibly on defense, but also continued their counter-attacks. The more we played, the worse it got. We showed neither tactical variations nor harmony in defense. Our attacks weren't convincing. It is one thing to fly like a whirlwind at the rivals' net; it is another thing to score.

Yes, the outcome of this struggle was decided by one goal The Americans were triumphant. In an interview with reporters, Brooks explained that he and his team had been using Tarasov's tactics in games as well as in the practices.

The goalkeeper Craig, in the coach's opinion, played brilliantly. His reliability was the base of the victory. "Regarding the Soviet team," Brooks remarked, "they did not play their usual game, but rather a primitive style. They made thirty-six shots on goal to our sixteen, but they couldn't create any real opportunities to score."

Holding my head in my hands, I sat alone for a long time, going over again and again everything that had happened. Volodia Krutov came back from supper, but when he saw my state of mind, he tactfully left the room, leaving me alone again. Could I have prevented those goals? Yes, they weren't terribly difficult shots. What went wrong? Could it be that our veterans wanted too much to be three-time Olympic Games champions? That could be the reason. Sometimes excessive effort can stiffen, transforming itself into its opposite.

It is awful when you can't live up to the expectations of many people. It is so painful.

I don't think I should have been replaced in that game. I had made so many mistakes already, I was confident that my play would only improve. Volodia Mishkin is an excellent goalie, but he wasn't prepared for the struggle, he wasn't 'tuned in' to the Americans. To replace somebody during a game is always difficult, especially in such an important game as that one.

What was left? On the last day of the Olympic Games, the

American team defeated the Finns 4-2, and thus repeated the 1960 American Olympic team's success at Squaw Valley. We beat the Swedes 9-2, and had to settle for the silver.

When our plane landed at the Moscow airport, the crowds came to meet us and carried some of the other athletes away on their shoulders. The skier Nikolai Zimyatov was the major hero of the Olympics that year. We were demonstratively shoved aside and left unnoticed. And rightly so! But then, what counts as success in sports is relative. The silver medal doesn't mean a thing to the hockey fan – give him gold only! We had been accustomed to this ourselves for decades.

Many years have passed since Lake Placid. Little by little, we have erased from our memories the sad details of our 'jail term'. Almost all the meetings there have been forgotten. But the game against the Americans stands out clearly in my mind, as if it was only yesterday: Schneider shoots from a sharp angle . . . I skate towards him, hesitating; he appeared so suddenly, and logically speaking, he should pass to his teammate . . . Johnson is one on one with me. Danger, tension – but I've won many such duels. So many times, so many bullets I've saved, and now – was it nerves? One thing I know for sure: I couldn't have played any worse. But there's no use in crying over spilt milk.

It would require four years of persistent work, waiting, bruises, victories, and failures to regain the title of Olympic Champions at the next Games in Sarajevo. But there will be more about that later.

15

TO THE RINK BY AMBULANCE

Fate was hard on me at that time. Perhaps, if I'd left the game and retired from sports, no one would have said a bad word about me. By then I had two Olympic gold medals and one silver medal in my collection. I had been named the Most Valuable Player in Soviet hockey three times and had received a lot of other honors as well.

I had enough other concerns. I was studying by correspondence at the Military-Political Academy. My children were growing up but I didn't have much time to spend with them. Dimka was ready for Grade One. Little Irishka was too serious for her age. Relatives said that she was just like her father.

I could have retired but I didn't. In the first place I would have considered retirement to be a sign of weakness, like a retreat in battle. I could never retreat. Second, I wanted to prove that my failure overseas had been an accident – a single episode that would never happen again. I had enough strength left and I was eager to fight again.

However, it was Volodia Mishkin who went to Sweden as the first string goalie in the Swedish Cup tournament and he played very well. I was the backup. Let this season be over soon, I thought. Time would pass, I'd get some rest, and everything would be as it was before.

That summer we went to visit my wife's grandmother in Vishny Volochyok, 250 kilometers northwest of Moscow. We spent our entire vacation there, picking mushrooms and berries, and taking long hikes in the woods. The place was beautiful; there were lakes, rivers, and mountains all around us. And what fishing! Even a newcomer to the area couldn't come back without catching a fish. A holiday in a place like that heals many wounds.

Of course the south has its charm too with the sea and the sun. But at the resorts in the south there is always a schedule for breakfast, lunch and dinner as well as for getting up and going to bed. As a hockey player one becomes fed up with strict schedules. As well, there are always so many people at these resorts. Everyone, it seems, wants your company, inviting you to parties and other celebrations. And if you refuse, they whisper behind your back that you are stuck up or arrogant.

It never occurs to people that when hockey players are on vacation, they do not value the same things as others. Throughout the year a hockey player can never relax nor can he forget about the gruelling schedule he must follow. I used to look forward to my twenty-four day annual holiday like a child looks forward to receiving a present.

That's why a holiday in Vishny Volochyok was so good. We stayed in a big village house. We drank fresh milk. By seven each morning the 'Tretiak team', Tania, Dimka, Irishka and I, were up and on our way to the lake. Someone always brought

back a basket of mushrooms and a jar of berries for dinner.
I always came back with fish. In the evenings I set up a samovar
and drank tea with my wife's eighty-six year old grandfather.
He told me what it was like in the area before the Revolution
and how they fought for Soviet control in the region. He was
obviously very proud to have me as his guest. And I was happy
too. I was happy that there was such a house in Vishny
Volochyok where I was having a wonderful time.

* * * * *

In the first game of the 1980 Isvestia tournament against the
Czechs, our net was defended by Volodia Mishkin. Our national
team lost that game by a score of 5-4. They put me in goal
for the second game and I played as hard as I had in my younger
years. We won that game 5-2 and went on to win the tournament. But that wasn't all. The tournament organizers named
me as the best goalie.

Did that mean that my luck had finally returned? As I said,
fate was hard on me. And how hard. A month and a half later
we went to the city of Gorky for a regular league game. Carrying my huge bag of equipment in front of me, I stepped off
the bus in front of the hockey arena. As my right foot hit the
ground I felt a sharp pain. I let out a yell and my teammates
rushed over to see what had happened. Half the team had gone
down those steps without incident. I had somehow managed
to put my right leg directly into a hole on the sidewalk. When
the results of the X-rays came back it was clear – a fracture.
And the World Championships were a month away.

The doctors told me that my leg would be in a cast for at
least a month. When I arrived home on crutches, Tatiana started
to cry. "Finally your hockey has come to this," she said. "It's
left you crippled." But her grief soon turned to joy when she

realized that I would be at home for at least a month.

For the first week I enjoyed a complete rest. There was no way, however, that I was prepared to give up. I called the club and told them that I was ready to start training. From then on, everyday, I went down on my crutches to the entrance to our apartment building where an ambulance stood waiting to take me out to the Army training club. Each day for an hour to an hour and a half, I sat with my catching mitt on a stool in front of a hockey net which had been set up in the gymnasium while Viktor Kuzkin fired tennis balls at me with a racket. Not only did this help me to maintain my skills, more importantly it helped to rebuild my self-confidence.

Tikhonov ordered that a rowing machine be delivered to my home. The machine took up half of the room. At first my children were delighted but their enthusiasm quickly cooled off when they discovered that exercising on such a machine was very hard work. I worked for hours with those mechanical oars.

I still wasn't fully convinced that I could be ready in time for the World Championships but I decided that it was worth the struggle to try. And I had a role model by the name of Valery Kharmalov. Kharmalov had gone into hospital with fractures much more serious than mine but even as he lay in that hospital bed he began to prepare himself to return to the ice. Doctors argued about how many years he would need in order to walk properly again. They didn't even discuss the possibility of him playing hockey. Yet Valery, as soon as he could stand, came to practice. The doctors were right about one thing. Kharmalov limped for the rest of his life. But how well he played hockey!

I also thought of Alexander Maltsev who was plagued by injuries throughout his career. What kind of patience and courage he must have had to keep coming back time after time. There are many amazing examples of self-sacrifice in the history of sports.

Three weeks later my cast was taken off and I was on the ice almost immediately. I knew right away that my injury had set me back. Even Tatiana, watching me play on television, noticed the uncertainty, the hasty tumbles to the ice and other uncharacteristic movements.

There were only a few days left before the World Championships. I went to Tikhonov and told him that I probably wouldn't be ready in time and that I didn't want to let the team down. His response surprised me. "Yes, we can see that you're not in shape," he began. "But there's still time. You can catch up. We believe in you."

If he had answered differently or not sounded so confident, perhaps I really would have given up. But his words gave me a second wind. I told myself that if they believe in and count on me, then I will get myself into shape. The rest is history. I went to the 1981 World Championships in Sweden with our national team and played in every game except the last one, which didn't matter anyway since we'd already clinched the gold medal.

Guy Lafleur and Larry Robinson joined the Canadian national team in Sweden for that tournament after the Montreal Canadiens had been knocked out of the Stanley Cup playoffs that year. I remember a reporter asking Lafleur why he thought the Russian team was so strong. "We could talk about that for a long time," replied the famous professional. "But I can answer you in one sentence. They are great patriots."

He hit the nail right on the head.

The next season began incredibly early. By September we had to be in top shape for the second Canada Cup tournament. Before we went overseas we played two games against the

Swedish National team which had been reinforced with such great players as Salming, Hedberg and Nilsson who were playing with North American professional clubs. The stands were packed with fans. The Swedes had obviously missed their stars. We played on shortened ice surfaces in order to prepare for the smaller Canadian rinks. We also played two games against the Finns. We won all four games.

On the flight to Montreal I thought a lot about the first Canada Cup tournament in 1976. Our debut in 1976 wasn't successful. Now, five years later we were going overseas again, not to experiment but to win. We also had to convince those who questioned our championship status even after we won the World Championship. In some western newspapers there were several miserable attempts to cast aspersions on our victory because of the absence of the best professional players on both the Swedish and Finnish teams.

I also thought about our relationship with North American hockey. I was only an infant when Soviet players went overseas for the first time. However Anatoly Tarasov told me stories about how our players were received in Canada and the United States. What foolish and ridiculous questions they were asked about things like snowshoes and bears. Some people even tried to touch them, just to make sure that Russians were made of the same dough!

But I also recalled how Moskovites reacted when the Canadian professionals came to Moscow in the fall of 1972. They swarmed around the exit of the Palace of Sports; they sat around the clock at the entrance to the Intourist Hotel on Gorky Street, waiting for the Canadians to show up. And when they caught sight of the professionals they reached out for autographs and stared wide-eyed. The names of the players were pronounced with great respect – each of them a legend to the Moscow hockey fans.

During the player introductions before the first game in Moscow in 1972, Phil Esposito slipped and fell as he was being introduced. The spectators were stunned. This was the great Esposito. How could he fall? Most likely Phil pulled this stunt on purpose just to receive the sympathy of the fans and to break the tension in this very official atmosphere. As a matter of fact I'm sure he did it on purpose. He smiled at the crowd and perhaps only then they realized that these professionals were ordinary people too; they could cry and they could smile just like us. The audience burst into applause and their faces shone.

To get to know each other we have to meet. To trust each other we have to conduct a dialogue, not only in the auditoriums of the United Nations, but on the hockey ice as well.

For all hockey players the Canada Cup is a very special tournament. I'll explain why. The strongest national teams consider the World Championships and the Olympics to be the most important competitions and all their training is aimed at preparing for those tournaments. On the other hand, the North American professionals worship the Stanley Cup as the most important and prestigious championship. Even though we play the same hockey, life dictates its own rules to us which, within the limits of existing tournaments, means that regular games between the best professionals and amateurs cannot be held.

The Canada Cup is a different story. Without a doubt, all the brightest stars from around the world are gathered there. The Swedish and Finnish players, who play for North American professional clubs, return to play for their national teams. The coaches of those teams can show their stars off; but they can't make excuses when they lose either. As I understand it, the Canadians and Americans attach great significance to this tournament, assuming, not without grounds, that it provides an opportunity to see and to test new strategic concepts in the world hockey arena. Our Czech friends readily participate in the Canada Cup because they regard it as a great opportunity to evaluate their young players. Justifiably, they think that if a player can show well in the Canada Cup then he can be relied upon in any future battles.

Finally, let us not forget about the fans on both sides of the ocean. For them, these games between the strongest professional and amateur teams are the most delicious spectacle.

Prior to the start of the 1981 Canada Cup we played an exhibition game against the Canadians in Edmonton. We lost that game. Our hosts used a new tactic. Wayne Gretzky, the Edmonton Oilers' sharpshooter, loomed for a long time behind my net. Naturally my attention and that of our defensemen switched to him. Meanwhile, one of the Canadian forwards, usually Gilbert Perrault, snuck into position in front of the net, took an exact pass from Gretzky, and... . The Canadians worked this maneuver to perfection. It probably took them many practices to polish this technique but, at least at first, it paid off in goals. As the tournament progressed we finally came up with the 'antidote': we had to keep Gretzky from quietly skating behind the net. We tried it and it worked.

There was a new generation of players on the Soviet team. A whole constellation of outstanding hockey stars had left the team, leaving Valery Vasilyev, Alexander Maltsev and myself as the only 'oldtimers'. However, the youth that joined the team were no slouches either. Their play exhibited an original style and their characters were solid.

At the World Championships in Prague in 1978, the talents of Makarov became apparent to the world. Two years later, in Lake Placid, Krutov showed his sparkling gifts. Now, in the 1981 Canada Cup, everyone was talking about the brilliant skills and courage of Igor Larionov. Igor doesn't look like a hockey super star, particularly when you see him next to a six-foot giant like Larry Robinson. How deceiving appearances can be! Larionov showed such a passionate thirst in battle, such magnificent skills, that he became a genuine hero of the tournament. In the final game of the Canada Cup, which brought us together with our hosts, Igor outsmarted Robinson for the opening goal. It was a goal that amazed not only the spectators, but half of the players on the ice.

But I'm getting ahead of myself. We opened the 1981 Canada Cup series as we had five years before with a game against Czechoslovakia. It was an unusually tight game that ended in a 1-1 tie. Our next game, against the Swedes, wasn't an easy one either. For much of the game the score was even. We had a 4-3 lead in the third period when Kent Nilsson got into position in front of the net and then proceeded to miss the open corner. That was the turning point. Maltsev put the game out of reach with an unbelievable goal from an impossible angle in the corner. We won the game 5-3.

Our next game was against Team USA. Before we left the Soviet Union our fans had told us that we could give up the Canada Cup but we had to beat the Americans. Hockey lovers couldn't get over our defeat in Lake Placid the previous year. The American net was defended by Tony Esposito who, for the sake of participating in the Canada Cup, had actually changed his citizenship. There were many players from that 1980 Olympic gold medal team as well. They were anxious to play, to convince the world that their Olympic victory had not been an accident.

Tony let in four pucks that night while I let in just one. But at what cost! At the end of the second period I was so dizzy that I could barely drag myself to the dressing room. I was literally seeing stars. Only with great difficulty did our doctor manage to revive me enough to finish the game.

Our next game, with the Canadians, really didn't decide

anything. Both our teams had already earned berths in the semi-finals. I was given a rest. The Canadians were in the best shape possible. Gretzky, Bossy, Perrault and their teammates won the game 7-3, to the noisy excitement of the crowd. After this game the Canadian fans were sure that the Cup would once again be theirs.

Our team took the loss calmly. We watched the videotapes of the game several times, examining details of key situations and finally determining what to do against the cunning tricks of Gretzky. We didn't panic, nor did we overestimate our chances. We were confident.

We beat the Czechs in the semi-finals while the Canadians beat Team USA. And now the finals. Once again we found ourselves in the giant Montreal Forum. Once again the concrete walls shook from the roar of thousands of fans. The Forum was thirsty for a Canadian victory. The whole of Canada was in front of their TV screens for the second final in the history of the Canada Cup.

If someone had told us before the game that we would win by an 8-1 margin, none of us would have believed it. The Canadians were strong and they had the advantage of home ice. The majority of fans were absolutely certain of a Canadian victory. The day before the game the newspapers wrote that the outcome would depend most of all on how well Tretiak played. I gave my all in that game, and so did the rest of our guys.

What's the matter with the Canadians? I thought. Presumably they were over-eager; they wanted so much to make a brilliant showing in front of millions of their fans. In the early going they had numerous scoring opportunities but they couldn't put the puck in my net. Usually professionals fight to the end, no matter what the score, but once we'd scored a few goals, I saw something I'd never seen before – the Canadians seemed to give up. They hung their heads and, like an army given the order to surrender, they lost their hearts. I felt sorry for their goaltender, Mike Liut. His team had left him to be torn to pieces by our forwards. The fans were in a rage. The final score was 8-1.

Back home in Moscow, I met an elderly neighbor. "Aren't you Tretiak, sonny?" she asked.

"Yes I am," I replied.

"Let me kiss you," she said. "You know when you were playing those bastards, I blessed the TV set, and when you overcame them I even cried. You can't imagine how I felt when they played our national anthem in victory."

16

LEAVING BUT STILL
BEING THERE

At the beginning of 1984 I made a firm decision that I would play to the end of the season and then leave. It was time. People were trying to persuade me to stay on the team, insisting that I was still needed, that I still had some resources left. But my decision was firm.

I had never wanted to leave hockey before; I had always felt that I was strong enough to be reliable in the net, no matter whom we played, Canadian professionals or a second division team. However, strength has its limit. My skills were still with me and my reflexes hadn't lost their sharpness, but my nerves had worn out. Sometimes I couldn't sleep at night. I had to see a doctor to get a remedy. It was getting harder and harder to 'tune-in' to the game. When somebody on the ice played too roughly against me, I could hardly hold my anger. "You'd better go before I do something to you!" I would say to the offending player, and he would look at me in astonishment because for many years, everyone had known me as as easy-going fellow.

Frankly speaking, I could have left a year earlier, but I wanted to repay to my fans (and myself) the debt for the defeat in Lake Placid. Olympic Games, after all, are only held once every four years.

In the four years that had passed since Lake Placid, we never left the ice defeated. We were World Champions three times, we won the Canada Cup and Izvestia tournaments – in a word, luck was on our side. We waited for the Olympics to come, and trained with no regard for our own health. Our coaches tried to consider all possible circumstances to prepare the team to fight to the last drop of strength. For Soviet hockey, those upcoming Olympic Games were especially important. Either we would regain the title we lost four years before, or...

We didn't have any doubt that we would get the title back. But the strong desire to win can sometimes bring about the opposite result. It makes you stiff, binds your arms and legs, and doesn't let you display all your real potential. A similar situation hampered the Canadians at the Forum in 1981.

I'd like to give credit to the Yugoslavs who were the hosts of the Games. They were well prepared to meet guests from all over the world. Everything was thought out in detail, both the organization of daily routine and the competitions. There was a spirit of celebration, of peace, friendship, and mutual understanding. This is the way the Olympic Games are supposed to be. As far as I could tell, everybody was happy with the Yugoslavian hospitality in Sarajevo.

Again, as eight years ago, I was a standard bearer for the Soviet Olympic team. I was probably honored because there were no other athletes participating in the 1984 Olympics who had participated in four Olympic Games in a row. Or perhaps it was meant to have a special psychological effect: to show the hockey players that everybody was counting on their victory. Yes, in comparison to the skiers, speed skaters, and figure skaters, we were competing for only one medal, but it was highly valued by the fans.

The hockey teams were divided into two groups. One group included the national teams of the USSR, Poland, Italy, Yugoslavia, West Germany, and Sweden. In the other group were Czechoslovakia, the USA, Finland, Canada, Austria, and Norway. We all agreed that the Czechoslovakian players were lucky because they had stronger rivals, which meant that they had the potential to improve with each game.

Ten players from our team were participating in the Olympics for the first time. Nine had been silver medal winners at Lake Placid. I was the only one who had enjoyed the fruits of Olympic victories, both in Sapporo and Innsbrück.

Our first game in the Olympic tournament was with Poland. In the 1976 World Championships, when we had also played Poland in our first game, some of our young hockey players had gone out on the ice with too much confidence. Before we came to our senses, four pucks were already in our net. No, we would not repeat that mistake here.

I took my usual place in the net, looked around as always, and calmed down. The main thing is to get started.

The start of the tournament didn't bring us any disappointments, but Tikhonov wasn't happy; he thought we weren't scoring enough. He probably thought that the players were unconsciously saving themselves for decisive games. The Olympic distance is long, you have to play every other day, and you have to play prudently.

We wondered whether we would get the chance to play the Americans in Sarajevo, or whether our fate in the tournament lay in another direction. We knew that the 1984 USA Olympic team had prepared thoroughly for the Games; they had played about eighty games, including games with Krilya Sovetov and the USSR second team. We studied videotapes of these games carefully, paying close attention to their European-style passing and puck control. Before we left for Sarajevo, I talked to Alexander Tyzhnykh, who played on the second team. Sasha had a very high opinion of the Olympic champions: "Technically, they are very well-equipped. The team has character. But, I have no doubt that you will win."

In Sarajevo, American tourists prematurely bought out tickets for the finals, convinced that there would be a repeat of what happened four years ago, that it would be *their* finals. There was a big fuss surrounding the USA national team before the Olympics, and for the first few days after the opening. A lot of this came from overseas, and from the players themselves, who were giving brave interviews to anyone who would listen. If it was so, we thought, it meant that the Americans were not so confident in themselves. A really strong person never brags about it.

Before their first game against Canada, the Americans launched a psychological attack, accusing the Canadians of having two former professionals on their team. The Americans achieved what they wanted; those players were forbidden to participate in the Olympics. On the other hand, it infuriated the Canadians tremendously. They swore to 'tear apart' these upstarts, and kept their word. The score was 4-2 for Canada.

The next game for the Americans was with Czechoslovakia, who remembered their defeat by the USA team four years ago in Lake Placid. This rematch was considered one of the best games at the Sarajevo Olympics. The Americans didn't back down, but the rivals were strong too. I had a feeling that, physically, both teams were almost equal, although the Czech players were superior in technique to the Americans. The

Rusnak line single-handedly beat the Olympic champions, scoring four goals.

For the USA national team, the Olympics ended in a tie game with the Norwegians. It was a real shock. In a burst of disappointment and rage, the former champions smashed their sticks to smithereens on the ice and wrecked the furniture in their locker room. I could not understand that incident. You have to lose with honor, too.

All the other athletes at the Olympics had already finished their competitions, received their share of rewards and punishment, celebrated and sobbed out their grief. Only we, the hockey players, still could not afford to think about anything else but victory. As had happened many times before, the main game brought us face to face with our old acquaintances, the Czechs.

The Czechoslovakians had taken the process of changing generations more painfully than we had. It was as if the great players of the seventies had taken with them something very important to the character of the team. I clearly saw that their young players were not satisfied with silver medals, which we invariably left to them. But I also saw that they weren't psychologically ready to defeat us. I guess they didn't have enough self-confidence.

We went out on the ice on the last day of the Olympics, knowing that our gold medal, if we could win it, would give us first place in the unofficial all-team score. We had to try hard.

Tikhonov gave general directions for the game. Then he asked me to step aside: "Vladik, I am afraid I might overdo it. Gather the team by yourself, and have a heart to heart talk with the guys, without putting too much pressure on them." The coaches were no less worried than we were. Tikhonov and Yurzinov had pinched faces, their cheeks were sunken.

The forthcoming game was a review of their strenuous four-year effort. Were they on the right track or not?

We got together with the team. I talked to them as the oldest and most experienced: "Guys, all the Olympic games have been very interesting for the viewers, but you know how our fans are waiting for our hockey victory. I can see that many rookies are nervous. It's only natural. It is the fourth Olympic competition for me, but I am as nervous as I was the first time. It is important for us to help each other, and to quickly correct our mistakes, if there are any."

I took a good look at the familiär faces, thinking about how hard it had been for them in their last days! Makarov, Larionov, and Tyumenev were finishing the tournament with heavy injuries. Our team doctor, Boris Sapronenkov, was run off his legs restoring our players to health. A few days later, he commented in an interview with a newspaper: "Some time ago, I worked with skiers and I can't say that they don't have endurance. But hockey players have endurance of a special kind. I am talking about the ability to endure pain and injuries. I'll put in a few stitches during the intermission, and they'll go back out on the ice as if nothing happened. That's what kind of people they are, our guys. They don't pay attention to trivial bumps and bruises. There is an opinion that if you haven't got any, you haven't played your best."

After our meeting, some sports managers also expressed a wish to talk with the team, and with each player separately – to raise the morale, so to speak. But that would have psyched the players up too much, and that never did any good. Tikhonov was firm on this issue, and didn't give in to any appeals or persuasions. As an experienced psychologist (and a good coach definitely has to be an experienced psychologist), he could see in our faces the complete inner concentration of each player, each mind directed selflessly to the task at hand. This kind of intrusion could have provoked irritation and stiffness in the younger players. I remember Tarasov never let anyone, no matter what his rank, near the team before an important game. Tikhonov did exactly the same.

I won't describe the game in detail; it's still within recent memory. The score was 2-0. It wasn't the most interesting game in terms of a show, but it was an outstanding duel in terms of inside tension. The goalkeeper Sindl was good in the first period, but couldn't save his net from a sharpshooter's blow by Kozhevnikov. Kozhevnikov, by the way, had been included on the Olympic team at the last moment. A wrist shot by Krutov was successful in the second period. Two errors by the Czechoslovakian defense – two goals for us. And our defense played flawlessly that day.

Before the game, all we could think about was how joyful it would be if we won. And now we had our victory. We had recovered the title of Olympic champions. Our fans in the stands were triumphant, and we were supposed to be joyful too. But there was no strength left for joy. All had been spent on the ice of the Olympic hockey rink.

After the awards ceremony ended and we were on the bus, Fetisov stood up and shouted, "Hurray!" In full voice we all began to sing a song of victory.

Yes, I said firmly to myself, these Olympic Games will be the last for me. I'll just play to the end of the National Championships, and that's it.

There seemed to be no outward reasons for me to leave. I played as confidently in Sarajevo as I had in my best years. Our Army team broke away from our opponents long before the end of the season, and, with only one defeat, lead Spartak by twenty-eight points! Nobody could blame me for anything. From the outside, everything was as always – the season went on quite well.

But I knew that I was leaving, and the coaches knew it too. By some unspoken agreement, we didn't talk about it until the very end of the season. I played in almost every game, both for my club and for the National Team.

Yes, everything went on as usual. I was playing, and defending the net no worse that I had for the last fifteen years. I was honestly exhausting myself in practices. I lived in my room at our Army Club training camp in Arkhangelskoye, carrying out all the requirements of the stern order of the day; rising time, workout, breakfast, practice, dinner, practice, supper, free time, bedtime. But I was already looking differently on this life. I understood that soon, nothing of this would exist for me, and that every day I spent there had a special value.

A long, long time ago, when I was very young, I watched Loktev, Alexandrov, then Firsov, Ragulin, and Mishakov retire. At the time, I thought I'd be playing forever. From my point of view, veterans were people from another age. I called Brezhnev 'Uncle Volodia'. And now, unwittingly, I had become a veteran myself. I was the oldest player on the Central Army Club, and many of the rookies called me 'sir'. How strange it was that many of those rookies of the Central Army Sports Club had never seen Firsov, Ragulin, or Mishakov on the ice.

I left because I was very tired. I'd played fifteen years with the Army Club and the National Team without a break. Backup goalies came and went, as did three generations of forwards and defensemen, but through four Olympic Games, all the important games with the professionals, all the World Championships, all the Izvestia tournaments, it was I who played in the net.

Now I can admit that it was very difficult for me to be a number one goalie for fifteen years. It was such a load. Over ten years ago, I was asked, "If you had to start all over again, would you walk into this mine field again?" All over again.

At that time, I didn't know what to say. And now? I don't feel sorry for the years left behind. They were beautiful, but I can relive them only in my dreams. Would I do it all over again? I feel goosebumps on my skin when I think about it.

I am not complaining. I wanted it, it was my life. But towards the end, I would drag myself to the locker room during the intermissions; I was dizzy, my feet felt like they were made of lead. The fans didn't see it, all they saw were my saves. That is how it should be; we did not play for ourselves, but for our fans.

I said goodbye to the old park in Arkhangelskoye. Exactly sixteen years before, I had stepped timidly over the threshold of a wooden one-storey pavilion, which, at that time, housed the Army Club players. Now, the club and the management are located there.

Every corner of that old park is familiar to me. There is a spot, on the bank of the Moskva River, where I liked to sit down, fishing rod in hand, hypnotized by the movement of the float. There were a lot of fish in the river and in the mill pond – roach, carp and bream. Once, Kolya Adonin and I were fishing there, and such a huge perch got away that I fell into the river trying excitedly to catch it.

The hill holds yet another memory. This was where Tarasov, during our athletic training, made us run up and down the hill, up to our waists in snow.

Some of our most loyal Army fans were actors. They liked to come to Arkhangelskoye. For many years, we had astronauts, authors, and scientists as our friends. War veterans, legendary heroes of our Motherland, said parting words to us before hard battles. This was also a part of life in Arkhangelskoye, and a very important one. We wanted to work even harder after those meetings. It is a wrong to think that our distinguished guests were only there to broaden our knowledge; personal contact with truly interesting and bright people is always spiritually enriching. It compels one to pull together, and be even more committed to one's goals.

But let me return in my memoirs to those paths of the famous park, which lead me again to the wooden pavilion. There is the source of everything that ever became of me in later life. During my career there, I usually shared my room with one of the other goalkeepers, but this changed in the last years. The management of the team tried to accommodate me in a single room. It was not quite the tribute to my merit that it may seem. I never asked for privileges; indeed, I though it was better to have a roommate than to be alone. But our doctor decided that it would be better for me to prepare myself for the games. He could see how my nerves were giving out.

A lot has changed in Arkhangelskoye. Players now live in a three-storey brick building, where there is a sauna, doctors' offices, and video recorders. But the traditions of Loktev and Firsov remain, and this is one of the reasons for the club's continuing success.

Of the players with whom I had started, none remained. It was difficult, especially during leisure time. The young players had their own interests, their own tastes in movies and music. There was no feeling of camaraderie in fishing, playing chess, or watching movies. Most of the time I spent talking with our masseur who was closer to my own age. Sometimes I visited the political worker Yuri Danilov, who had helped me prepare for tests at the Military-Political Academy some time ago.

Yes, it was time to put my skates in the closet, to let others follow in my footsteps. I didn't believe that all the best had gone by; life doesn't end with a final whistle. On the contrary, the old man from Vishny Volochyok, whom I mentioned before, expressed himself very definitely on this point. ''You showed yourself on the ice not badly," he said. "You didn't slip. But that was a game. Now you are going to be a political worker, and I think this job is more important."

Good-bye, hockey. Sooner or later, it had to happen, but it was better that it happened no sooner and no later. I left the ice with a feeling of having fully accomplished a duty. The satisfaction was not in the awards I won, but in all the years that I honestly and conscientiously served my club, my nation, our Soviet sports.

Many times I participated in solemn ceremonies in arenas around the world, where our flag was raised and our stately Soviet anthem played in honor of our victories. It was in these moments that we truly felt our belonging to the great Soviet country, our great people, our land – that is where we got the strength for our glorious victories.

My friends were always beside me. It is a great happiness to take part in a cooperative accomplishment. Fate gave me the most talented mentors. Each of them, from Tarasov to Tikhonov, left a significant imprint on my athletic and personal development.

I bow to my fans, who gave me their warm support all these years, as if they were sharing with me their strength, hope, and optimism. What would I have been without these loyal friends!

I looked back into my past, turning over in my mind episodes of brilliant hockey battles, feeling again on my lips the salty taste of the sweat of practices that I relived in my imagination.

For me, it was all, and all of it is with me forever.

17

TRETIAK, VASILIEV, AND MALTSEV –
An Unforgettable Farewell

On December 22, 1984, I went out on the ice for the last time, and took my place in the net. It was a special game – a farewell game. International hockey was saying good-bye to the defenseman Valery Vasiliev, the forward Alexander Maltsev, and me, the goalkeeper. We had all started at about the same time on the major league teams and on the National Team. We had known each other for fifteen years. And now, together, we were leaving the ice. Naturally, each of us was nervous. It was our last game and that's why we wanted to play well and to demonstrate our best skills.

We had very serious rivals. For the first time, Soviet players were playing against a European combined team made up of the best athletes of the national teams from around the continent, who were participating in the Izvestia tournament in Moscow.

We knew that we were supposed to play only ten minutes

of this game. Then the game would be stopped, and an official ceremony would begin. I hadn't played for about six months, and I had practised persistently for the last two days, according to my individual plan, to be in good shape. To remain unbeatable in this last game was a matter of special honor for me.

In the dressing room I quickly put on my mask to hide from my teammates the fact that I was worrying more than usual. The announcer addressed the public: "Vladislav Tretiak is defending the net . . . on defense, Valery Vasiliev . . . playing forward, Alexander Maltsev. The puck was dropped, and it spun on the ice like a top. I calmed down right away. I finally found my confidence when I beat off a heavy attack. No matter how hard our rivals tried to score, they couldn't do it.

Vasiliev and Maltsev also maintained their style in that last game. Valery was always an example of hockey power for us. Bobby Hull once confessed that when even he saw Vasiliev approaching, he wanted to get rid of the puck as quickly as possible. As for Alexander Maltsev, Chernishev, an honored coach of the USSR, once remarked: "If Maltsev had been a soccer player instead of a hockey player, he probably would have been no less famous than Kruiff, the 'Flying Dutchman'."

In that last game, we saw them again as we had always known them. In the second half of our ten-minute period, Valery Vasiliev nailed a persistent European forward to the boards, took the puck away from him, and quickly directed it to Maltsev. Everyone wanted very much for Maltsev to explode, to outsmart the defensemen, and to score easily. And he did explode and outsmart the defensemen, but instead of shooting, he suddenly passed to Svetlov, who was in a much better position. Even the opponents' goalie didn't expect such a turn in events, and soon we heard the announcement: "Sergei Svetlov opened the scoring, with assists from Valery Vasiliev and Alexander Maltsev."

The fans gave Maltsev a long ovation. Even in the last game, he followed his usual tactic – team work. And this particular goal was like passing the baton to our young players.

When the ten minutes were up, the famous Soviet referee, Dombrovsky, who was also participating in his last game, stopped the play. Both teams left the ice, and only the three of us remained at center ice. We were presented with awards from the Central Committee of the Communist Youth League, the Sports Committee of the USSR, the Sports Committee of the Ministry of Defense, the Central Council of Dynamo, the Executive Council of Moscow City Hall, the Soviet Peace Fund, and the International Federation of Ice Hockey. There were speeches by the pilot-astronaut V. Aksyonov, two times a Hero of the Soviet Union, and by the three-time Olympic champion swimmer, Vladimir Salnikov.

Then I was asked to make a speech. I had prepared and memorized my speech ahead of time, but when I went up to the microphone on the Luzhniki ice, I felt that I couldn't present the speech that I had learned. I decided to say exactly what I was feeling at that emotional moment, even if it wasn't as smooth.

We left hockey. Our farewell game ended with the victory of the Soviets over the European team by a 7-3 score. To us, it meant that there were players who would continue our glorious tradition. All proceeds from the game went to the Soviet Peace Fund.

And that's it. So closed the last page of my sports biography. Now, I am sitting in front of a blank piece of paper. Is it worth it to continue this book? Will the story about my life after hockey be of interest to readers?

A few years have passed since I was a goalie. I lead a completely different life. Is it really that different? Certainly the things I do each day have changed, but the meanings, the goals, and the purposes are still the same: to work for the well-being and glory of Soviet sports, to develop high moral qualities in Soviet athletes.

Even to this day, people ask me if I am sorry that I left hockey, if I wish I was on the ice again. My answer is, "No!" I have never had the desire to put on my goalie mask again. Am I tired of hockey? Probably. Even now, I haven't learned how to relax and watch a game. I worry during the game, and not just as a fan. After watching a game, I feel the familiar tiredness in my muscles, as though I had been playing. However, as a spectator, I do not get the satisfaction of a job well done and that is when I have regrets.

At a recent meeting I was asked how many awards I have. I answered that I have around a hundred, but the persistent fan wanted me to be more exact. I had to confess that I didn't know the exact number. I never kept count. I accepted them, so to speak, as one huge medal. When I returned home, curiosity overcame me – let's count them! But counting awards turned out to be harder than counting fish after a successful fishing trip; every award triggered a flood of memories. I spent almost half my weekend counting my medals, but I never did finish.

People say that hockey is a whole life. I agree. But real life is even more varied, more interesting, and harder than my favorite game. I had a sharp, unforgettable feeling when I left the ice; I suddenly realized how much of the joy of day to day living I was missing. I looked forward to having a lot of free time, and doing all the things I enjoyed, but had denied myself for the sake of hockey. I would be able to be at home more, to spend time with my family, go to the theatre, movies, fishing . . . Indeed, before, I had to be away from home very often. I found out about the birth of my daughter during an American tour. I remember when I used to come home and ask my son, Where's your daddy? He would lead me to the TV set or to my photo.

Why doesn't my son like hockey? He probably didn't have enough of my attention in his early childhood, and he disliked what, in his opinion, was an obstacle which prevented us from being together. Although Dima plays basketball at our parental insistence, he unfortunately shows no special interest in this sport. His gentle nature is not suited to rough sports.

Irishka, on the other hand, could be a good athlete if she wanted to be. She is a persistent, go-getter of a girl. However, she started to take a preparatory course at the Moscow Choreographic College and perhaps she will be a ballet dancer in the future. In any case, at the age of nine, she already watches ballet with great pleasure. I, too, have become a real ballet lover. In the last year and a half, my wife and I have seen almost the whole repertoire of the Bolshoy Theatre.

And there is still not enough time. A whirl of new events keeps me even busier than I was the ice.

In the summer of 1984, Viktor Tikhonov asked me to help him to prepare Soviet goalkeepers for the next Canada Cup. I agreed with pleasure, because I considered it very selfish to leave the hockey arena and bury all the knowledge and experience that I had gained over many years.

I tried to teach them everything I knew, to open all my secrets to them, all my exercises and methods. I told them how to find out by watching a forward's eyes what his next move would be. I shared the subtle details of psychological training. I spoke about intuition, without which no goalkeeper can expect success. Everybody practised willingly and learned their lessons fast. Later, I was very proud of Volodia Mishkin, who was named the best goalkeeper of the Canada Cup.

Tikhonov asked me to help him on several more occasions, and I was always ready to help my team. Once, an acquaintance of mine came to one of those practices. "This is very good," he said, "Why don't you start coaching seriously, full-time?" There is an opinion among sports fans that yesterday's champion will be tomorrow's good coach. Alas, real life often proves this to be wrong. Not too many athletes are transformed into good coaches. I don't want fans to look at me with regret and sigh, "He was such a good goalkeeper and yet he became such a bad coach." That is what often happens in real life.

Some time ago, I found a quotation by M.I. Kalinin in one of the textbooks, which seemed to be very appropriate: "Sports is a good thing; it makes a human being strong. But sports is an auxiliary subject, and to transform it into the goal itself in bare recordsmanship, doesn't do any good . . . . Sports has to be subjected to general tasks of Communist education. We develop and prepare not narrow-minded athletes, but citizens of Soviet society, who are supposed to have not only strong hands and good digestive systems, but, in the first place, very wide political horizons and organizational skills." These are remarkable words!

When I left the ice, I was offered a job almost immediately with the political department of the Central Army Sports Club. I accepted the offer without hesitation. At first, I was acting as a senior instructor of international relations. Then, I was appointed Political Deputy Chief of the sports games department. Neither position was probably very important on the scale of our Army sports, but let me tell you, each held a lot of responsibility.

When I began I worked twelve hours a day, helping to insure the smooth organization and operation of international competitions. Although this job was not suited to my academic qualifications, it was nothing to complain about. The numerous and varied duties of a senior instructor of international relations allowed me to understand the organizational problems of sports, and to obtain a wide range of practical habits, without which I would have got into difficult situations in the future.

At the same time, I decided to take a course in English. I would run to the teacher at night, and zealously learn new words and grammatical rules. How many times during our foreign trips had I felt sorry that I didn't speak the language! It wasn't laziness that had prevented me from learning English before. Studying a foreign language requires a lot of concentration and attention, and at that time I concentrated all my attention on hockey; it took all my effort.

When I was named Political Deputy Chief of the sports games department a few months later, my duties were changed slightly. I was responsible for all political-educational work among sports players. These sports, I would say, have a very high profile.

Soccer alone means a lot. In 1984, Army soccer players finished so poorly that they were forced to leave the first division. They couldn't change the situation in the following season either. The reason for their poor performance stemmed from a crisis that the team had been suffering for a long time. Now we had to change it.

In April 1985, I was sent south to where the soccer players were finishing their pre-season training. I wanted to be with them, to examine them closely, to feel the strong and weak sides of the team. To be precise, it wasn't the sort of team that I had become accustomed to on my own hockey team – a team with many years of traditions, succession of generations, and a sense of pride in the honor and traditions of the Army Club.

The majority of the soccer players were wearing the T-shirt with the Central Army Club logo for the first time, and they had come to us from many different places. Now, those diverse young men had to be united into a team, which was supposed to regenerate the past glory of Army soccer. At that time they had only one thing in common – youth. The average age was twenty-two years. Certainly they had the skills, but even if they could all play like Pele, they could not play well unless a collective will was formed among them. It was necessary for players to have faith in each other, for coaches to have faith in players, and for the whole team to have faith in a big goal. A team without faith is like a team without a soul.

There, in the south of the country, I was trying to kindle the flame of faith as much as I could. Of course, I told the guys mostly about hockey traditions: Tarasov's lessons, our Komsomol meetings before major games, in-house newspapers, meetings with fans, our friendship, how to tolerate pain and fight to the end. I saw that what made the strongest impression on the soccer players were stories about the courage of my friends.

When I told them about how our players fought on the ice with heavy injuries – fractures, bruises, torn ligaments – how after some games, several of them at once were admitted to the hospital, disbelief was written all over the faces of my listeners, as if to say, no, it couldn't have been like that. But it was, and if the young Army soccer players would not only believe me, but also draw the right conclusions for themselves personally, the spectators would be applauding them too.

The season of 1984/85 turned out to be a difficult one for the Army Club hockey team. Fetisov wasn't playing because of his injuries. Injuries were also following Drozdetsky, Vasiliev, Zubkov, Gerasimov, and Babinov. On the other hand, a strong opponent appeared before the Army players – the Moscow Dynamo, coached by our former mentor, Yuri Moiseev. First of all, Yuri brought discipline to the team. He inspired confidence in the players, and ignited their ambitions. Moiseev went through the schools of Tarasov and Tikhonov.

Hockey held no secrets from him. He aimed his pupils for first place only. The struggle between the Army Club and Dynamo turned out to be intriguing. Dynamo lead all the way, and was closer to the gold medal of the USSR Championship than ever before. But they couldn't last to the finish.

Our club, in fact, had more potential. The Army club tied the second-to-last game with Dynamo, 2-2, and two days later, literally crushed them by a score of 11-1. I sympathized with Mishkin very much; he played the whole season steadily, and now, what a finish! His own teammates left him to be torn to pieces by the Army players. Such a score can be psychologically traumatic for a goalie.

The final duel was in Kiev. To become the USSR champions, the Army players had to beat the local team, Sokol. I was with the team, and I saw how nervous everybody was. The long season was behind them. Everything would be decided in only one game. The Army Club hadn't been in such a crucial situation at the finish of the USSR season for a long time.

After the first period the Army players were losing, 3-1. But then, they started to play like champions are supposed to play. They played the kind of hockey for which our club was always famous: fast, precise, daring. After the game the members of the Red Army Team were photographed on the ice as Champions of the Soviet Union. For the first time in many years, the photograph didn't include me.

The next season, Army players took a lesson from their rivalry with Moscow's Dynamo, improved their training, and lead the league from the start. They had already won the championship six rounds before it ended. Some newspapers and magazines hurled reproaches at the Army players because they played too well, as if all the troubles in our hockey existed because of the Army Club. Supposedly, coaches of the Army team had drained other teams of talented players and that was why nobody could compete on the same level as the champions.

I flatly disagree with such an assertion. Firstly, many of the pupils of the Army Club now play in other clubs around the country; there are tens, if not hundreds of them. Secondly, not only the Army Club, but all other major teams started to recruit players from different cities a long time ago. As strange as it may sound, only the Army Club was blamed publicly for that.

Looking at this problem from another point of view, I am convinced that many of today's hockey players would not have become stars if they had remained with their former teams. The Army Club Hockey School is, in a way, an academy of our hockey. There is nothing amazing about that; many players from other clubs want to come here. And furthermore, there is nothing to prevent Dynamo or Spartak from having such an academy themselves.

As a political worker, I supervise plans for educational work on teams. I see my task as being to make physical education a component of communist upbringing, the aim of which is to form a new human being, which harmoniously combines in itself a spiritual richness, moral purity, and physical perfection.

I remember the enthusiasm with which we discussed articles about the fight against alcoholism with our team. This is a very topical and emotional issue for everyone, including athletes. How many of them were ruined by the 'Green Dragon'? It's bitter to recall.

Right after the formation of the All Union Volunteer Society of Sobriety, I was chosen to be a member of the board representing all the athletes of the country.

If alcoholism is our obvious enemy, there are vices which cannot be recognized so easily. These include vanity, mercantilism, and egocentricity. One of my acquaintances, a reporter, told me a story. He went to the airport to meet our shooters, who won the world championship. The whole team had performed very well, but in individual competition, misfortune got one of the team leaders. The reporter expressed his regrets regarding the misfire. He said, "It's too bad you came back without any awards." "Without awards?" the athlete complacently and defiantly objected. He pointed to a box of Japanese radio equipment; "This is my main award."

It is a shame that there such people, opportunists of sports. They transform the noblest occupations into objects of profit.

My position – political worker of an army sports club – is very responsible. Athletes are, in fact, on the main line of the ideological fight of two social systems. Our athletes have to prove constantly that they are not only the strongest and most talented, but, more importantly, they must let the world know that behind them is the strength of Communist ideals, the all-triumphant truth of our Soviet morality.

Recently, the party organization of our Army Club entrusted me with the very important and responsible assignment of preparing deserving people for enrollment in the lines of the Communist Party. I try to talk thoroughly with each applicant; I want to know what reasons motivate an athlete to take this important step in his life, and whether he could represent our Communist Party with dignity.

An acquaintance of mine, with whom I played for some time on the same team, asked me once, not without wonder: "Tell me Vladik, what kind of enjoyment do you find in meetings with fans? You never refuse to make a speech. And you have to prepare yourself for every speech you make. So many unnecessary worries." I will repeat now what I answered him then. In this case, I do it not for personal pleasure, but as a duty before my country and hockey fans. They trust us, look up to us, and, with their selfless labor, create excellent conditions for our practices and competitions. This is our civic duty, if you'll permit me, and I strive to discharge my duty the best I can.

I take care to answer every question that comes from the audience. After I've answered them, I go home and analyze what questions I've been asked because it helps to learn the interests of the audience and accordingly correct my speeches. The most diffucult task is to speak in front of kids. I usually tell them how I came into hockey, how I practised, what interesting things happened to me on ice. I purposely don't tell them how I did at school, I wait for them to ask me. And it always comes, not one, but several similar questions. Then I tell in detail how good I was at school, otherwise my father would never let me go to practice.

At the end of one meeting, one of the boys sent me a note: "I always thought that only thugs could become real hockey players. I didn't register for the hockey team because I don't like to fight. Now I am going to register and play like you."

And now, I want to tell about one more side of my post-hockey life. But why post-hockey? We are talking about work directed at consolidating peace and mutual understanding between all nations – weren't all the previous years dedicated to this cause? The ice of hockey arenas brings people together – it's warm ice.

Sheremetyevo International Airport. I was sitting in a comfortable easy chair in the waiting room, listening to the announcements over the loud speaker. Planes from different airlines around the world were landing – Prague, Vienna, Montreal, Frankfurt, Stockholm. I wondered how many cities on our planet are connected with my hockey memories. In ten or fifteen minutes, I would board my plane to Zurich.

"Mister Tretiak?" I took my eyes off the newspaper and

saw an older couple smiling at me warmly. "How do you do, Vladislav!" I am used to the fact that even perfect strangers recognize me and say hello. I rose from the chair and warmly shook hands. By their accent, I guessed that they were foreign, most likely Canadian or American.

"Of course you don't remember us, Vladislav," said the man. "You gave us your autograph in Vancouver after the game with the best stars of the NHL in 1972. The play of the USSR team made such an impression on us! We like hockey and we decided to learn the Russian language in order to know more about your country and your hockey. Now, we are in Moscow as tourists. And how are you? Where is your mask and hockey stick?"

"I am not playing anymore. I left the game."

"Yes, we heard about this. Canadian newspapers reported this sad fact but they also reported that you have been invited to play in the NHL, and that they promised to pay several million dollars. Have you turned them down?"

Here, I suppose I should explain where the rumor about my possible contract with the Montreal Canadiens came from. This subject kept reappearing on the pages of Canadian newspapers for almost two years. It all started when once, overseas, I was asked what NHL team I would like to play for, if such an opportunity arose. The question was simply hypothetical, and I casually answered, the Montreal Canadiens. As it appears, the reporter who interviewed me turned out to be rather irresponsible, to put it mildly. Newspapers printed sensational headlines: "Vladislav Tretiak would like to play in Montreal after ending his hockey career!"

You have to understand that nothing like that ever crossed my mind! We protested to the Canadians about this irresponsible reporting, but it was to no avail. They took the bit in their teeth and ran away with the story. What was most amazing was that the management of the Montreal club believed the media. Serge Savard rubbed his hands together and spoke about the deal as if it was certain.

The January 17, 1984 edition of the *Toronto Star* warned the manager of the Canadiens against excessive optimism. However, Savard himself told a reporter, " My experience in racing taught me that there is no chance of winning unless you enter the race." Furthermore, in June of 1983 during the NHL amateur draft, Savard included my name on the list of Montreal Canadiens selections. This was done to outstrip all possible competitors from other clubs. Generally speaking, they were selling the bear skin before catching the bear.

I never for a moment considered playing in the NHL. It wouldn't suit me, as an officer and a Soviet citizen, to wear the uniform of a North American professional player. This fuss continued for some time. The rumor reached me that the proposed salary offer had risen to an amount that had never before been offered to any professional player. Then they understood the hopelessness of this deal. But the story followed me, resurfacing here, in a Moscow airport, during a conversation with my fans.

"I have other plans and concerns," I told them. "I am a member of the Athletes' Commission of the International Olympic Committee, and I am flying to Switzerland to participate in a regular session of IOC." "Have a nice trip. We are for peace and friendship too," said my new friends. I gave them my good-bye autograph.

It was a pleasant meeting! Although nothing special was said, it was a very heartwarming experience. Before, when I used to play hockey, I knew that our play helped to consolidate friendship between nations, but now, since I have become a member of the IOC Commission, I see it in another light.

In 1981, I spoke for the first time in front of prominent

figures of the International Olympic Movement at the XI Olympic Congress in Baden-Baden. I spoke of the importance of preserving Olympic traditions, and of cherishing the atmosphere of friendship which allows people to meet with each other, to exchange opinions, and to discuss common problems.

I was just beginning to play when our athletes were first discovering American hockey, but I know what a cynical and hostile reception they got overseas. Hatred of our social system has been fed into the minds of people in capitalist countries since their childhood. I remember a stupid cartoon I once saw on American TV. Imagine a small globe on which, over mountains and through oceans, from the wilds of Russia, runs an awful and mad bear. It had a shining hammer and sickle on its forehead, and it carried nuclear bombs and missiles in its paws. The message was clear: to save yourself from such a monster, you had to arm yourself and kill it.

I recall one of my first meetings with North American fans. I was approached by two Canadians on a street in Montreal who said to me: "There are many rumors about your country. There is talk that you are organizing international terrorism, provoking the western world to war and aggression. You are the first Soviet person we have ever met. Please tell us, is there any truth in this gossip?"

What could I say to these people who had never heard anything good about my country? I smiled and asked them instead, "What do you think, do I look like a terrorist to you?" "No, you don't," answered the Canadians with confusion. "Well, if you could see my other countrymen," I continued, "you would have the same opinion. Only crazy people can dream of war now." The conversation lasted for no more that two minutes, but those Canadians will remember it for a long time.

One more observation: After our first game with the professionals they refused to shake our hands. In the NHL, the custom of shaking hands was foreign, even in friendly games. Now, under the influence of our players, professionals have also adopted the tradition of being friendly to each other, no matter what the results of the game are.

As you remember, the first series of games in 1972 between the Soviet National Team and the best stars of the NHL consisted of eight games. Four of them were held in Canada, the other four in Moscow. I have already said that the Canadian goalie Ken Dryden wrote a book about his impressions of those games. Most of the book is dedicated to the actual games, but when Dryden describes the games in Moscow, he includes his impressions of walking around our capital.

The Canadian goalie describes in detail his visits to Red Square, the Kremlin, Lenin Hills, and the Bolshoy Theatre. He had heard a lot of tales about this city before coming here, and he admired the beauty of this huge, modern city and was surprised by the accommodations: "Our room at the hotel Intourist turned out to be quite acceptable. The whole team was immediately invited to dinner in a room specially designated for us on the second floor. To our amusement, we were served an excellent beefsteak."

Walking around Moscow between games and practices, Dryden makes one nice discovery after another. It turns out that the Russians have a store, GUM, which is one of the largest shopping centres in the world. "We saw a huge tsar-cannon," writes the author, "it's too big to be able to shoot from it." I have often wondered whether Canadian fans, after reading this book, still believe in idiotic cartoons about the mad Russian bear? I think not. In Canada, where almost the whole population is interested in hockey, this frank book by their goalkeeper was very popular.

That year, Moscow's hospitality made Canadian professionals – I am not talking about fans – take a closer look at their hockey. In the NHL, rudeness was considered an almost necessary quality in players. On the other hand, Dryden tells about the dirty play of the Canadians on Moscow ice with a feeling of shame and guilt. He adds at the end of the book that the coaches were wrong to instruct them to play in such a manner.

And do you remember how respectfully the North American spectators stood before the game, when their famous singers were performing in Russian the anthem of the USSR? After the game, the police could hardly hold back the crowds of autograph seekers and well-wishers who sought to shake hands with someone from our team. "It's hard to win over a good team," wrote one Philadelphia newpaper after our victory, "but it's harder to win sympathy from their fans."

In front of hotels where we stayed, there were always several dozen fans. People came up to us on the streets and in airports, congratulating us for victories, consoling us for defeats, thanking us for a good game, wishing us new successes. Once, the management of the NHL asked our team to hold an open practice at the Montreal Forum. The arena was almost filled to capacity. Twelve thousand people showed up, and we practised to the accompaniment of their applause. We were introduced as though we were playing a real game. After the practice, we scattered all over the arena and signed autographs for about an hour.

I remember an interesting event in Calgary. We were almost all on the bus, when a woman with two small children ran up to coach Tikhonov and said that she needed to see Tretiak. "Let him shake my children's hands, so that they may grow as talented as he is," she pleaded. I stepped off the bus and took the boys in my arms. A photographer from a major newspaper appeared beside us. The next day, the newspaper featured a huge picture with the caption: "Children in safe hands".

I can assure you that the majority of Canadian fans feel respect for the Soviet team and Soviet hockey. The best example of these good feelings is a story about the 1981 Canada Cup. As many will remember, in the final game the National Team of the USSR literally knocked the hosts off the ice with an 8-1 score. Immediately after the game we received the main trophy of this competition – a cup in the shape of the Maple Leaf cut in half. It was made of pure nickel and weighed forty-nine kilograms. We took the trophy to our dressing room and began discussing the best way to deliver it home to Moscow to show our fans.

Suddenly, one of the tournament organizers, Alan Eagleson, came to us and said that the Cup had to be left in Canada, in the Hockey Hall of Fame. We wondered why. In every other international tournament the trophy remains with the winning team until the next playoffs. But nobody would listen to our arguments. Our way out of the dressing room was already blocked by hefty policemen. We were forced to give the Cup back to our not-so-hospitable hosts.

Shortly after we returned home, some very nice news came from Canada. A Canadian businessman by the name of George Smith, who is now very well known to our hockey fans, made an appeal through a newspaper to all Canadian fans, with a proposal to make an identical Cup for the Soviet team. To do this, he asked all who were interested to send no more than a dollar. He received enough money to make two Canada Cups.

Soon after, this trophy was presented to the winner – the National Team of the USSR – to keep forever. Reporters called it 'the Cup of the Canadian People'. This award is of special value to us because, first of all, we won this Cup in an honest fight, and second, because it was presented to us by thousands of Canadian fans sincerely, from the bottom of their hearts.

Incidentally, since then 'The Snowman' – the organizer of the Izvestia tournament – invites George Smith and his family to the competitions. Smith accepts the invitations with pleasure and always brings with him thousands of letters from Canadian fans, who send their best wishes to Soviet fans. That kind of correspondence solidifies the friendship between our two countries. In 1982 the same George Smith organized a trip to Moscow for veterans of Canadian hockey, to meet with our hockey aces of past years.

"I would have been happy to bring our best professionals to this tournament, but I am not as rich as the NHL who, in pursuit of profits, doesn't want to interrupt the game schedule to send a real team to Moscow," said Smith in one of his interviews.

Fans often ask me if I have friends among foreign hockey players. Of course I do. I can name Czechoslovakian goalies as well players of Swedish and Finnish National teams among my friends. During the tournaments we sometimes visited each other and spent our spare time together. We also found a common language with many Canadian professionals – as I mentioned before, Bobby Clarke, Bobby Hull, Wayne Gretzky. . . .

The top scorer in the NHL for the past several years, Wayne Gretzky, reminds me in some ways of our Igor Larionov. Slim and active, he absolutely does not look like a professional ice-gladiator. Almost every year he rewrites the NHL record book. I think one of the main reasons he is able to do that is that he plays our kind of hockey – creative, combinational, full of surprises. One of his favorite forwards was Valery Kharlamov. He claims that he learned a lot about hockey by watching Kharlamov and Yakushev.

In 1982 Wayne came to Moscow for the first time to

participate in the shooting of a documentary film about hockey. He brought along his whole family to our capital; his mother, his father, who works as a hockey coach, his three younger brothers, his girlfriend, and even his girlfriend's mother. And, of course, he brought the film crew. The movie they intended to shoot was entitled *Champions*. In this movie, they wanted to show a warm and friendly relationship between the best forward of the NHL and the best Soviet goalie.

Gretzky also came to Moscow on a diplomatic mission; he had a letter from the Prime Minister of Canada, Pierre Trudeau asking for support in the creation of the movie. The letter stressed that this movie would consolidate the friendship between Canada and the USSR. And we tried to help him as much as we could.

Wayne wanted to know more about our country, and he definitely wanted to show all the beauty of Moscow and its historical sites, which are very dear to all Soviet people, in the movie. We laid wreaths on the grave of the Unknown Soldier in front of the Kremlin wall, and visited the Lenin's Tomb. We saw the sights of the Kremlin and visited the Bolshoy Theatre, where we watched the ballet "Spartacus", and later talked to the dancers. And what a warm welcome was given to us at the circus! We were even invited into the ring during the performance.

The movie script called for us to go to the Moscow Subway, which can truly be considered one of the best in the world. At first Wayne seemed scared, almost like a kid. But then he became a little more confident. The cameramen shot Mayakovsky Station. I said to Wayne, "Let's ride the train. I will show you other beautiful stations – real masterpieces." But he flatly refused. Maybe the stereotype of North American subways – where gangs of murderers, thieves, and rapists rule – frightened him.

We went to Luzhniki, to the Olympic sports complex on Mir Boulevard, to the Olympic Village, and to the bicycle course in Krilyatskoe, which Gretzky especially liked. There are many scenes in the movie of us on bicycles.

However, this movie was primarily about hockey players. Gretzky wanted to try out the Moscow ice. I proposed to hold an exhibition practice with our boys. Wayne, as well as his brothers, expressed a wish to take part in it right away. There was an interesting moment: Gretzky couldn't do a somersault on ice, but to our boys it was no trouble at all. I showed him how I practised, and explained why I did particular exercises.

Then the practice was continued by Wayne's father. He was once a mailman, but he taught himself the hockey methods from Tarasov's book. He was Wayne's first coach, now he is training his younger sons.

In the evening we all went to my home, where my family and I welcomed our guests in the Russian tradition, with bread and salt. A conversation about books and paintings didn't interest Wayne. He looked over my library, of which I am very proud, with indifference. He also refused an invitation to visit the famous Tretiakovskaya Gallery.

Gretzky came to life however when he saw my awards. With great care, he took my Order of Lenin in his hands, and asked the cameraman to be sure to film the moment. I showed him another order, the Friendship of Nations, and remarked that if he came to Moscow more often, told the truth about our country, and fought for peace, he too could be honored with such an order. Gretzky smiled and said that he would try.

Wayne's younger brothers became so friendly with my kids that when the time came for them to say good-bye, the children even cried. It's too bad that the cameramen didn't shoot that farewell scene.

The movie was released in North America and was a big

success. Even though some of the episodes could not be included, I think it turned out well because it showed the warm, friendly, and trusting atmosphere which accompanied the visit. After he returned from Moscow, Gretzky held several press conferences, where he gave very high praise to our players and our country. Soon after that, he was recognized as the Athlete of the Year in Canada and the USA.

Yes, sports can bring all nations together.

I remember our game in Philadelphia against the Flyers during the North American tournament in 1979. We knew that the people there were especially hostile to Soviets. Organizers of the competition provided extra guards for our team to avoid incidents. We were warned that walking on city streets was not safe at any time of day. As soon as we finished our supper and went to our rooms, all access to our floor was blocked by FBI agents.

Not long before the beginning of the game, we received a phone call from a 'well-wisher', warning us not to go to the game because there was a bomb in our dressing room. Police asked us to wait to let them check to see if this was true. They searched for a bomb, but nothing was found. We received permission to prepare for the game, although a couple of sharpshooters remained at our door. This story may sound like a cheap hoax, but for us it was a nerve-wracking experience. However, it did not affect our play in the end.

When we came out on the ice, I immediately understood that the public were not only against us, they hated us. We played, trying not to pay attention to the reaction of the viewers. We played correctly, efficiently, and with refinement. We won deservedly. Unbelievably the Philadelphia fans, who were ready to tear us to pieces before the game, appaluded us after the game and the next day a local newspaper wrote, not without bitter irony, that in sixty minutes the Russians had changed the minds of a few thousand Philadelphia residents.

During trips abroad, our athletes often have to hold what almost seem like press-conferences for local media. The questions are not always the most harmless. Here, for example, is one that I was asked: "Is it true that participation of your representatives in international sports federations is aimed at the indoctrination of Communist ideology within these federations?"

This was ridiculous but I had to say something, and my answer was: "It's unlikely that international sports federations elect Soviet representatives as their presidents, vice-presidents, chairmen of different commissions and committees, or simply members, to let themselves become 'reds' under their influence. You can be sure that during sessions of the executive committee of the International Gymnastics Federation, its president, Yuri Titov, doesn't preach Marxist ideology. Rather, he discusses exclusively the questions concerning the development of the sport of gymnastics in the world today, and in the future. And you can also be sure that if Soviet representatives on the International Olympic Committee fight for purity of Olympic ideals and therefore speak out against participation by South African racists in international sports, that they have the support of all the progressive forces in the world of sport."

The media in the USA was very agitated when they found out about the first tour of Soviet hockey players in North America. They wrote that, together with hockey, we would supposedly bring to their country Communist ideology, and would make them believe that our Soviet way of life is the best. I'd like to say that we are not carrying out any ideological sabotage. Regarding popularization of our way of life, naturally we speak the truth about our country; the truth which, regrettably, is hard to swallow in the west. The strength of the Soviet athlete's personality comes from the sense that his glory and his success, is the success of his team and his fellow citizens.

Once I read remarkable words in a book dedicated to Soviet Olympic athletes: ". . . success in international sports shows, first of all, the moral and material welfare of the country, as well as the high cultural standards of the people, massive development of sports, and strong support for the sciences of the human being. Our Soviet athlete is a plenipotentiary representative of our great Motherland, and by his success all the world judges us!''

The last years of my hockey career coincided with the sharp deterioration of Soviet-American relations. Because of the USA administration, economic, cultural, trade, and sports contacts were eliminated or reduced to a mimimum. Our hockey players were among a handful of Soviet representatives who maintained constant relations with their American colleagues. I am glad that this small flame of friendly relations between our two great nations wasn't extinguished.

In Canada, after a series of games between the USSR National Team and NHL clubs, a reception was held to celebrate our victory. One of the Canadian there said, "The ice in the hockey arena is special; it warms the hearts of people." I'd like to add that it also helps us to understand each other better.

I was days away from finishing this book when the XXVII Communist Party Congress was held. Like all Soviet people, I impatiently opened the newspaper every morning. The Congress demanded that all of us revise all our attitudes toward life in order to make socio-economic acceleration a reality.

A big sports gala celebration was held by tradition for delegates of the Congress at the Olympic sports complex. I confess, on that Sunday in March I was feeling, not sad, but somehow out of place. For the first time, I went into the arena in the veterans' line. I was standing beside other famous champions whose names are known to all the world. People applauded us generously. I thought to myself that the best days of my life were those spent on the ice, not in full dress like now, but in heavy hockey gear, dripping with sweat. Those days were so painful and so hard, it made my stomach turn, but all was compensated by the happiness of victories. And what a great joy it was!

18

RENDEZ-VOUS '87

In early 1987, a Canadian publisher asked my permission to publish my memoirs and I had no objections. The publisher asked me to conclude the book with an account of the events in my life in the last few years and particularly to share my impressons of Rendez-vous '87 which was held in Quebec earlier this year. I do so with great pleasure.

During the first few months of 1987 it seemed to me that I spent more time in Canada than I did anywhere else. In the first three months I travelled overseas no less than three times, and each trip was memorable in its own right.

Over the Christmas and New Year's holidays, Tatiana and I were invited to a pre-Olympic hockey tournament in Calgary featuring the national teams of Canada, Czechoslovakia, the USA and the USSR. This was to be a dress rehearsal for the 1988 Winter Olympics. Before I continue, I'd like to point out that the facilities there are excellent. Calgary has prepared itself very well for the Olympics. Each sports venue has been constructed with due regard for the latest achievements in architecture and design. Everything is beautiful, comfortable and pleasing to the eye. I think that Olympic athletes will be very happy with the Games in Calgary, not only because of the architecture but because of the goodwill and open-mindedness of the people of Alberta. Albertans do not seem to be preoccupied with an interest in making as much money as possible from the Olympics (I recall Lake Placid, 1980) but rather with a desire to make the Games better and more joyful than others. Canada has a spirit which makes it one of the most sports-minded countries in the world.

Before the final game of the tournament, which was between the Czech and Russian teams, my wife was invited to drop the puck for the ceremonial face-off. This was the first time I had ever known a woman to be entrusted with this duty. Tatiana had never been on a hockey rink before in the presence of thousands of spectators. She was so nervous her knees were trembling. She dropped the puck and came back to our seats but her worries weren't over. "Maybe I've jinxed the game," she whispered, taking her seat beside me. I thought for a moment. If Tatiana brought bad luck, which team was it destined for? I didn't have to wait long for an answer. The Soviet national team lost the game and Tatiana became very upset. She was positive that Tikhonov would blame her for the defeat and swore that she would never do another face-off again.

That was the only unhappy episode. The rest of our trip was wonderful. We celebrated the New Year in Edmonton at the home of my old friend Wayne Gretzky. At 2:00 in the afternoon, which was midnight in Moscow, Wayne, his girlfriend Vicky Moss, Tatiana and I raised our champagne glasses. Everyone was happy. We talked about Wayne's visit to Moscow.

He said that he would like to play in an eight game series between Canada and the USSR like the one in 1972.

With a mysterious expression on her face, Vicky motioned to me with her hand. "Come here," she said, "there's something I want to show you." She led me to a closet where she opened the door to reveal at least a hundred different pairs of shoes. "Wayne collects them," she said. I still don't understand whether he wears all of them or if he just collects them the way other people collect stamps.

Gretzky is still the greatest hockey player in the NHL and I recently learned that his team, the Edmonton Oilers, won the Stanley Cup for the third time. Wonderful!

Back in Calgary we watched a real rodeo and visited an Indian reserve where, to my surprise, they had a hockey arena. Another memorable thing happened to me in Calgary. I was captured by my fans and spent no less than three and a half hours signing autographs – an absolute record for me!

From Calgary we flew to Toronto where I gave a press conference. Immediately I was asked what I thought about the brawl that occurred between the Canadian and Soviet teams at the world junior championships. I answered that, in my view, such behavior did not fit well with either team since they represented the world's two greatest hockey countries. I blamed the referee for the incident. It was obvious that he was unqualified to handle a game like that. "Hockey is a man's game but that doesn't mean it has to be transformed into a street fight," I said. I tried to finish on a diplomatic note by saying that I hoped this unfortunate event would not sour the mood before the wonderful festival which Rendez-vous '87 promised to be.

Interestingly, I later read an interview with Alan Eagleson who also said that the main cause of the brawl was incompetent refereeing. "The game was already out of control ten minutes after it began,'' Eagleson said. ''The refereeing was ridiculous.''

It wasn't very long before I was back in Canada again, this time in Quebec City. Everywhere there was an atmosphere of a grand international festival. Even the air seemed impregnated with the spirit of Rendez-vous. The Soviet hockey players were accompanied to Rendez-vous '87 by soloists of the Bolshoi theatre, the rock group Autograph, and, for 'dessert', the Soviet Army song and dance ensemble. People at the first show may have been shocked when they saw on stage two hundred soldiers in full Soviet military uniform which is the usual stage dress of the ensemble. I was worried myself. I wondered how such a mass landing of Soviet army troops would be accepted in Quebec. Judging by American movies, which are shown in Canada, Russians do nothing but sharpen their knives and dream about establishing collective farms in Texas and rebuilding California. What if these Red Army soldiers should suddenly jump down from the stage and begin raping Quebec's women? Probably to the astonishment of some viewers, nothing like that happened. The Soviet soldiers began to sing and dance and performed so well that the audience gave them a long standing ovation.

During Rendez-vous articles from the Hockey Hall of Fame in Toronto were brought to Quebec and put on display at a museum. I spent one-and-a-half to two hours each day at this museum signing autographs and answering fans' questions.

I met some old friends there too – players from the 1972 Team NHL. Fifteen years ago the spirit of competition, along with the distrust for one another, most of which was generated by officials and the media, prevented us from socializing like civilized people. Now there was no trace of the old antagonism. We had become wise and kind. We looked at one another's aging faces and couldn't hold back the laughter, thinking about what bullies we had been in 1972. There was a press conference at a museum at which Brian Mulroney, the Prime Minister of Canada, was present. I presented him with a Russian balalaika which Mulroney attempted to play for the benefit of the press photographers.

I'd like to add a few more words about the Hockey Hall of Fame. Back in Moscow I watched a television program which had been made while we were in Quebec. The report on the Hall of Fame was illustrated by old news footage. What thrilling pictures I saw – Maurice 'The Rocket' Richard; the early history of the Stanley Cup, a huge, paunchy, glittering trophy that looks like a Russian samovar; the timid skating, weak shots and baggy looking gear of hockey players in the last century. As well, there was an interview with Guy Lafleur and commentary by Tikhonov. "I like your guys," the former NHL star began. "They can and like to practise. They are stronger physically. Your training process is more highly developed. One of our main problems in Canada is related to the number of injuries that occur in the junior leagues; a lot of talented boys end up being forced out of hockey," Lafleur concluded. Tikhonov commented: "If I were them I would forbid hitting until the age of fourteen and concentrate on the development of technical skills." Finally there was an item about the Montreal Canadiens, a team that has won the Stanley Cup twenty-two times.

It would be wonderful to have a museum like this in the Moscow. I will see what I can do about it.

Rendez-vous featured two games between the NHL All-Stars and the USSR National Team. As a guest of the festival and a sports ambassador of the Soviet Union, I participated in the ceremonial face-offs for both games, in the first game with Jean Beliveau and Gordie Howe, and in the second with Guy Lafleur and Mark Johnson, who had been the captain of the 1980 US Olympic Team in Lake Placid.

Both the NHL and Soviet teams were afraid of losing two games. One loss would not be too bad, but two... I think even before the tournament started both rivals had subconsciously agreed that the ideal result would be for each team to win a game. Adding to the international spirit of the tournament, the NHL team had a lot of European players from Sweden and Finland. "I've never seen anything like this before," I commented to Gretzky. "Me neither," he replied.

On the way to the first game we got into an accident when a clumsy guy in a Lincoln Continental hit our limousine. It was the first car accident in my life and we were lucky to get out without any injuries.

The first game was extremely close. With only five minutes to go, the score was tied 3-3 but the Soviet team, in an effort to break the deadlock, forgot about defence and were punished by allowing a goal. In that game both goaltenders, Fuhr and Belosheikin, played extremely well but, as usual, the star of the game for the NHL team was Wayne Gretzky with his precise passing and his play behind the net.

Before the second game the NHLers were in a cheerful mood. First of all, they already had one victory which gave them a great psychological advantage. Second, the referee was Canadian too which had a certain impact, regardless of how unbiased he was. The NHL team came out on the ice with the same line-up they'd used in Game 1 and they seemed confident of their forthcoming victory. Nevertheless, our guys weren't intimidated and the game ended in a 5-3 victory for the Soviet team. Gretzky was named the best NHL player and received a luxurious new Chrysler. The Canadians were particularly impressed by Valery Kamensky, number thirteen on the Soviet Team. Valery is a young and relatively unknown player and may be someone to watch in future international competition.

At the end of the tournament, Governor-General Jeanne Sauve, presented each team with a trophy. The Soviet captain, Viacheslav Fetisov, took the prize from Mme. Sauve and, without thinking, gave her a kiss. This may have violated the usual protocol but I think it expressed better than anything else the feelings and the gratitude of all those who participated in Rendez-vous '87.

Yes, it was an incredible festival. The program included tasting dishes of international cuisine, fashion shows by the most famous designers, concerts, a carnival, and sports competitions. The list of honorary guests included the great Brazilian soccer player, Pele; the American basketball player, Wilt Chamberlain; the Belgian cyclist, Merx; the Canadian skier, Nancy Greene; Jean Beliveau; the Russian gymnast, Kim; and many others. This alone made Rendez-vous an event of international proportions.

Canadians certainly know how to have fun. One morning in Quebec City I was awakened with an invitation to attend a beauty pageant. "What is it?" I asked suspiciously. "You will see when you get there," I was told. In the hotel to which I was taken reigned the most beautiful women I have ever seen. Almost immediately I was asked to confirm that in answer to the question: "Where do the most beautiful girls in the world live?" "In Quebec," I answered without blinking an eye. On the spot I was honored with a kiss and I was thankful that my wife wasn't around.

My next trip to Canada occurred in March and was related to my participation in a series of games between Soviet and Canadian oldtimers. It was hard to believe that fifteen years had passed since we first met on the ice. How ruthless time is! Without exaggerating, the games between the Soviet and Canadian stars in 1972 opened a new era in the history of hockey. Now, from a distance of fifteen years I can clearly see that series as the brightest, most exciting event in the chronicles of the game. It is unlikely that there will ever be anything to match it.

In our country hockey pushed everything else aside, even the events of the '72 Munich Olympics. Fans literally held their breath waiting for the results of the first game in Montreal. For the majority, the biggest question was by how much the Canadians would tear us apart. It bears repeating that our fans truly believed that Canadians could pierce the boards with their shots. The Canadian players wore halos; each of them was a legend; and most of all, they inspired fear.

Oh what games those were in September 1972! What passions they inspired! Time has now erased from my memory everything unessential or accidental (for example, the breaches of rules and the brawls) leaving only the most important memories of the happy moments in that exciting, intense and fierce struggle. The Soviet team won three games, tied one and lost four. We scored thirty-two goals and allowed thirty-one.

And now, after all those years, the NHL Oldtimers' Association had decided to gather the participants of that memorable series for three games in Hamilton, Montreal and Ottawa. In their invitation to us, our hosts stipulated two conditions: There should be no less than twelve players from the 1972 team, and the Soviet team definitely had to include Tretiak! At the time I hadn't picked up a hockey stick for a long time. My weight was the same, but except for tennis, I hadn't played any other games.

After only three or four practices, we once again flew our familiar route – Moscow-Gander-Monteal. There were many stars from the seventies on our team. Unfortunately, Mikhailov, Petrov and Maltsev couldn't come, but nearly all of the rest of the stars of that show fifteen years ago barely gathered the necessary hockey gear and were ready to play. The mood was less than confident. We knew that the Canadian veterans had been practising and that they even held their own tournaments. I'm afraid that most of us don't even do our morning exercises anymore.

We were also worried that there wouldn't be any interest among the fans. Surely, after all those years they had forgotten about us. Our worries, however, were groundless. There were reporters waiting for us when we touched down at Gander – a sure sign that this was, indeed, serious business.

One reporter asked me what had happened to Valery Kharlamov's children. I readily answered that his daughter, Begonita (named after Valery's mother who was of Spanish origin) is in grade three and is training to be a gymnast. His son, Sasha, is in grade five and plays hockey in the Central Army Sports Club. By the way, another Valery Kharlamov, a nephew of the great hockey star, plays on the National USSR junior soccer team. Valery's former teammates have not forgotten that his children were left orphans. We always bring them presents from our trips abroad and we are always interested in how they are doing at school and in their chosen sports.

People in Canada constantly asked questions about Kharlamov. It didn't matter that six years had passed since his death. Even time cannot erase the memory of this great player and fine man. Before every one of the oldtimers' games the players and spectators paid tribute to Kharlamov by observing a minute of silence.

There is an excellent souvenir program which was published for the Oldtimers' series. In it are words of welcome from Canadian Prime Minister Brian Mulroney, Sports Minister Otto Jelinek, and Alexei Rodionov, Soviet Ambassador to Canada. There are also color photographs which show the most memorable events of the Superseries of the century, and portraits of its participants. It is interesting to compare those old photos with their subjects so many years later. Unfortunately, time has shown no mercy. These gentlemen have seen a lot in their lives, and it shows.

Dennis Hull went completely bald, although it didn't prevent him from behaving like a boy in our company – endlessly joking and making fun of everybody. During the official dinner at the Château Laurier, Hull approached the microphone to make a toast. His words were interrupted by laughter when he suddenly pulled a bunch of table knives from his pockets and threw them to the ground. It was a hilarious moment. Perhaps he wanted to say that he didn't need any bad feelings towards the Russians; as the Russian proverb says, "Don't hold a stone under your coat."

Paul Henderson was also there. He is the man who upset us on September 28, 1972 by scoring the deciding goal for the Canadians with only thirty-four seconds left in the game. I had always remembered him as persistent, always ready for a fight. There was rarely a scuffle which Henderson did not initiate. Now, I saw a modest, almost timid forty-four-year-old man with a calm voice and meek expression. "What happened, Paul? Are you ill?" "No," answered Paul, with a melancholy smile, "everything is all right. I now work at Athletes in Action, a charitable Christian organization which helps athletes to build their relationship with God." "It is really difficult to imagine you as a priest!" I said, astonished. Henderson smiled with understanding; "I played hockey until 1981. I had everything – money, fame, fans. But then I experienced a breakdown, a crisis. I turned to religion, and it supported me like a crutch."

Yvan Cournoyer had not changed as much as the others. He was still the same; active, kind – one of the boys, as they say. On the ice, he still skated faster than anybody else, and he never seemed to tire. Now he has his own restaurant in a suburb of Montreal, and our 'over-the-hill gang' ate there three times a day. On the first day, Yvan gave me a friendly tap on the shoulder, "It's good to be back together again, isn't it?" Of course it was! We were the most unique sports rivals in the world – divided by nothing, but united by much. Whoever thought of this series for veterans deserves the prize!

Stan Mikita, a forty-seven-year-old golf club manager from Chicago, told me that he tries to skate with a hockey stick at least once every two weeks. "These veterans' games have brought me one of the greatest joys in my life." "He's right," confirmed forty-nine-year-old Frank Mahovlich, now the owner of a Toronto travel agency, "The main benefit of this series is that we see each other. My feelings about you are a lot better than they were before."

My meeting with my old friend Bobby Clarke, now thirty-seven years old and the manager of the Philadelphia Flyers, was very joyful. I also found out that Ron Ellis was now breeding race horses, and that Gary Smith was a sheriff in Ottawa. We had endless conversations; we reminisced more this time than in all my other trips to Canada put together.

The Canadians, in turn, were interested in our lives as well: How were we? How were our families? How much money did we make? Once more, we came to the conclusion that we all shared the same problems, concerns, and anxieties.

In contrast to the former professionals, the majority of whom had not tied down their lives to hockey, almost all my friends who had finished their sports careers weren't far from the ice. Many of them were coaches, managers, or directors of sports facilities. Viacheslav Starshinov, on the other hand, went into science; he is now the head of the faculty of physical education at one of the Moscow institutes. Evgeny Zimin is a sports commentator on television.

Now, I will tell you about the results of this series: Our hosts won the first two games, and the last one was a tie, 8-8. All three games kept the spectators on the edge of their seats, especially the final one, which ended in a tie despite going into overtime. I honestly thought, much to my regret, that since we were meeting again as aging veterans, both parties would behave peacefully on the ice, without rivalries or strong passions. Boy, was I wrong! It didn't come to blows, but the rest was like fifteen years ago. I could already feel it in the first game, when I had to beat off twenty shots in each period. This is a fight to the death, I thought, wiping the sweat off my forehead.

I was deeply touched by the warm welcome I received from fans in different cities. When I went out on the ice of the Montreal Forum, the people there gave me a long ovation that brought tears to my eyes. It has been a long time since I was a famous goalkeeper. Now, I am an ordinary man, like anybody else. And yet, you remember me; you still like me. I remember you too, my friends, and my heart is with you.

In Ottawa I accidently ran into my old acquaintance, Dmitri Shapiro, the Moscow mathematician who is known in Russia as a leader of the first ever skiing expedition from the coast of the USSR to the North Pole and then to Canada in 1979. He was planning another such expedition which, as far as I could judge from the reaction of the newspapers, had met wide support here in Canada. Dmitri told me that hundreds of Canadians had expressed a wish to participate in it.

The expedition team wanted to start at the end of February of 1988, from the Russian island of Severnaya Zemlya and, three months and seventeen hundred kilometers later, finish on Ellesmere Island. Canadians and Russians would live side by side, sharing the same tents, eating from the same pots. I asked how they would overcome the language barrier. "That isn't the main problem," said Dmitri, "We are already learning English, and the Canadians who are accepted will have to learn Russian." "So what is the main problem?" I asked. "The main difficulty is not to make a mistake in the process of selecting participants. As you know, our group has existed for many years, and we are confident in each other. The selection of Canadians is basically by lottery. How can we foresee the behavior of a stranger in an extreme situation? There will be no replacements out there. We have to live and work together for three months."

Let it be a joint expedition through the arctic ice. Let the Winter Olympics be in Calgary. Let Canadian students come to our country more often on missions of peace, and let Canadians enjoy the performances of our singers and dancers. Let hockey players, scientists, and public figures meet. To break such contacts would mean to once again breed mistrust, from which there is only one step to hatred.

Not long ago, Soviet TV showed an American movie, *The Day After.* It was a realistic fantasy about an exchange of nuclear strikes. I thought, How fragile is peace in the world! The human race is walking on the edge of a terrible disaster, and we must join hands and form a strong human chain to keep from falling into it. We hockey players not only entertain you with our play, but also carry out a very important human mission. I promise that I will be faithful to that mission.

I am ready to come to Canada as a coach of a school for young goalkeepers, which will soon be open in our country. I am ready to receive Canadian guests in Moscow. There is nothing more important now than preserving peace in the world.

It is the truth. Who would not agree with it?

EPILOGUE
Around Him A Magic Field

We would like to end Vladislav Tretiak's book by publishing some of the comments made by different people at different times about this remarkable goalkeeper.

Vitaly G. Erfilov, his first coach:

Only the unknowing fan would think that all this impressive equipment could protect the goalie from getting hurt by the puck. You can imagine how it feels to a boy – not a man – when a solid rubber disk hits him with a speed of more that a hundred kilometers per hour. I have seen how even adult players have lost consciousness because of the pain, but sometimes it seemed to me that Tretiak was charmed; even in his childhood years he never complained when he was in pain. Only in the dressing room, when I saw his bruises and scratches, did I understand what his silence cost him.

And despite all this, hockey always brought joy to

Tretiak; it was his life. He would not be Tretiak if he did not try to bring into the game something new, unexplored. While still on the junior team, he was already the first of our goalkeepers to play further from the net, and he proposed a new technique to deflect low pucks. In all his inventions, Tretiak used his excellent skating skills, as well as his great intelligence and courage, without which his skills would be impossible.

And then success came. In 1968, the young goalie playing on the junior National Team became a European champion. After that tournament, Vladik refused to take a well-deserved rest. The next day he returned, when everybody thought he would be resting at home, and played in a game between senior teams for the Moscow championship. After that game, he could barely stand on his feet. The next day he travelled through the whole city with his favorite sports bag full of heavy goalie gear, to play on the intermediate team. He knew we didn't have a worthy substitute, so he had to play without taking time off to rest.

Shortly after that, Anatoly Tarasov accepted Tretiak to the Central Army Club team.

Anatoly Tarasov:

Before our National team went to Canada at the end of 1969, all the coaches except myself and Arkady Chernishev spoke out against including Tretiak on the National team.

Our colleagues talked passionately, but not very convincingly: "He is young, too young; he might not withstand the test; there is no need to hurry..." But nobody could say that Tretiak was weak, that he didn't have skills. He had shown his best at the USSR Championship and at the Moscow International Tournament.

What was our faith in this young player based on? On his absolute diligence, his fanaticism. I saw in Vladik a fine athlete, whose clever moves were successfully combined with quick reflexes. This young man could already value friendship and advice from older people, and could analyze a situation.

And we succeeded. Tretiak went to Canada. He played well in almost all the games, and in Montreal he met the legendary Jacques Plante. This great Canadian presented Vladik with his stick, and the happy rookie didn't let it out of his hands all the way back to Moscow.

Ken Dryden, former Montreal Canadien goalie:

It's hard not to be amazed by what Tretiak does to us. It seems like we are talking and thinking about him more than any other Soviet hockey player.

This is what Eddy Johnson said about Tretiak: "The pressure doesn't bother him at all. Look at him – here he let in a very easy goal, but he seems very calm. And that's not all. So many times he prevents rebounds. Here, the puck got caught in his pads and everybody waits for it to fall down on the ice, but nothing like that happens."

It would be interesting to know how he would have done in the NHL. For now, I can simply admit that even today he handles the best players of the NHL. I was not the only one who thought that when our boys opened fire on him, he would start to look towards the dressing room door. I supposed that our guys would simply crush him. No way! He's only twenty, but look what he does to us!

Vera Tretiak:

I always used to meet Vladik and the team at the airport after their trips abroad. And always, the head coach Anatoly Tarasov came to me, kissed my hand, and thanked me; "I am very satisfied with your son." Now that Vladik is married, his wife Tania meets him, and my husband and I wait for them at home.

I know how much time my son spends practising and how hard he works. All the fame and recognition haven't spoiled him. He is still the same – as easy-going, joyful, and kind as he was in his school years.

Of course, I worry about him – trips, flights, endless pucks flying at my younger son with awful speed. The best forwards in the world try to shoot right through him.

I wouldn't say that Vladik has become quieter with years. He is a restless type, especially during a game. As he says himself, "I have to be this way, no matter who our opponents are." It might not be very noticeable from TV screens and arena stands, but I know my son's character.

Grigory Mkrtchan, veteran Soviet goalie:

Tretiak's play is more developed because it combines the best styles of both the Soviet and Canadian schools of hockey. He skillfully divides the play at the crease from the play far from the goal line. He is always ready to beat off the most powerful and exact shots, and figure out the most difficult combinations. Unlike Canadian goalies, who deflect pucks after powerful shots, Tretiak saves the puck, thus eliminating the danger of rebounds.

Tretiak is the strongest of all. Not only is he unusually talented, but he also practises more often and more thoroughly than others. He is incredibly hard-working. He does not simply sweat through the practices, he invents a new exercise at every one; he is always in search. In a word, he takes a creative approach to his practice. I would call Vladislav the most reliable goalie in the world.

Anatoly Firsov, veteran Soviet star:

By the time he was twenty-three, Tretiak had won all

imaginable awards for an athlete. Some famous athletes have left their sports without receiving such titles and honors as Tretiak did even as a boy. But this did not spoil or change him. He did not become arrogant or capricious, and he never asked for special privileges. There are many hard-working and talented athletes, but very few can pass the fame test. Tretiak passed it with flying colors.

Y. Brykin, referee:

When we are in the midst of events on the ice, we hear the remarks of the players, so naturally each referee knows what can be expected from each player. I am not going to characterize each player, but I would like to talk about goalies.

Some goalies always try to poke the skates of forwards with their sticks, and when they stumble over the stick of a forward, they take an offensive stand and demand that the referee punish the forward, or else they take the law into their own hands.

I have taken the puck from Tretiak's catcher many times, and each time I was amazed at his remarkable calmness and respectful attitude towards opponents. I have never heard rude words from him, even when the rivals were clearly violating the rules of the game. I noticed that his calmness had an influence on 'dirty' players. They were surprised by Tretiak because he did not become outraged and fight back. Tretiak put them in an awkward position and, as a result, achieved respect, even among the favorites of 'dirty play'.

Valery Kharlamov:

I know how Tretiak worries about failures. But when it is necessary, he can force himself to forget them and play with such spirit that it seems like the season just started, and he is in the net after a month of rest.

When the forward gets a breakaway, it is almost always a sure goal against any goalie except Tretiak. I was convinced of that during the practices when, at the end, I asked Vladik to stay a little longer to polish up some techniques. Tretiak was always willing to work overtime; that is how he is on the ice. Beyond the arena, he is a happy, friendly guy, my closest friend. He is demanding of himself, and a man of principle towards his friends.

Viktor Tikhonov, head coach of the Soviet National Team:

I don't like to single anyone out, and I don't like to use such a phrase as 'heroic deed'. But what Tretiak did in the last season cannot be called anything but a sports feat. His overall attitude towards work cannot be matched; this has always been so. But life put Vladik to the test. Not long before the World Championships, he broke his leg. He was replaced by a young goalie, Alexander Tyzhnykh. Nevertheless, Tretiak didn't miss a practice. Viktor Kuzkin, an Army team coach, sat on a bench in front of Tretiak's net and shot tennis balls to keep his reflexes up.

Vladislav didn't lose his skills, precise movements, reflexes, or goalie intuition. Even though he wasn't great in the games before the Championship, we were all convinced that he had to go to Sweden. It was necessary for him to know that we believed in him. As you know, Tretiak was the best goalie at the World Championships, and he was named the best player in Europe and the USSR in 1981. He certainly deserved it.

Garry Kasparov, world chess champion:

Of all the athletes, for me the number one champion is Vladislav Tretiak. Although our sports history is not short on names of famous athletes, the name Tretiak has an epochal character. This unique man was the greatest hockey player of the last decade. Canadians react only to one name – Tretiak. For me, Tretiak is an example of a man who not only knows his sport brilliantly, but shows his skills with an unusual artistry. Unfortunately, I have never met him personally, but I am certain of one thing – around him is a magic field.